# Teaching Multicultural Literature in Grades 9–12: Moving Beyond the Canon

# Teaching Multicultural Literature in Grades 9–12: Moving Beyond the Canon

Arlette Ingram Willis, Editor
University of Illinois at Urbana-Champaign

Christopher-Gordon Publishers, Inc.
Norwood, MA

# Credits

Every effort has been made to contact copyright holders for permission to reproduce borrowed material where necessary. We apologize for any oversights and would be happy to rectify them in future printings.

All student work is used with permission.

Christopher-Gordon Publishers, Inc.
1502 Providence Highway, Suite #12
Norwood, MA 02062
(800) 934-8322

Library of Congress Catalog Card Number: 97-78321

Printed in the United States of America

10 9 8 7 6 5 4 3 2 1                    02 01 00 99 98

ISBN 0-926842-73-0

# Contents

## Chapter 3
## Celebrating African American Literary Achievements ......... 37
*Arlette Ingram Willis*

## Chapter 4
## A Continuing Journey: The Puerto Rican Reality as Viewed From the Narrative ................................................................. 83
*Antonio Nadal* and *Milga Morales-Nadal*

## Chapter 5
## Asian/Pacific American Literature: The Battle Over Authenticity ............................................................................. 101
*Sandra S. Yamate*

## Chapter 6
## Contextualizing Native American Literature ...................... 143
*Anna Lee Walters* with *Debbie Reese*

## Chapter 7
## Storying in the Mexican American Community:
## Understanding the Story Behind the Stories and
## the Cultural Themes Shared in Chicano Novels .............. 169
*Sylvia Y. Sánchez*

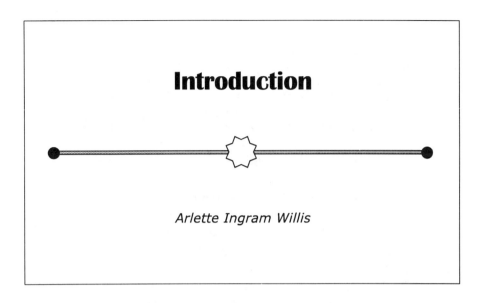

# Introduction

*Arlette Ingram Willis*

> *It takes strength to remember;*
> *it takes another kind of strength to forget.*
> *It takes a hero to do both . . . Heroes are rare.*

James Baldwin, 1960

I recently received a letter from a former student who was struggling to include multicultural literature in her school's curriculum during student teaching. Here is an excerpt from her letter:

> I am teaching junior year English at American High School. I am teaching one "regular" and two "honors" American Literature classes and a combination American Literature and History class. My curriculum includes the Puritans through the pre–Civil War period. I have to teach *The Crucible, The Scarlet Letter,* Hawthorne, Thoreau, and possibly *The Adventures of Huckleberry Finn.* For the most part my co-op teachers seem energetic and sympathetic to my situation, although I haven't really gotten a chance to talk to them about their philosophies and thoughts on education-related issues. I have to admit that I'm not really thrilled with the literature line-up, and I was wondering if you

> could suggest not only books but methods and ideas I could use to teach these novels and authors, as well as any other supplemental reading I could use for this particular period of American literature. I want to give the kids the most diverse and interesting look at literature, but I can't help feeling that this time period constrains me. This is definitely due in part to the fact that when I've studied this material I've only been taught the standard authors, but I'm hoping there's more out there that I'm not aware of.

This former student had completed a methods course I teach that offers students an introduction to learning and teaching multicultural literature. What I find particularly meaningful in this letter is her desire to expand her students' notions of "American literature" (one of the goals of my course) and her commitment to making a change in the way "American literature" is understood and taught. Furthermore, her instructional dilemma indicates that she wants to know how to begin to extend the very entrenched system of Anglicizing early American literature. Her willingness to undertake this stance supports the work of critical theorists who maintain that to continue to teach as we were taught will only perpetuate the status quo. Her position also suggests that by teaching multicultural literature one can challenge dominant ideologies, present multiple voices and experiences, and demystify the intersection of history, culture, privilege, and power relations. Moreover, learning and teaching multicultural literature can create opportunities for shared understandings and greater inclusion of literature written by underrepresented groups within the current curriculum. We can move beyond the canon.

This student, however, represents only a small number of undergraduates who have the opportunity to enroll in preservice multicultural literature courses. It is widely acknowledged that "teachers need additional cultural and social knowledge as they work with increasing numbers of students from varied cultural and linguistic backgrounds" (Diamond & Moore, 1995, p. xi). Where will teachers obtain the needed information? This book is designed to offer sociohistorical information to teacher educators, inservice teachers, and preservice teachers and to introduce students and teachers to the rich tapestry of multicultural literature that is available. It is also designed to be used in a multicultural literature survey course that can open to university preservice students, as well as secondary students, a world of literature that is not always present in their literature anthologies. The historical and cultural information presented in each chapter provides a foundation for understanding the literature of underrepresented groups. Additionally, this book may serve as a reference that presents a broad array of information about the history, culture, and literature of groups traditionally underrepresented in American literature anthologies. This is not the first such book to attempt to capture a broad array of multicultural history, culture, and literature in one text. However, the collective scholarship of the authors and practitioners has produced a truly unique text.

Finally, this book is an attempt to bring together the literature written by people of color living in the United States and its territories that reflects their histories, language, culture, and experiences. The diverse groups represented are all Americans: African, Asian/Pacific, Caribbean, Mexican, Puerto Rican, and Native. Though different in country of origin, culture, and language, each group has experienced the harsh realities of oppression in the United States from the forced abandonment of its language and culture to the assimilation into a Euro-American way of life in order to survive. However, each group also has miraculously been able to gain literacy skills, record its American experience, and produce a plethora of literature. Victoria Earle Matthews (1895), cited in Gates & McKay (1997), a turn-of-the-century African American female author, observed that

> unless earnest and systematic effort be made to procure and preserve for transmission to our successors, the records, books and various publications already produced by us, not only will the sturdy pioneers who paved the way and laid the foundation for our Race literature be robbed of this just due, but an irretrievable wrong will be inflicted upon the generations that shall come after us. (Cited in *The Norton Anthology of African American Literature*, p. xxvii)

Each group represented herein has experienced its own unique struggle for literacy and freedom. The early writings of each group attests to its struggle for literacy and its quest to publish and share people's lives, voices, and thoughts with others. Fortunately, many individuals were able to have their thoughts recorded for prosperity.

The collective writings of many men and women make multicultural literature alive today for all to enjoy. Their works illustrate the unique melding of diverse cultures with Euro-American culture in the United States and its territories. Literature produced in the past, present, and future will continue to challenge the resistance to the inclusion of works by non-Whites in school curricula.

## Book Overview

This book was created to extend our knowledge and understanding of the contexts in which the literature written by people of color living in the United States and its territories, often missing in secondary curricula, should be learned and taught. The inclusion of this literature in secondary curricula will move literature beyond the canon to include the works of many underrepresented Americans. Literary critic Henry Louis Gates, Jr.'s, reflection on the power of story in the lives of African Americans can be extended to the power of story revealed through the literature contextualized and reviewed in this book from an insider's perspective. I believe his quote captures the heart of what we are saying. Gates (1993) argues that "telling our stories" is an important element in the survival of a culture. He puts it this way:

> The stories that we tell ourselves and our children function to order our world, serving to create both a foundation upon which each of us constructs our sense of reality and a filter through which we process each event that confronts us every day. The values we cherish and wish to preserve, the behavior that we wish to censure, the fears and dread that we can barely confess in ordinary language, the aspirations and goals that we most dearly prize—all of these things are encoded in the stories that each culture invents and preserves for the next generation, stories that, in effect we live by and *through*. And the stories that survive, the stories that manage to resurface under different guises and with marvelous variations, these are a culture's *canonical* tales, the tales that contain the cultural codes that are *assumed* and *internalized* by members of that culture. (pp. 17–18)

Included in this volume is a collection of writings by outstanding authors and practitioners who discuss multicultural literature for grades 9–12. Collectively, the chapters offer readers a smorgasbord of information and understanding about various aspects of multicultural literature (novels, plays, ballads, and essays). In chapter 1, Cameron McCarthy offers an overview of the state of multicultural education and its evolution into the curriculum. His work is followed by Linda Spears-Bunton's explanation in chapter 2 of the place of multicultural literature in the curriculum.

Chapters 3 through 8 form the heart of this volume and offer a sociohistorical framework for understanding the literature of select cultural groups: African Americans, Puerto Ricans, Asian/Pacific Americans, Native Americans, Mexican Americans, and Caribbeans. Each chapter is a tribute to the rich treasury of multicultural literature available for learning and teaching the literature of diverse groups. The voices of many long gone speak to the reader from the selections discussed. Due to space limitations, all possible works are not included, but that is not to be misunderstood as a judgment of the worthiness of those omitted. Each contributing author attempts to offer racial, ethnic, and cultural insider perceptions that provide respect for the history, culture, values, and beliefs that are qualitatively difficult to assume others know. Personal style dictates the authors' mixture of biographical, political, social, economic, and cultural material. The selections of pieces to include was the province of the individual authors; thus the voices that are included are merely representative of a myriad of ways in which the chapters could have been written. The selections included are, in the authors' opinions, works that are meaningful and appropriate for secondary school readers. Each of these chapters concludes with references.

Certain themes have emerged, although this was not an intended goal, that reflect the individual and group struggle for personal identity in a foreign land and the desire to maintain cultural identity and affirmation while transgressing the waters of acceptability within Euro-American mainstream culture. Other themes that emerge throughout can be understood on a continuum that ranges from the struggles with dual and multiple cultural identities, the denial of cultural referents, and the masking of cultural difference to the embracing of dual and multiple cultural identities, the celebration of cultural referents, and the highlighting of cultural differences.

The final chapter, chapter 9, offers readers practical applications for the information in the preceding chapters about learning and teaching multicultural literature in colleges or university classrooms and in a high school classrooms. This chapter attempts to move beyond discussions of literature and illustrate how two educators have taught multicultural literature in their classrooms in ways that have challenged students to acknowledge and address the multiple voices and experiences found in literature. Their desire to make multicultural literature a welcome and necessary part of the curriculum, however required a great deal of time, research, reading, dialogue, and commitment.

There is an appendix to this chapter that shares a multicultural reading list I distribute to my college students. Please recall that every title on this list is not appropriate for high school students. There are some titles that have been "planted" for students to discover for dialogue about appropriateness, censorship, and authenticity.

# References

Diamond, B., & Moore, M. (1995). *Multicultural literacy: Mirroring the reality of the classroom.* New York: Longman.

Gates, H., & McKay, N. (Eds.). (1997). *The Norton anthology of African American Literature.* New York: Norton.

Mathews, V. (1895). Cited in Gates & McKay (1997).

Mullane D. (Ed.) (1993). *Crossing the danger water: Three hundred years of African-American writing.* (p. 249). New York: Doubleday.

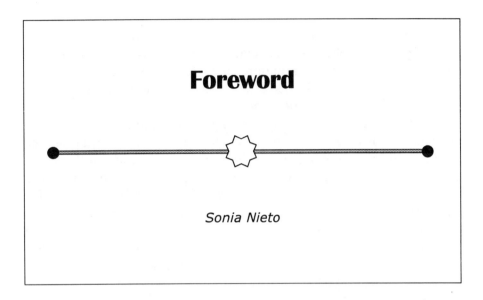

# Foreword

*Sonia Nieto*

At the age of 16, during the summer between my junior and senior years in high school, I started working at my first formal job. It was at the neighborhood branch of the Brooklyn Public Library in East Flatbush and my job was to shelve the books returned by patrons, a task that facilitated my exploration of the entire building. I was happy to be immersed in the library, a place I had always loved. One day, as I was shelving in the psychology section, I came across a book that stopped me in my tracks. The title was something like *Mental Illness Among Puerto Ricans.* I picked it up and checked it out immediately so that I could take it home. Unfortunately, when I got home, I found that the book was a technical presentation of particular mental illnesses among Puerto Ricans and the language and subject matter were both well beyond my comprehension. Disappointed, I returned the book the next day.

As I reflect on this experience, it becomes very clear to me that what excited me about this book was not its subject matter but its subjects. The fact that it concerned Puerto Ricans was thrilling to me. As a child and young woman, I had *never* read a book—a children's or young adult book, a book in English or Spanish, a book in school or out—that focused on Puerto Ricans in any way. Imagine my excitement, then, when I finally found a book that made mention of my people. Never mind that the book was hopelessly inappropriate for a sixteen-year-old, that its subject matter was depressing, or that its discourse was technical; what mattered was that, here at last, there was a book that made me and other Puerto Ricans visible. After all, if we were in a book, we *had* to be important.

I wish I could say that my experience is a thing of the past, but regrettably this is not the case. There are still too many young people who search in vain to see themselves and their families reflected in the books they read and in the stories they hear. There are many more young people who do not even know they should be searching for such books; for them, stories are about other people, never about them or their families or communities. *Teaching Multicultural Literature in Grades 9–12: Moving Beyond the Canon,* by Arlette Willis and her skilled coauthors, will serve to bridge that terrible gap, a chasm that still exists for many young people who are invisible and silent in U.S. literature. Fortunately for us, the subject matter, level, and discourse of this book are much more appropriate for the concerns of young adults than was the book about mental illness that I found many years ago when I was sixteen.

The abyss between students' home lives and their school lives, however, cannot be negotiated by simply incorporating multicultural literature into the existing curriculum; to do so would place the new curriculum within an assimilationist ideology that negates the very essence of the literature. The stories of the communities that are the subject of this book—American Indians, African Americans, Mexican Americans, Puerto Ricans and other Caribbeans, and Asian/Pacific Americans—emerge from complex histories rooted in domination, conquest, and colonialism. As such, they need to be understood not only within the U.S. mainstream historical context, but also within the sociopolitical and historical context of each of the groups themselves. That is precisely the major contribution of this text: Each of the authors makes the case that it is not enough simply to add a few poems or short stories or novels to the canon; it is necessary, at the same time, to forge the connection between the lived histories and the current realities of the people represented in the literature. Denying painful and harsh realities will not make them disappear. Although teachers are often reluctant to discuss issues such as oppression and domination in their classrooms, these conversations are unavoidable if we are serious about making room in the curriculum for all our students.

I often ask my graduate students to consider the "So what?" question when reflecting on curriculum, pedagogy, or any other school policy or practice: That is, what does it mean for students in classrooms? How will it influence their education? So what? The chapters in this book speak to this question by making the connection between what Professor Willis, in her Introduction, has so eloquently called the connection between "literacy and freedom."

Opening up the curriculum to a more diverse literature not only enriches all students by giving them a broader perspective; it also provides them with a more complete and honest history in general. Therefore, it seems to me that another dimension of this book that warrants mention is how the authors collectively dare educators to go beyond multicultural literature as a hodgepodge of books unrelated to real life. Instead, educators are challenged to begin the process of multiculturalizing the curriculum by beginning with themselves— questioning their own biases, assumptions, and incomplete knowl- edge—to then take a critical look at their classrooms, communities, and the society in general in order to understand and confront the ideology in which schools are immersed. Too many times, it is an ide- ology that limits the life options of young people based on their race, ethnicity, or social class. It is, in sum, an ideology that must be chal- lenged, and incorporating the stories of those who have been misrep- resented in U.S. literature is a way to begin to do this.

In the end, all students, regardless of their identity, will benefit from this approach. Arlette Willis and her coauthors have written a book that can have an immense impact on students, their teachers, and even the world beyond school walls.

# Chapter 1

# Multicultural Education, Minority Identities, Textbooks, and the Challenge of Curriculum Reform

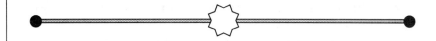

*Cameron R. McCarthy*

While developments have taken place in contemporary popular culture toward a certain radical eclecticism—a postmodern sensibility in the areas of art, architecture, music, and literature that in some ways brazenly absorbs third world and ethnic influences—the school system, particularly the school curriculum, remains steadfastly monolithic. For example, while popular artists such as David Byrne and Paul Simon directly incorporate Afro-Brazilian and South African styles into their music (e.g., their CDs *Rei Momo* and *Graceland*), and while minority artists like Spike Lee, Julie Dash, and the Afro-Asian Black Arts Movement in England have begun to influence new ethnic themes in television and film culture, American educators have responded with a decided lack of enthusiasm for cultural diversity and, at times, with a sense of moral panic to the demands for a ventilation of the school curriculum (O'Connor, 1990). Over the years, this administrative hostility to diversity has propelled minority agitation for multiculturalism in schooling.

Driven forward by demands from racially subordinated groups for fundamental reforms in race relations in education and society, and by the efforts of mainstream educators to provide practical solutions to the problem of racial inequality in the United States, multicultural education emerged in the late 1960s as a powerful challenge to the Eurocentric foundations of the American school curriculum (Pinar, Reynolds, Slatterly, & Taubman, 1995; McCarthy, 1995). Multiculturalism is therefore the product of a particular historical juncture of relations among the state, contending racial groups, educators, and policy intellectuals in the United States that occurred when the discourse about schools became increasingly racialized. From the first, African Americans and other minority groups emphasized a variety of transformative themes, insisting that curriculum and education policy address the vital questions of the distribution of power and representation in schools and the status of minority cultural identities in curriculum organization and arrangements.

It should be understood that minority cultural identities are not fixed or monolithic but multivocal and even contradictory. These identities are indeed "fluid" and are theorized here as the effects and consequences of the historically grounded experiences and practices of oppressed minority groups and the processes by which these practices and experiences come to be represented, reconstructed, and reinvented in daily life, school, the workplace, the electronic media, textbooks, and school curriculum. Minority identities are therefore defined in the context of inter- and intragroup conflicts and in the context of encounters and struggles with dominant White groups.

Within the last two decades the transformative themes in the multicultural movement have been steadily "sucked back into the system" (Swartz, 1990). As departments of education, textbook publishers, and intellectual entrepreneurs pushed more normative themes of cultural understanding and sensitivity training, the actual implementation of an emancipatory multiculturalism in the school curriculum and in pedagogical and teacher education practices in the university has been effectively deferred. (*Emancipatory multiculturalism* is the critical redefinition of school knowledge from the heterogenous perspectives and identities of racially disadvantaged groups—a process that goes beyond the language of "inclusivity" and emphasizes relationality and multivocality as the central intellectual forces in the production of knowledge.) Indeed, within the past few years, there has been a virulent reaffirmation of Eurocentrism and Western culture in debates over the school curriculum and educational reform (Bloom, 1987; Hirsch, 1987; Ravitch, 1990; Herrnstein & Murray, 1994). The dominant school curriculum therefore exists as a powerful symbol of the contemporary American educator's willful retreat from the social and cultural heterogeneous communities that now surround the school in every urban center in this country.

In this chapter, I will situate the topic of multicultural education in the context of current debates over Eurocentrism and "Westernness" and the way in which these discourses are consolidated in the textbooks used in American schools. I will conclude by offering some suggestions for curriculum and educational reform that can help to facilitate an emancipatory multicultural education project and the fostering of minority cultural identities in an American identity.

Educators and textbook publishers have, over the years, directly participated in the trotting out of a particularly cruel fantasy about the story of civilization in general and American society in particular—one in which the only knowledge worth having and the only stories worth telling are associated with the handiworks of the bards of Greece and Rome. Within this frame of reference, art, architecture, music, science, literature, and democracy are portrayed as the fertile products of Europeans and their Caucasian counterparts in the United States. It is, as Aime Cesaire (1983) would say, "a funny little tale to tell." It is, in fact, the essence of our school knowledge. Through the school curriculum and its centerpiece, the textbook, American schoolchildren come to know the world as having been made by European ancestors and White people in general. This world that schoolchildren come to know is overpopulated by minorities and third world people—a world, according to Allan Bloom (1987), "brought to ruination" by these peoples of other lands.

Contemporary conservative writers have sought to reinvigorate these myths. Bloom, for example, maintains in *The Closing of the American Mind* (1987) that it was the protests of African American students and women in the 1960s that brought this country's university system and its curriculum to the present nadir. The reason we are doing so poorly with respect to the Japanese, others maintain, is that we let the underprepared masses into the universities in the 1960s (Herrnstein & Murray, 1994). Others, such as Diane Ravitch (1990), contend that although the American populace is diverse, the primary cultural and institutional coherence that currently exists in our society is unequivocally European in origin. It is the durability of these European values of order, democracy, and tolerance, Ravitch maintains, that has protected "us" from the cultural chaos that afflicts countries in Eastern Europe, the Middle East, Africa, and Asia.

> The political and economic institutions of the United States were deeply influenced by European ideas. Europeans' legacy to us is the set of moral and political values that we Americans subsequently refined and reshaped to enable us, in all our diversity, to live together in freedom and peace. (p. 20)

These kinds of remonstrations get us nowhere beyond nostalgia and its obverse, cynicism. Here we can find no real solace—no new ground to help guide us through the events and challenges of the present era. This rather Philistine reassertion of Eurocentrism and Westernness is itself a wish to run away from the labor of coming to terms with the fundamental historical currents that have shaped this country—a wish to run away from the fundamentally "plural," immigrant, and Afro–New World character that defines historical and current relations between minority and majority groups in the United States (Gates, 1992; Jordan, 1985, 1988). To claim a pristine, unambiguous Westernness as the basis of curriculum organization—as Bloom, Hirsch, Ravitch, and others suggest—is to repress to the dimmest parts of the unconscious a fundamental anxiety about African American and other minority identities and "cultural presence" in the distinctiveness of American life. The point I want to make here is similar to the argument that Toni Morrison (1992) makes about Western literature in her brilliant book, *Playing in the Dark*: There is nothing intrinsically superior or even desirable about the list of cultural items and cultural figures that are celebrated by traditionalists like Hirsch and Bloom.

It should be remembered that at the end of the last century, the English cultural critic Matthew Arnold did not find it fit to include in "the best that has been thought and said" any existing American writer (Arnold, 1888, 1971; Czitrom, 1982). This powerfully reminds us that what is "Western" is not synonymous with what is "American," no matter how much some people may believe this. It also reminds us that the notion of Westernness is a powerful ideological construct—one thoroughly infused with ongoing social struggle over meaning and values (Bernal, 1987). What is Western is therefore highly problematic, as June Jordan (1985) has argued. Do we, for instance, want to say that Ernest Hemingway is in and Toni Morrison is out? Where is the line of "Western" to be drawn within the school curriculum? Where does Westernness end and Americanness begin?

No wonder, then, that schools and universities have been hostile toward the cultural identities of students of African American, Asian/ Pacific American, and Latino backgrounds. No wonder, then, that we are experiencing everywhere in this country what observers are calling a resurgence of racism and intolerance in educational institutions (Giroux, 1996). The school system still effectively marginalizes minority youth in access to instructional opportunity, access to an academic core curriculum, and so on. Our educational institutions are not genuinely multicultural or integrated even at those institutions that are formally desegregated. As Linda Grant (1984, 1985) has shown in her ethnographic studies of desegregated schools, there is de facto segregation at these schools in terms of access to teacher time and the general availability of material resources in the school setting. Yet in terms of organization, the concentration of African American and Latino students in dead-end, nonacademic tracks contributes to their failure and structurally facilitates the disorganization of their identities through a process of selection and labeling that disproportionately designates them as "underachievers" and "at risk."

## The Textbook

Nowhere is this marginalization and suppression of minority cultural identities more evident than in the textbook industry. Minority history is absent in school texts, and emancipatory indigenous scholarship is excluded from the process of textbook production. But changes in the contents of textbooks are only one aspect of what is necessary for meaningful reform toward the goal of a genuine multicultural curriculum and school experience for all students. There is also a need to look at the entire range of elements in the institutional culture of schools, the constraints of and barriers to teacher ingenuity, and the educational priorities set by district offices, building principals, and teacher education programs in the universities. In all these areas, emancipatory multiculturalism, as a form of what Henry Giroux (1985) and George Wood (1985) call *critical literacy*, is now suppressed.

Let us now look at the relationship of the textbook and the text-book industry to multicultural education. Textbooks themselves embody real-life relations of representation, production, and consumption that tend to suppress minority identities and reproduce the inequalities that exist in society. By "representation," I am not simply referring to the presence or absence of pictures of minorities in textbooks. Rather, I mean the whole process of who gets to define whom, when, and how. Who has control over the production of pictures and images in this society? Textbook production is an important dimension of a much broader social and political context in which minorities, women, and the physically and mentally disabled have little control over the process of the production of images of themselves. When incidents like the LAPD's beating of Rodney King occur, for example, Black people do not have equal access to the media to tell their side of the story. So too in the case of textbooks.

In an essay entitled "Placing Women in History: Definitions and Challenges" (1975), feminist historian Gerda Lerner maintains that, with respect to the treatment of women, contemporary textbooks present "compensatory" or "contribution" histories of the experiences of women in the United States. By *compensatory history*, Lerner means that dominant history textbooks tend to identify and single out what she calls "women worthies." The kind of history of notable women celebrates the achievements of individuals such as Jane Addams, Elizabeth Cady Stanton, or Harriet Tubman. But history of this kind still tends to marginalize the broad masses of minority and working class women. As such, these compensatory textbooks, while more inclusive than earlier books, are not exemplars of emancipatory or transformative scholarship.

This notion of compensatory history is also pertinent to the treatment of minorities in textbooks. In history, social studies, literature, and other discipline-based textbooks, minorities are added into an existing "order of things" (Foucault, 1970). Half a page here and half a page there discusses slavery, Harriet Tubman, or "The Peaceful Warrior," Martin Luther King, Jr. There is no systematic reworking or restructuring of school knowledge, no attempt to present history from an alternative, minority perspective. This fragmentary approach is also evident in the treatment of the peoples of Africa, Latin America, and Asia. For instance, the editors of *Interracial Books for Children Bulletin*

(1982), in an in-depth review of a "representative sample" of 71 social studies textbooks used in the 1980s in American schools, report the following:

> Central America is entirely omitted from many of the most common world geography, history, and "cultures" textbooks used in U.S. classrooms. Thirty-one U.S. history texts were checked for their coverage of Central America. Seven of these do not even mention Central America. Fifteen texts limit coverage of Central America to the building of the Panama Canal, and most of these books ignore or mention only in passing the U.S. military intervention that led to the acquisition of the canal. . . . Not one of the 31 texts discusses the continuing involvement of the U.S. government—sometimes overt, sometimes covert—in Central America. (pp. 2–3)

The U.S. imperialistic presence in Latin America is often narrated in a highly mythological discourse in which the U.S emerges as the good Samaritan. The natives of South America cannot do without our "help." U.S. paternalism is not only what the Latin Americans want, it is what is needed "down there" to keep hostile foreign powers from swallowing up the region and threatening "us":

> For a long time, the United States has been interested in Latin America. First, we have a large trade with our Latin American neighbors. They send us products that we need and enjoy, such as tin, copper, coffee, bananas and chocolate. In turn, their people buy many products from the United States. Second, the United States has tried to keep the Americas free from foreign control. If a strong and unfriendly nation controlled the nations near us, it would be a threat to the safety of the United States. (Schwartz & Connor, 1986, p. 39)

This highly ethnocentric approach to textbook history and social studies is stabilized by a language of universality and objectivity. In this way, the textbook is a central site for the preservation of a selective tradition in the school curriculum—one that pushes minorities and third world peoples to the outside, to the edge, to the point of deviance. But perhaps the most pernicious feature of this dominant approach to school knowledge and textbook preparation is the tendency to avoid complexity and conflict. For example, in King and

Anderson's *America: Past and Present* (1980), a fifth-grade social studies text used in Wisconsin's elementary schools, the only sustained discussion of the experiences of African Americans is in the context of slavery. But even the topic of slavery is treated in a perfunctory manner, and the relations between Whites and Blacks on the slave plantation is described in benign terms, free of the violence that characterized the slaves' daily existence. Complete with supporting illustrations of "life on the plantation" that makes it look like a California wine orchard with the slaves living comfortably and snugly in their cabins, the authors of *America: Past and Present* describe life on the plantation in the following terms:

> On any plantation you visited in the South you would find that all of the farm workers were black slaves. Southern plantations came to depend on slavery. By 1750 there were more slaves than free people in South Carolina. On the plantation you visit, the slaves live in cabins near the fields. Since the slaves get no money for their work, they depend on their owners for clothes and food. The food is mostly salt pork and corn. Some of the slaves have tiny plots of land where they can grow vegetables. (pp. 149–150).

It is interesting to compare this description with the writings of indigenous authors such as Vincent Harding in *There Is a River* (1983), or C. L. R. James in *The Black Jacobins* (1963). For example, in his discussion of slavery in Haiti, James draws on this eyewitness account:

> A Swiss traveler has left a famous description of a gang of slaves at work. "They were about a hundred men and women of different ages, all occupied in digging ditches in a cane-field, the majority of them naked or covered with rags. The sun shone down with full force on their heads. . . . A mournful silence reigned. Exhaustion was stamped on every face, but the hour of rest had not yet come. The pitiless eye of the Manager patrolled the gang and several foremen armed with long whips moved periodically between them, giving stinging blows to all who, worn out by fatigue, were compelled to take a rest—men or women, young or old." This was no isolated picture. The sugar plantations demanded an exacting and ceaseless labour. (p. 10)

Harding, on the other hand, draws attention to another dimension of plantation life that is normally given short shrift in the history textbooks used in our schools: Black liberation struggles. He makes the following contention about the impact of these struggles on the planter-mercantile class in colonial America:

> But it was not in Virginia and South Carolina alone, not only among white Southern society, that the fear of a black quest for freedom existed; the same attitude permeated much of Northern colonial life. In the Northern colonies blacks had already given evidence of their struggle for freedom. As early as 1657 Africans and Indians in Hartford "joined in an uprising and destroyed some buildings" in the settlement. Such incidents were regularly repeated. (p. 31)

In sharp contrast to the works of Harding and James, the bland, nonconflictual writing that one finds in many textbooks is in part the product of a highly routinized approach to textbook production. As publishers work to maximize markets and profits, textbook writing has become increasingly more of an assembly-line process in which multiple authors produce submissions that are checked for quality control, readability, and overly conflictual issues by keen editorial staffs (Apple, 1993). When the textbook finally becomes a finished product, it is often uninteresting and unchallenging to students and teachers alike. By bargaining away issues that might offend state adoption committees and conservative interest groups, publishers and textbook writers contribute to the marginalization of cultural diversity and the suppression of minority history and identities in textbooks.

## Multicultural Reform

As I indicated earlier, the textbook is only one aspect of a broad set of practices that impact on the institutional environment of the school. School critics and government officials are now talking about curriculum reform without recognizing the pivotal role of the classroom teacher. Thus, curriculum reform proposals such as "critical thinking," "scientific literacy," and "problem solving in mathematics" are coming from the outside—researchers, politicians, and the business sector—to teachers as slogans, in some cases already packaged and teacher-proof (Apple, 1996). No matter how well meaning many of these new proposals are, there is a real risk of the loss of teacher autonomy in the classroom.

Mobilization for multicultural education reform must therefore follow a very different path. Initiatives in the area of multicultural education must be situated in the context of broad structural and organizational reform in schooling. In most urban centers in this country, teachers presently work in school settings in which one or more of the following is true:

1. They are underpaid (McCarthy, 1990a, 1995).
2. The principal, except in a number of exemplary circumstances, is subject to enormous administrative demands that impact on his or her effectiveness as an instructional leader. Excessive administrative demands directly limit the building principal's involvement in instructional improvement, whether it relates to critical thinking, multiculturalism, or some other curriculum reform (McCarthy & Schrag, 1990).
3. There is considerable institutional isolation. Teachers complain of not having the time to meet and plan, and such collaboration is not explicitly encouraged or materially supported (McCarthy, 1990a). Consequently, there is little peer supervision or collegiality.
4. Despite the rhetoric of "restructuring," school district offices are driven by a narrow concept of excellence, accountability, and educational achievement. Critical issues such as the need for multicultural reform in education are not given priority status (McCarthy & Schrag, 1990).

Of course, it is important to recognize, as Steven Purkey and Robert Rutter (1987) argue, that not all urban schools are beset by these barriers to critical teaching and learning. Some schools do have dynamic and progressive learning environments in which teachers pursue critical and emancipatory goals (Bastian, Fruchter, Gittell, Greer, & Haskins, 1986; Apple, 1996). But in a general sense, it can be said that educators in urban centers in this country have been presented with a crisis of legitimacy concerning the project of multicultural reform. In a society where the government has clearly reneged on the promise of racial equality made during the Kennedy and Johnson administrations, educators are being bombarded with new and contradictory demands. They are being asked to generate an ethos of harmony and equality while simultaneously having to respond to increasing governmental pressure to foster competitive individualism in schools. This emphasis on competition is reflected in the dominant role of standardized testing in pedagogical practices and the narrow range of classroom knowledge that is actually taught in the urban classroom setting. Teachers feel compelled to be conservative about what they teach, and multiculturalism, in this context, is regarded as a "supplement" to a school curriculum that is oriented toward "the basics."

In other ways, too, the federal policy in the last two decades of cutting back on financial support for the education and overall social welfare of low-income students has sent a message that has been destructive for the education of minorities. The message is, "To hell with equality. We want to compete with the Japanese." In a period when resources are becoming scarce, the gap between winners and losers is widening. Black and Latino youth have fallen victim to a system that says, "You are not a priority. You do not really matter." These developments are part of the bitter legacy of the Reagan and Bush era. In many respects, however, the Clinton administration has not offered any respite from the pattern of disinvestment in the urban centers that was initiated by Richard Nixon.

Ironically, all this is occurring at the same time that school populations are becoming more ethnically diverse. In the largest school systems in the country, the majority of students are now minorities ("Here they come," 1986; Hacker, 1995). Indeed, current demographic projections indicate that by the third decade of the 21st century, a third of the American population will be minorities. This demographic change raises profound questions about school knowledge—particularly, the wisdom of maintaining dominance of a Eurocentric curriculum in our educational institutions. The Eurocentric curriculum is, in a manner of speaking, being overtaken by events. These developments should not lead to paralysis but to action for comprehensive reform in schooling. Multiculturalist proponents should not merely focus on curriculum content but should introduce broader brush strokes of educational reform that would promote structural reorganization in schooling. Such structural reorganization should involve as a first priority the restoration of the professional space of the teacher and the full integration of, and guarantee of equality of access to instructional opportunity for, minority and underprivileged children. For the multicultural curriculum to be fully realized in the school, the following specific initiatives are absolutely critical:

1. Preservice teacher education programs at universities and colleges across the country must systematically incorporate critical multicultural objectives into their curricula and field experiences.

2. School districts and school principals must set diversity as an explicit goal and seek ways to integrate it into the organization of the curriculum and the institutional life of the schools. Right now multiculturalism is treated as a side topic that is mentioned only during Black History Month and on International Women's Day.

3. Multiculturalism should not be limited to the present understanding that all we need to do is to add some content about minorities and women to the standard curriculum. Multiculturalism must involve a radical rethinking of the nature of school knowledge as fundamentally relational and heterogeneous in character. In this sense, for example, we cannot fully understand the Civil Rights Movement in the United States without studying its effects on the expansion of democratic practices to excluded groups in Australia, the Caribbean, Africa, and England as well as in the United States itself. For that matter, we cannot properly understand the development of European societies without a full understanding of the direct link between Europe's development and the underdevelopment of the third world. For example, at the time that the French were helping to bankroll the American Revolution, two thirds of France's export earnings were coming from its exploitation of sugar cane plantations in Haiti (James, 1963).

4. Such a reworking of school knowledge must go a step further toward a reconsideration of the privileging of Eurocentric perspectives in the curriculum as reflected in, for example, the "famous men" approach to history. The new multicultural curriculum must go beyond the "language of inclusion" toward a "language of critique" (Giroux, 1985, 1996). This would centrally involve the affir-

mation of minority identities and perspectives as the organizing principles for school knowledge. In this manner, schools would be sites for multicultural curriculum reform and pedagogical practices that are truly liberating.

5. Teachers must be centrally involved in reworking the curriculum and reorganizing the school in ways that give them a sense of professional autonomy and ownership of curriculum changes.

6. There is a vital need to revise the K–12 exam system in this country that now places an overwhelming emphasis on standardized, multiple-choice, and short-answer tests. Also, it is absolutely critical that these exams begin to reflect the emphasis on multiculturalism that I have argued for in this chapter. At present, there is little incentive for teachers to teach and for students to learn more about minorities and women if these topics are not reflected in testing.

7. Concerning textbooks, there is a need to involve minority and third world scholars and teachers in the production of school knowledge in the textbook industry at every level—from textbook writing right through to editorial and managerial decision making.

8. Finally, let me return to a theme that I stressed elsewhere at the beginning of this chapter: *The multicultural ethos in schools will only be fully realized when minority and underprivileged students have access to an academic core curriculum on par with their middle-class and White counterparts.*

Multicultural curriculum reform must therefore mean that we think about all these things. It should not simply mean incremental changes in curriculum content but should involve a wider scope of educational, pedagogical, and curriculum reforms. These reforms should help to enhance the participation of minority scholars and classroom teachers in the production of school knowledge rooted in minority cultural identities and to facilitate equal access to an academic core curriculum (that is critical as well as multicultural) for minority and underprivileged youth, who are now significantly excluded from these critical educational experiences.

## Summary

In this chapter I have sought to call attention to the urgent need to rethink the current privileging of Eurocentric ideas in our contemporary American school curriculum. I believe that this Eurocentric emphasis is misplaced in light of the rapid diversification now taking place in school populations all across the United States. A fundamental place to start rethinking is the school textbook and the entire process of textbook production. Nevertheless, this is not enough to ensure that our students will have a genuinely emancipatory multicultural experience in schooling. As I have maintained, multiculturalism must involve a wider range of educational change that addresses the professional needs of the classroom teacher and the burning issue of equality of access for minorities to the academic curriculum. The needs of teachers and minority students must be understood as critical organizing principles in the movement toward multicultural curriculum reform as we enter the 21st century.

## References

Apple, M. (1993). *Official knowledge: Democratic education in a conservative age.* New York: Routledge.

Apple, M. (1996). *Cultural politics and education.* New York: Teachers College Press.

Arnold, M. (1888). *Civilization in the United States: First and last impressions of America.* Boston: Cupples & Hurd.

Arnold, M. (1971). *Culture and anarchy.* Indianapolis, IN: Bobbs-Merrill.

Bastian, A., Fruchter, N., Gittell, M., Greer, C., & Haskins, K. (1986). *Choosing equality.* Philadelphia: Temple University Press.

Bernal, M. (1987). *Black Athena: The Afroasiatic roots of classical civilization: Vol. 1. The fabrication of ancient Greece 1785–1985.* New Brunswick, NJ: Rutgers University Press.

Bloom, A. (1987). *The closing of the American mind.* New York: Simon & Schuster.

Central America: What U.S. educators need to know. (1982). *Interracial Books for Children Bulletin, 3,* 2–3.

Cesaire, A. (1983). *The collected poetry.* (C. Eselman & A. Smith, Trans.) Berkeley, CA: University of California Press.

Clayton, R. (1971). *Mexico, Central America, and the West Indies*. London: John Day.

Czitrom, D. (1982). *Media and the American mind: From Morse to McLuhan*. Chapel Hill, NC: University of North Carolina Press.

Foucault, M. (1970). *The order of things: An archeology of the human sciences*. New York: Pantheon.

Gates, H. (1992). *Loose canons: Notes on the culture wars*. New York: Oxford University Press.

Giroux, H. (1985). Introduction. In P. Freire, *The politics of education*. Boston: Bergin & Garvey.

Giroux, H. (1996). *White noise: Racial politics and the pedagogy of Whiteness*. Unpublished manuscript, State College, University of Pennsylvania.

Grant, C., & Sleeter, C. (1989). *Turning on learning: Five approaches for mulitcultural teaching plans for race, class, gender, and disability*. Columbus: Merrill.

Grant, L. (1984). Black females "place" in desegregated classrooms. *Sociology of Education, 57*, 98–111.

Grant, L. (1985). *Uneasy alliances: Black males, teachers, and peers in desegregated classrooms*. Unpublished manuscript.

Hacker, A. (1995). *Two nations: Black and White, separate, hostile, unequal*. New York: Ballantine Books.

Harding, V. (1983). *There is a river*. New York: Vintage.

Here they come ready or not: An *Education Week* special report on the ways in which America's population in motion is changing the outlook for schools and society. (1986, May 14). *Education Week*, pp. 14–28.

Herrnstein, R., & Murray, C. (1994). *The bell curve*. New York: Free Press.

Hirsch, E. D. (1987). *Cultural literacy: What every American needs to know*. Boston: Houghton Mifflin.

James, C. L. R. (1963). *The Black Jacobins*. New York: Vintage.

Jordan, J. (1985). *On call: Political essays*. Boston: South End Press.

Jordan, J. (1988). Nobody means more to me than you and the future life of Willie Jordan. *Harvard Educational Review, 58*(2), 363–374.

King, D., & Anderson, C. (1980). *America: Past and present*. Boston: Houghton Mifflin.

Lerner, G. (1975). Placing women in history: Definitions and challenges. *Feminist Studies, 3*(1–2), 5–15.

McCarthy, C. (1988). Reconsidering liberal and radical perspectives on racial inequality in schooling. *Harvard Educational Review, 58*(2), 265–279.

McCarthy, C. (1990a). *Being there: A math collaborative and the challenge of teaching mathematics in the urban classroom*. Magnolia, WI: Wisconsin Center for Educational Research.

McCarthy, C. (1990b) *Race and curriculum*. London: Falmer Press.

McCarthy, C. (1995). The problem of origins: Race and the contrapuntal nature of the educational experience. *Education/Pedagogy and Cultural Studies, 17*(1), 87–105.

McCarthy, C., & Apple, M. (1988). Race, class and gender in American educational research: Towards a nonsynchronous parallelist position. *Perspectives in Education, 4*(2), 67–69.

McCarthy, C., & Schrag, F. (1990). Departmental and principal leadership in promoting higher order thinking. *Journal of Curriculum Studies, 22*(6), 529–543.

Morrison, T. (1989). Unspeakable things unspoken: The Afro-American presence in American literature. *Michigan Quarterly Review, 38*(1), 1–34.

Morrison, M. (1992). *Playing in the dark: Whiteness and the literary imagination*. Cambridge, MA: Harvard University Press

O'Connor, J. (1990, April 29). On TV, less separate, more equal. *The New York Times* (Arts & Leisure), p. 1.

Pinar, W., Reynolds, W., Slatterly, P., and Taubman, L. (1995). *Understanding curriculum*. New York: Peter Lang.

Purkey, S., & Rutter, R. (1987). High school teaching: Teacher practices and beliefs in urban and suburban public schools. *Education Policy, 1*(3), 375–393.

Ravitch, D. (1990). Diversity and democracy: Multicultural education in America. *American Educator, 14*(1), 16–48.

Schwartz, M., & Connor, J. (1986). *Exploring American history*. New York: Globe.

Swartz, E. (1990). *Cultural diversity and the school curriculum: Context and practice*. Paper presented at the Annual Meeting of the American Educational Research Association, Boston.

Viadero, D. (1989, May 24). Schools witness a troubling revival of bigotry. *Education Week*, p. 1.

Will, G. (1989, December 18). Eurocentricity and the school curriculum. *Morning Advocate*, p. 3.

Wood, G. (1985). Schooling in a democracy: Transformation or reproduction. In F. Rizvi (Ed.), *Multiculturalism as an educational policy* (pp. 91–111). Geelong, Victoria, Australia: Deakin University Press.

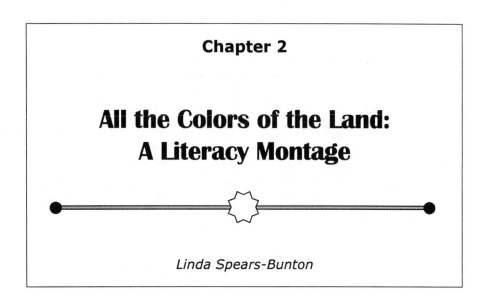

# Chapter 2

# All the Colors of the Land: A Literacy Montage

*Linda Spears-Bunton*

## Teaching the Heart and the Head: The Village Transforms Pedagogy

Teaching literature through multicultural perspectives is logical as well as eloquent if our aim is to transform classrooms, schools, society, and individual minds and hearts. If our sights are on the higher ground—knowledge, understanding, honorable pedagogy, and sustained learning and literacy practices—multicultural literature experiences point us toward that higher ground. Sharing story experiences, listening, and trying to understand textual and extratextual referents involve cognitive and affective choices that set the stage for transformed ways of seeing the world and possibilities for enhanced learning, literacy, and living. Transformation makes continual personal demands on our time, our ways with words, and our choices; it is a conscientiously critical and creative process.

Quintessentially different from reforming what is and what has always been, transformation necessitates an informed willingness to take risks. Poignant challenges of reified knowledge and taken-for-granted assumptions are critical to the transformation process. For example, if I reform or reshape a piece of tin, I can make it something externally different, aesthetically pleasing, and intellectually stimulating. Yet the chemical composition of the tin will remain unchanged. Transformation seeks to change not only the shape of institutions and their attendant ritualized race, gender, and class behaviors but also the social fabric that created those institutions and sanctioned those behaviors in the first place. Shifts in the locus of control are reasonable but not seamless because transformation involves the replacement of ineffective and inequitable elements in our social, political, educational, and ethical fabric with chemically different elements. These include (a) a disposition to develop multiple literacies in teachers and students, (b) equitable and regular participation in literacy activities, (c) partnerships in the meaning-making process, and (d) a respect for honoring difference. Within the community, these are created and constantly evaluated for their effectiveness in elevating society as a whole and in assisting individual members of society in the quest to transcend the boundaries of class, race, gender, ignorance, hopelessness, learned helplessness, and institutional short-sightedness.

Transformation speaks for inclusion; it garners an expansive, critical literacy intent upon empowering readers to engage in respectful and scholarly discourse about reading the "word and reading the world" (Freire, 1986). Multicultural literature study is inherently transformative; it can be the great equalizer rather than the center of the great divide. Multicultural literature speaks with the voices inscribed by the infinite boundaries of human possibilities—the stories of humanity as told by itself. It is necessary and sufficient if American school children are to be grounded in the principles of a democratically organized society.

Notable by-products of transformation in minds, hearts, and curricula minimally include the following: (a) demonstrably more teacher work, (b) more actively engaged learners in more diverse intellectual learning environments, (c) more reading, writing, thinking, listening, and speaking, (d) more choices, and (e) fundamental changes. Perhaps the inexorable movement toward valuing all humanity and the knowledge we create, combined with the requisite and perennial learning, reading, questioning, and unlearning, leads to resistance to transformation. Resistance narrows and obscures the path; it inhibits literacy acquisition and promotes retrogressive social action. Resistance limits the aptitude of the village to come together, raise our children, and move forward toward habits of mind and heart that encourage literacy and reward inquiry with civility and honesty. Multicultural literature should cause learners to consider perspectives, values, possibilities, and dreams of others while simultaneously reseeing and repositioning the image we have constructed of ourselves. This can be disquieting for ideologies based on dominance.

## Voices From the Bottom: Canons on the Deck

Consider the canon, the officially sanctioned set of literary texts judged to be standard and universal. Historically charged with the responsibility of transmitting cultural history and perpetuating the dominant culture's attendant suppositions of morality, aesthetics, and traditions (Applebee, 1974, 1996), the canon has been assiduously guarded. Its composition has been defined and delineated by those who rule, who traditionally have not been people of color or women. There was little impetus to seriously consider the cultural perspective of "Others" (Morrison, 1992). The multicultural debate is part of the process of challenging hegemony and moving toward a more honest and egalitarian curriculum that befits a democratically organized society. The classics—presented in class anthologies, from the Planters and Puritans to Hemingway, and in Great Books— represent one version of American values, aesthetics, ethics, and truth. Students and teachers may read these texts and wonder where African American, Asian/Pacific American, Latino, and Native American people were living and what they have been doing since the birth of our nation; students may graduate from high school and college without ever hearing the voices of the "Others." Curricular invisibility and marginalization of people of color and women may not appear problematic to dominant members because the canon, as the singular or majority "text" in school curricula, is a persuasive agent of cultural and intellectual domination, restricting all learners to a narrow view of the world (Freire & Macedo, 1994). Speaking with the voice of those who have conquered, the canon has the power and the presumed authority to silence and to exclude the majority of minority voices (Anyon, 1983; Apple, 1982).

Nevertheless, reading, interpreting, and analyzing diverse literary texts and making judgments about the appropriateness of the behaviors of fictive characters are important skills of empowered and critically literate readers. Moreover, exploring a multiplicity of cultural perspectives and participating in cultural exchanges adds to readers' repertoire of responses about books, differences, and people and leads to an expanded literacy (Au, 1993; hooks, 1994). So what is the problem? Why isn't everyone who is interested in the development of higher order literacy enthusiastically transforming English and Language Arts curricula? Why do some teachers fret that students might be missing something if they explore the theme of coming of age, identity, and courage by reading Parks' *A Choice of Weapons* (1986), Anaya's *Bless Me, Ultima* (1972), George's *The Talking Earth* (1983), Santiago's *When I Was Puerto Rican* (1993), Wharton's *Summer* (1979), and Namioka's *April and the Dragon Lady* (1994)? The possibility that such a multicultural unit of study might be a watered-down curriculum is a very real concern to many teachers with traditional, canonical English backgrounds. Implicit in this issue is the relationship between power groups and conflicting ideologies in our society (Baker, 1988; Freire, 1986; Freire and Macedo, 1994; Gates, 1992; Rabinowitz, 1987). Knowledge created and formalized by minority groups in daily living and in literary texts may be seen as embodying less value, meaning, or intellectual rigor than knowledge formalized by elite groups. Nevertheless, multicultural curricula extend access to literacy and, critically important, expand the quantity and quality of literacy and literature learning (Applebee, 1996; Au, 1993; Dyson, 1993; Spears-Bunton, 1996).

## Affective Dialectics and Reader Response

Multicultural literature expands the definition of basic literacy because readers engage in multiple images and perspectives with which to think, dream, and play. Multicultural-literature experiences instill the disposition in communities of readers to weigh new knowledge against old knowledge, taken-for-granted assumptions and to question the attitudes and behaviors that accompany reified knowledge.

Multicultural-literature experiences situate readers to respectfully consider (and reconsider) the world views and human exigencies of others. A multicultural perspective labels no part of humanity as trivial; it unsilences humanity's voices, and it seeks and welcomes opportunities to include and honor diverse cultural ways of creating knowledge and metaphorical ways of understanding (Pugh, Hicks & Davis, 1997).

Affective reader response can initiate powerful meaning formations for individual respondents and a community of readers. The notion of cultural consciousness establishes a distinction between being talked to and being talked about. "Talked about" implies a one-way monologue—that is, being seen through the eyes of others, which offers an inadequate and distorted self-consciousness (DuBois, 1961). In the traditional canon, people of color and women are described and talked about by others. For example, Morrison (1992) has argued that

> the presence of Blackness in America has fed white literary imaginations for centuries. For the most part, the literature of the United States has taken as its concern the architecture of a new white man. . . . Playing in the dark, the constructed white man is able to position himself against a choked Africanist presence. Black characters exist at the pleasure of and to serve the needs of their white creators; rarely do the characters in these texts express their vision of the world in ways that reflect an authentic Blackness. (p. 15)

Being "talked to" suggests a dialogue—an exchange of ideas, feelings, and responses; it is an interactive relationship with shared understandings and references. Gaps, or information that the narrator or storyteller leaves out, may be filled in culturally appropriate or inappropriate ways (Genette, 1980; Steffensen, Joag-Dev, & Anderson, 1979). However, both appropriate and inappropriate cultural extensions of a literary text provide teaching and learning occasions for extending readers' cultural knowledge, especially among a community of readers that is managed by a teacher who actively encourages student discourse. In teaching to transform the curriculum, it is necessary to consistently seek ways to explore conflicts and contradictions with students, not to silence or intimidate them but to make conflict the subject of debate and learning.

Clearly, the practice of mentioning "Others" only at a specific time, such as Black History Month, and occasionally adding *a little something* African American, Asian/Pacific American, Caribbean, Hispanic or Latino, and Native American, is innocuous. Regularly occurring, shared, and respectful discourses tend to make plain the sometimes rough places inherent in our society of social, cultural, racial, gender, and class differences. A transformed curriculum defines "Others" as all humanity—the simultaneous symphony and cacophony of the human voice across time and space. The goal of a transformed curriculum is to help novice learners learn to learn, read, write, and think independently and use that knowledge to embrace and rescue humanity. Clearly, the teacher is a critical element in the journey toward curricular transformation. It is equally clear that a teacher who has claimed personal responsibility and a scholarly approach toward learning offers the best opportunity for adolescents to become empowered readers and learners.

# Teaching Multicultural Literature: The Teacher's Dilemma

The current educational debate focusing on the interrelationship of culture, literature, and literacy places English teachers in the center of two interrelated ancient debates: (a) what literature to teach, how to teach it, and how to get schoolchildren to read, learn, think independently, and love reading; and (b) the unresolved contradictions of a society that is founded on the ideology of human equality and democracy yet grounded in conflicting perceptions of race, class, and gender. Despite our best intentions and improvements, America is a raced and gendered society. Yet the traditional canon gives scant attention to issues that have powerfully shaped our nation's artistic, social, economic, and political ideologies, and it continues to influence the ways that we think about and treat people whom we define as "Others." Moreover, the social positioning of European Americans as an elite yet "unraced" group of people severely limits their attempts to understand the world and an individual's place within it (Frakenburg, 1993; Powell, 1996; Weiler, 1988). Within the multicultural debate, this very social positioning may also silence or obscure European American voices (Beach, 1997; Spears-Bunton, 1992). That is, while the effects of a monocultural curriculum upon students of color are rather obvious, there is a danger of overlooking the needs of the socially stratified elite to examine, articulate, and analyze issues that are complex and, for many, frightening. As an institution within American society, racism affects the oppressor as well as the oppressed. Overcoming historical and contemporary racist attitudes and dispositions requires cross-cultural knowledge, multiple experiences, a good deal of self-reflection, and an astute and courageous teacher/ambassador.

The notion of race is a powerful social and political force woven into the fabric and consciousness of American society. The United States is a racialized society in the sense that people are described and defined in language, law, and social policy in racial terms. Relationships between people are partially determined by our perception of what we think the other person is. A drop of African blood, for example, can be socially and politically important because we have been socialized to "know" the difference between racial groups and have internalized these differences into our cognitive processes (Aboud & Skerry, 1984; Rothenberg, 1988; Rotheram & Phinney, 1987). *Racialization* subjectifies "race" because it is based on the belief that the distinctive characteristics found in human beings determine their respective cultures and circumscribe their humanity (DuBois, 1961; Giroux, 1993).

The issue of cultural inclusiveness in course curricula has added responsibility and anxiety for overburdened English teachers, who must teach large numbers of students in small spaces and time slots and graduate or promote most of the students. Central to the multicultural debate is the issue that we can no longer accept in ourselves, our students, or our curricula, the taken-for-granted assumptions about our culture or about those we have learned to see as "Others" (hooks, 1994; Morrison, 1992). English teachers are charged by state, local, and commonsense mandates to construct and mediate literature curricula in an intelligent and equitable manner. Seldom is there "down time" for teachers to close shop and relearn, rethink, and retool curricula and pedagogy; rarely is there adequate support (i.e., material and human resources).

These issues are critical when we consider that our educational histories have led us across thousands of pages wherein we have read, memorized, and analyzed the literature and histories of the canon. We can argue earnestly that American English teachers have been sorely miseducated. However, arguing will not supplement our knowledge of the literature, culture, and history of marginalized Americans, nor will such arguments alone help teachers and students to negotiate the contradictions of race, class, and gender inherent in society and our classrooms. The task seems akin to building bricks without straw for the many teachers who want to construct symmetry in the curriculum because they believe that reading, thinking, and examining taken-for-granted assumptions about the "word and the world" can nurture fundamentally different human interactions that are based on respect, knowledge, and compassion.

Giroux (1993) argues that a critical ingredient for the success of understanding and managing multicultural curricula will by necessity include a critical examination of the issues of

> whiteness as a mark of racial and gender privilege, and raising the emotionally charged question of whether people are speaking within or outside a privileged space, and whether such spaces provide the conditions for different groups to listen to each other differently in order to address how racial economies of privilege and power work in this society (pp. 60–61).

Across the nation, we hear committed and talented teachers assert that they do not know where or how to begin.

Clearly, we must change the way we go about educating American citizens; yet because minority and majority Americans experience life so differently, each of us will engage in the problem with different needs, perspectives, and knowledge bases. Such differences are necessary, and treating these differences as subjects for reflection and scholarship is critical for the process and product of teacher learning. Teacher learning drives and sustains pedagogy and curriculum design. The paradigm for an antihegemonic response—rereading the "word and the world"—is established by the teachers who claim empowerment and authority for themselves, value the content of their learning and reading, and invite students into the process of constructing knowledge.

# Moving Mountains Out of Your Way: Teacher, Reader, and Scholar

A teacher's reasons for transforming the English curriculum must be both professional and personal because literature and literacy education is like a mirror and a window: We need to look in, as with a mirror, and out at the world, as through a wide window (Whaley & Dodge, 1993). Thus, it is important to make a self-assessment about what you know about African American, Asian/Pacific American, Latino, and Native American peoples. Concurrently, it is necessary to critically examine the source(s) of your prior knowledge. A simple way to begin is to survey the books, magazines, newspapers, works of art, and music in your home. Consider the films and television shows you watch and examine them for the kinds of images they present about people of color. Look at your network of friends and acquaintances and the social and cultural activities in which you regularly participate; examine this network in light of the ways in which it influences how you read the "word and the world."

Second, the teacher needs to make definitive plans to increase his or her knowledge of people of color, people whose first language is not standard Americanized English, and their literature. These plans need to be both long- and short-term, with a view toward increasing knowledge in discernible stages. One way to do this is to maintain a teacher reading and learning log. This log should be annotated with personal reflections on new reading and learning as well as notes of ideas for teaching. For example, if your home survey indicates that there are few books by and about African Americans, and your magazine and journal subscriptions do not include publications by African Americans, you've learned something important about your choices, and remedies are readily available.

It is important to recognize that the literary canons of people of color are vast and ever growing. Thus, it is easy to become overwhelmed unless you have a plan because you simply cannot read everything and at the same time teach. Begin where you are as an individual and a scholar. For example, if you are a woman, and you want to learn about Latino people and literature, begin by reading women's literature from these cultures. Similarly, if you have a passion for folklore, science fiction, mystery, poetry, drama, or short stories, immerse yourself in these genres from a different cultural perspective. In this way, you can enter worlds different from your own but at the same time use your knowledge of women or a certain genre as an initial reference point.

Many teachers are hesitant about teaching multicultural literature because they recognize that their educational and reading histories are limited, and they argue that one cannot teach what one does not know. I would argue that while it is not possible to teach what you do not know, it is certainly possible to teach what you are learning. I would argue further that shared learning among students and teachers enlivens and validates the learning and teaching enterprise. Chapters 3–8 in this book include titles that have been used and are recommended for use by secondary teachers.

Third, a teacher needs to make a conscious and conscientious commitment to transforming his or her classroom. For example, teachers new to infusing their curriculum with multicultural literature might begin with a focus on a single class, and within that class particular kinds of events—for example, literature teaching, learning, and response. The affective dimensions of response—specifically, readers' volition and motivation for engaging in or resisting the world of the text when juxtaposed against the cultural knowledge of self and others—are the ways in which the classroom teacher can address social and racial discontinuity through assigned class texts and classroom interactions.

## Curricular Transformation: Beginning Steps

There are three identifiable steps toward combating ignorance and transforming the curriculum. First, solicit recommendations for books that will provide background knowledge; these should include both fiction and nonfiction. Read for yourself as a scholar seeking knowledge and satisfaction; read as a teacher searching for suitable materials for your class. Select texts for teaching that provide the kinds of information and reading experiences you are seeking for your students. For example, many teachers assert, "I want them to feel and to understand what life was like in these circumstances at this time. Besides, I really like this one." (Caution: Examine your likes and dislikes.) A teacher's personal excitement about discovery—joy in learning—and the quality of the teacher's reading experiences become a critical and shared ingredient in the dynamics of the class.

Second, vow that you and your students will be better read and more knowledgeable at the end of this school year and even more so at the end of the next year. From the first day of school, share your excitement about your summer reading and learning with your students. Tell them they are going to study African American, Asian/Pacific American, Caribbean, Latino, Native American, and the traditional canonical literature in their textbooks. Speak directly and confidently. Make note of the students' responses; develop a system for "kid watching."

Third, share your reading and child-watching experiences within a small community. For example, you might utilize a free period for adult book-talk and verbalized reflections on the students, school, and community. Over time, this community can become a safe haven from troubled waters, providing emotional support, intellectual stimulation, and often comic relief.

By defining ignorance as a consequence of being improperly taught, teachers are able to situate the problem in a context that we understand well and that provides us with the autonomy and the authority for resolution. That is, if we as teachers reason that the teacher, not the text, is the final authority in the design and implementation of the curriculum, then we are empowered to adapt and to interpret the curriculum according to personal preferences, emerging learning, and the needs of the students. By situating multicultural literature centrally in the English curriculum, the classroom can become a site for individuals to act as agents for social change against a historical background of racial and sexual segregation, paternalism, and silence.

## Stepping to a Literate Tomorrow: Multicultural Lessons for Teachers

At many schools there is a subtle and contradictory mandate to avoid the mention of cultural or racial differences. It is understandable that in any school struggling against racial stigmatization, mentioning racial or cultural distinctions may be perceived as inviting conflict. What seems to be missing from this rationale, however, is rather obvious. Conflicts exist, simmer, and occasionally erupt, yet rarely are people given a scholarly opportunity to examine, discuss, and analyze their causes. Rather, people of color and European American people have lived side by side for several centuries and sometimes imitate each other in selective ways, but often they have skewed knowledge about each other. We need to realize that it is difficult to have respect and compassion for the human spirit that is clothed differently from ourselves without knowledge of the "Other's " song in his or her own voice. People need to be taught how to intellectually engage in conflict and contradiction and must be provided with models and multiple opportunities to practice and share what they are thinking, learning, and feeling. A multicultural curriculum demystifies the "race card" and robs it of its power to confuse and divide.

Transforming the curriculum occurs in overlapping frames rather than as fixed events. The process begins with a recognition of ignorance, a commitment to change, and the realization that it is neither necessary nor desirable to give up excellence in order to infuse the cultural perspectives of nondominant groups. This commitment, however, requires both subtle and radical changes in the way a teacher describes and defines the learning and teaching process. A concomitant initial step involves repositioning the teacher from one who transmits and transfers knowledge to one who shares and participates in the process of constructing meaning. This position involves constant reflection and the disquieting effect of trial and error. Repositioning involves the humbling recognition that as teachers we do not own and cannot control knowledge. Curricular transformation unfolds as part of the learning and teaching drama.

In the next step, the teacher presents him- or herself to students and colleagues as one poised to learn. Curricular transformation is a continual process throughout the school year. That is, multicultural literature is not an add-on, but rather *goes* on throughout the school year. In this way teachers may preserve continuity and consistency while allowing the curriculum to expand with new questions and learning.

Teachers can expand their sources of information and assistance by contacting the Pan-African, Latin American, Asian/Pacific American, and Native American Studies departments at the local university, using on-line services, and visiting and making friends with the local public librarians and the managers of minority-owned bookstores. In this way, teachers can establish contacts, resources, and references for themselves and their students.

Construct a context for engaging multiple perspectives. To this end, take inventory of the artifacts in your room and add posters of ethnically diverse athletes, actors and actresses, and writers, and add a world-justified map. Expand your curriculum by beginning with a critical examination of the materials on hand. For example, your study of African American literature might begin by using the *Negro Almanac*. Fill in the time lines provided in your anthology with information about African Americans, and note the omissions from the anthology with your students. In class discussions, engage students in discourse about African, Latin American, Caribbean, North American, and Asian civilizations prior to European invasion and colonization and the trans-Atlantic slave trade. Engage students in discourse about the inherent contradictions in Christianity (both Protestantism and Catholicism), ethics, national identities, and slavery.

## The Winds of Change: Students Respond to an American Dilemma

The use of multicultural literature provides opportunities for students to challenge taken-for-granted assumptions. These challenges become part of the classroom community discourse and lead to discussions of contradictions that are present in our society. As the reading continues, students begin to expand and elaborate upon their perceptions of cultural distinctiveness in literary texts. Recognition of survival efficacy is a recurrent theme among students of color and recent immigrants, and it suggests that the need to overcome difficult, race-specific obstacles is an important cultural expectation among these students. For example, African American students may readily focus upon self-discovery and self-understanding in relation to others. European American students, on the other hand, seem to start from an initial distancing and devaluing of the issues of cultural distinctiveness. That is, they may assert sameness or maintain silence. Over time and multiple reading opportunities, these students move toward the discovery of and respect for the unique humanity of others, and later focus on self-discovery in relation to others. This does not happen, however, without moments of anxiety.

## Open Floodgates: Overcoming Resistance and Reaching Understanding

Fear of what can happen when students engage in different perspectives, especially in a public community such as a classroom, is clearly a cause for consternation. However, we have ample evidence that silence and cursory mentioning does not resolve, and possibly escalates, the potential for conflict. For many reasons, fear drives resistance; but what is there to fear? In the case of classroom teachers, a common fear is the manifestation of hostilities. However, by responding directly and compassionately, a teacher can deal with racism and utilize expressions of racist behavior as an opportunity for teaching and learning rather than retreat.

Clearly, there is a deep well of emotionality associated with the issues of race, gender, and domination. Teachers fear divisiveness and the dangers inherent in losing control of student responses. However, like most people, students also fear the unknown and making mistakes. They need a courageous ambassador to light their journey into new territory and an attentive and safe environment in which to articulate emerging, sometimes faltering, understandings. For example, for some European American students, non-mainstream-students' alignment with and valuing of multicultural literature appears threatening. Some European American students may seem confused and resentful, particularly in the presence of an authentic Blackness/"Otherness" presented by the literature. An honoring of difference precipitates a shift in the locus of control and power from dominance to equality. Given the social positioning of Whiteness and maleness in our society, a time of disquietude is not surprising. Equality and symmetry have different meanings for people who come to it from the top than for those who come to it from the bottom. From a position of assumed superiority, equality may, for a short period of time, feel like a defeat, a loss of control, and an end to a way of life. Conversely, from the bottom, equality is an accomplishment and, as such, may invigorate self- and group esteem in tangible and subtle ways; it may cause changes in social and literary interactions.

## Race, Literacy, and Literature: Facilitating an Awakening

Response to and engagement with multicultural literature and the infusion of multiple perspectives into the curriculum provides students with opportunities for social commentary. This occurs when multiple perspectives become a regular, normative, and expected part of the learning and teaching enterprise. Transforming the curriculum necessitates treating tension and discomfort as subjects for scholarly inquiry. Student social critiques emanate from student discourse as the students participate in literary activities and examine the world views of particular texts.

Familiar conventional patterns and new observations gained from reading and responding to literary texts in a community of readers invite social comment. Moreover, an integrative approach to multicultural education is a wise strategy for teachers who want to foster both critical literacy and cross-cultural understanding. Curricular transformation is difficult because it challenges the mainstream critics whom Morrison (1992) describes as follows:

> Like thousands of avid but nonacademic readers, some powerful literary critics in the United States have never read, and are proud to say so, *any* African American texts. It seems to have done them no harm, presented them with no discernible limitations in the scope of their influence. (p. 13)

Curricular invisibility incubates ignorance and threatens the intellectual and social well-being of teachers and students.

Transformation of the curriculum takes place in the context of an emerging, reflective, and recursive process that includes the teacher's reflection on the purpose of schooling, the role of the teacher, and the role of literature in individual and social transformation. This process also includes the students, who are encouraged to construct rather than consume knowledge and meaning. Transformation of the curriculum suggests that human beings are perennial learners who require time, internal motivation, a supportive environment, a logical context for learning, and multiple opportunities to practice and test new knowledge against what is already known.

A multicultural curriculum is not a watered-down course of study; rather, students participate in more literary activities than is typical for public high school students. A culturally infused curriculum contains rich perspectives and depth of study as the learners engage with the texts, reflect upon their reading experiences, and then participate in ongoing discussions as a community of readers, learners, and thinkers.

Finally, the opening of the self to multiple perspectives is not a closed door or a fixed state that is either "us" or "them." Rather, I would argue that people can come to see the world with their own eyes and another's heart as they read, write, think, and share lived and vicarious experiences. Ultimately, however, the disposition underscoring the movement toward welcoming multiple perspectives— for participatory debate about human issues rather than a curricular filibuster—becomes a habit of mind for those who seek genuine critical literacy for themselves and their students.

## Toward an Empowered Literacy: Risk and Reward

Moving toward a more inclusive curriculum is not without risk. Tensions may be partially attributable to the historical reality of diverse cultures living side by side for several centuries and sometimes imitating each other in selective ways but rarely fully comprehending the extent and meaning of their differences. When the cultural dynamic created and vitalized by the community comes together, readers, texts, and social context cannot be easily appropriated and exploited by dominant groups. Further, those who have been socialized in language, social custom, and schooling accept, unexamined, the essential rightness and superiority of their cultural group, and they may experience an interlude of disquiet as new knowledge and emergent understanding unsettle the patina of privilege. Within the context of American social, cultural, and political history, people of color, particularly African Americans, have been cast as strangers and sometimes exotic (Abrahams, 1992). Thus, the presence of an authentic Blackness defined and described by culturally conscious African

American literary texts may confound and disturb European American notions of the self and the "Other."

In the same vein, children of color need the curriculum and the teacher as ambassador to assist them in their journey toward writing a revised understanding of America and their place in it. As Len, an African American male student, put it:

> If them dudes hanging over there on that corner could
> read something about their history and their culture,
> they would know that hanging on the corner ain't so
> cool. It ain't what Black is really about.

Students involved in sociocultural exchanges in an honest and safe environment can articulate and explore their understandings and receive support for their revisions.

Among well-intentioned European American students, the bestowal of White attributes—"They are like us"—bespeaks a socialization that both denies difference and denigrates the "Other." Statements such as "they are like us" are generous but biased, and they often emerge from student attempts to articulate in positive terms attributes that they have learned are negative. Such statements should be signals for the ambassador/teacher that work needs to be done.

When other perspectives are regularly sought, student responses became more layered; they include alternative perspectives provided by culturally diverse literary texts and readers. Giving "Other" perspectives a voice and a respected place in the curriculum seems to dissipate minority readers' anger and frustration while at the same time empowering them to ask questions of their teachers and peers. Hearing, sharing, and adding to the symphony of voices in texts and of people of color seems to dissipate European Americans' fear of difference while at the same time empowering them to question sociocultural relationships in their school and community.

A fundamental grounding in multicultural education can mitigate the superficial and simplistic knowledge of self and others that students acquire when the curriculum lacks substantive content. Simply mentioning difference or telling schoolchildren to "treat everybody right" fails to prepare students for participation in critical global discourse. Furthermore, silence does not resolve cultural ambiguity, contradiction, or conflict; it may even lead to further conflict. We should not think of multicultural education as something to be done for children of color only. Rather, multicultural education is critical for European American students, who need considerably more than "chitterling" knowledge, good hearts, and good intentions to survive the harsh reality of racism in their families and communities. Fortified with knowledge and free of fear and ambiguities, students can be powerful agents for change among the European Americans with whom they come into contact. The United States cannot afford to leave such children at risk.

In order for the transformation of school and society to occur, multicultural education must become a viable, proactive process of educating people for the 21st century. The practice of merely "mentioning" cultural differences and ignoring the basic content of the curriculum must be revised. The traditional chronological order of the American literature curriculum, with its emphasis on the emergence of the United States as a new, strong, and European American male nation, must likewise be revised because it is inadequate. Time ordering encourages teachers to cover material rather than to engage students in learning, and huge cultural omissions are often the result. A logical alternative is thematic ordering. In this way, students can look at the emergence of the United States as a nation from the perspective of those who did not conquer yet whose presence and voices have contributed to the greatness of this country. James Baldwin has argued that if we can change the way people think about the world, even a little, we can change the world. As we reread the "word and the world" through multicultural lenses, we come to live the change even as we participate in the process.

# References

Aboud, F. E., & Skerry, S. A. (1984). The development of ethnic attitudes: A critical review. *Journal of Cross Cultural Psychology, 15,* 3–15.

Abrahams, R. D. (1992). *Singing the master: The emergence of African American culture in the plantation South.* New York: Pantheon.

Anaya, R. A. (1972). *Bless me, Ultima.* New York: Warner Books.

Anyon, J. (1983). Workers, labor and economic history and textbook content. In M. W. Apple & L. Weis (Eds.), *Ideology and practice in schooling* (pp. 37–59). Philadelphia: Temple University Press.

Apple, M. W. (1982). The other side of the hidden curriculum: Culture as lived I and II. In M. W. Apple (Ed.), *Education and power* (pp. 66–134). Boston: Routledge & Kegan Paul.

Applebee, A. (1974). *Tradition and reform in the teaching of English: A history*. Urbana, IL: National Council of Teachers of English.

Applebee, A. N. (1996). *Curriculum as conversation: Transforming traditions of teaching and learning*. Chicago: University of Chicago Press.

Applebee, A. N. (1997). *Tradition and reform in the teaching of English: A history*. Urbana, IL: National Council of Teachers of English.

Au, K. H. (1993). *Literacy instruction in multicultural settings*. Fort Worth, TX: Harcourt Brace Jovanovich.

Baker, H. A. (1988). *Afro-American poetics: Revisions of Harlem and the Black aesthetic*. Madison, WI: University of Wisconsin Press.

Beach, R. (1997). Students' resistance to engagement with multicultural literature. In Theresa Rogers & Anna Soter (Eds.), *Reading across cultures* (pp. 69–94). New York: Teachers College Press.

DuBois, W. E. B. (1961). *The souls of Black folk*. Greenwich, CT: Fawcett.

Dyson, A. H. (1993). *Negotiating a permeable curriculum: On literacy, diversity, and the interplay of children's and teacher's worlds* (Concept Paper No. 9). Urbana, IL: National Council of Teachers of English.

Erickson, F. (1987). Transformation and school success: The politics and culture of educational achievement. *Anthropology & Education Quarterly, 18*, 335–356.

Frakenberg, R. (1993). *White women, race matters: The social construction of Whiteness*. Minneapolis, MN: University of Minnesota Press.

Freire, P. (1986). *Pedagogy of the oppressed*. New York: Continuum.

Freire, P., & Macedo, D. (1994). *Literacies of power: What Americans are not allowed to know*. Boulder, CO: Westview.

Gates, H. (1992). *Loose canons: Notes on the culture wars*. New York: Oxford University Press.

Genette, G. (1980). *Narrative discourse: An essay in method*. Ithaca, NY: Cornell University Press.

George, J. G. (1983). *The talking earth*. New York: HarperCollins.

Giroux, H. A. (1993). *Living dangerously: Multiculturalism and the politics of difference*. New York: Lang.

hooks, b. (1994). *Teaching to transgress: Education as the practice of freedom*. New York: Routledge.

Morrison, T. (1992). *Playing in the dark: Whiteness and the literary imagination*. Cambridge, MA: Harvard University Press.

Namioka, L. (1994). *April and the dragon lady*. San Diego, CA: Browndeer Press.

Parks, G. (1986). *A choice of weapons*. St. Paul, MN: Minnesota Historical Society Press.

Powell, R. (1996, Winter). Confronting White hegemony: Implications for multicultural education. *Multicultural Education, 4*(2), 12–15.

Pugh, S. L., Hicks, J. W., & Davis, M. (1997). *Metaphorical ways of knowing: The imaginative nature of thought and expression*. Urbana, IL: National Council of Teachers of English.

Rabinowitz, P. J. (1987). *Before reading: Narrative conventions and the politics of interpretation*. Ithaca, NY: Cornell University Press.

Rothenberg, P. S. (1988). *Racism and sexism: An integrated study*. New York: St. Martin's Press.

Rotheram, M. J., & Phinney, J. S. (Eds.) (1987). *Children's ethnic socialization: Pluralism and development*. Newbury Park, NJ: Sage.

Santiago, E. (1993). *When I was Puerto Rican*. New York: Random House.

Spears-Bunton, L. A. (1992). Literature, literacy, and resistance to cultural domination. In Charles Kinzer & Donald Leu (Eds.), *Literacy research, theory and practice: Views from many perspectives*. Chicago: National Reading Conference.

Spears-Bunton, L.A. (1996). Welcome to my house: African-American and European-American students' responses to Virginia Hamilton's *House of Dies Drear*. In Etta R. Hollins (Ed.), *Transforming curriculum for a culturally diverse society* (pp. 227–239). Mahwah, NJ: Erlbaum.

Steffensen, M. S., Joag-Dev, C., & Anderson, R. C. (1979). A cross-cultural perspective on reading comprehension. *Reading Research Quarterly 15*(1), 10–29.

Walker, A. (1982). *The color purple*. New York: Washington Square Press.

Weiler, K. (1988). *Women teaching for change: Gender, class and power*. South Hadley, MA: Bergin & Garvey.

Whaley, L., & Dodge, L. (1993). *Weaving in the women: Transforming the high school English curriculum*. Portsmouth, NH: Heinemann.

Wharton, E. (1979). *Summer*. New York: MacMillan Publishing.

**Chapter 3**

# Celebrating African American Literary Achievements

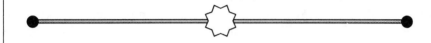

*Arlette Ingram Willis*

In this chapter I offer an introduction to the rich history and literary tradition of African Americans. As such, the chapter represents an attempt to meld together multiple historical and literary contexts with the literature of people of African descent in America. The more than 300 years of writings of African Americans reviewed in this chapter is by necessity selective. A complete review of all the literature written by people of African descent is beyond the scope of this chapter; the literature covered here is primarily fiction appropriate for students in grades 9–12. Therefore, other African American novels, which may well fit comfortably within the label *young adult* but are targeted for grades 6–8, are not included. Historically, the delineation between young adult and adult novels has not always been clear in teaching literature in schools. This is particularly true of the adult literature written by African Americans that is used in grades 9–12. I have selected what I believe to be the major writers and the most important works in each time period. My criteria for inclusion are works that are (a) historically relevant, (b) representative of a specific time period, (c) illustrative of the range of life circumstances and experiences of African Americans, (d) representative of unique cultural or linguistic use, and (e) appropriate for, and used in, grades 9–12.

This chapter is divided into seven chronological periods. A brief historical overview begins each chronological section. The historical overview, told from the perspective of African Americans within a general framework of U.S. history, is offered to help foster understanding and to contextualize the circumstances under which the literature was created. Moreover, the examination of the unique historical conditions in which African Americans lived helps to contextualize the literature produced during each time period and to illustrate the range and breadth of literature produced by African American writers throughout history. Additionally, the literature of each period is examined as it is reflected in the political, social, and cultural lives of the authors. Biographical information is interspersed when it lends a fuller understanding of the circumstances under which literary contributions were made and "within the context of the conditions of its production" (Smith, 1987, p. 5). Original works are used to illustrate the history, culture, language, and emotions of African Americans as expressed in their own time and in their own words.

An extensive review of African American young adult literature indicates that there was no literature written expressly for African American young adults until the 20th century. The roots of African American literature, however, began long ago in the villages of African people during the precolonial period, and this literature continues to influence the writings of African Americans today. This chapter begins by examining precolonial African roots of literature. Next, the earliest recorded writings of Africans brought to the shores of the "New World" are briefly reviewed. These early writings are followed by the literature of the antebellum period through the early 1900s. The literature of the Harlem Renaissance, the Civil Rights Era, the Black Arts/Black Aesthetic Movement, and the New Renaissance Movement of the 1980s and 1990s complete the chapter.

## The Roots of African American Literature

Recent scholarly research by Bennett (1982) and Van Sertima (1976), among others, records the presence of Africans in the Western Hemisphere as early as 1210. Most historians, however, do not acknowledge the presence of Africans until their participation in the expeditions of Spanish, Portuguese, and French explorers in the early 1500s. It is commonly believed that the vast majority of African indentured servants and, later, slaves were captured and brought to this country from the west coast of Africa. Franklin and Moss (1994) describe the precolonial region of Africa as existing from "the Mediterranean southward to the Gulf of Guinea and from the Atlantic eastward almost to the Nile, . . . the states of Ghana, Mali and Songhay, along with many lesser states" (p. 2). It is difficult to describe with any certainty the lives of Africans before their arrival in the "New World," as Africa, specifically precolonial West Africa, is a vast region. Although diverse languages and cultures existed among the various African nation states, there were some commonalties. Politically, groups were organized along the lines of limited monarchies with numerous advisors. This form of government offered considerable control. Contrary to popular media depictions of wild ungoverned savages, African people were peaceable folk who were governed by religion, rites, and laws.

The family served as the basic social organization. Extensions of the basic family unit included the clan (the allegiance to which was determined along matrilineal or patrilineal lines, depending on the specific clan) and the tribe. Family loyalty and ancestral worship were highly honored. Religions and religious practices included ancestral worship, magic, Islam, and in some northern areas of Africa, Christianity. However, on the whole Christianity was unknown in most of West Africa. Two important aspects of African religion were the prayers and songs used in worship.

The vastness of West Africa makes it difficult to pinpoint any one language as dominant; indeed, numerous spoken languages existed, but there were few written languages. The literature of West Africa during the precolonial period was predominantly oral in nature. The history and literature of the clan or tribe was as follows: "Handed down principally through the kinship group, the oral literature was composed of supernatural tales, moral tales, proverbs, epic poems, satires, love songs, funeral pieces, and comic tales" (Franklin & Moss, 1994, p. 23). Each kinship group had a griot (historian) whose express purpose was to preserve the memories of the tribe (history, law, and traditions). As Bell (1987) has observed, various forms of verbal art were used by Africans to "transmit knowledge, value, and attitudes from one generation to another, enforce conformity to social norms, validate social institutions and religious rituals, and provide psychological release from the restrictions of society" (p. 16). Many of these verbal art forms were retained when Africans were relocated to the "New World" and can be found in African American literature. Franklin and Moss (1994) suggest the following:

> The literary activities of Africans were tied up closely with their everyday lives. Oral literature, made up of tales, proverbs, epics, histories and laws, served as an educational device, a source of amusement, and a guide for the administration of government and the conduct of religious ceremony. (p. 25)

Although there are few written examples of the literature of Africans during this time period, what does exist suggests that when literacy was accomplished, the result was comparable to literature written by people in other parts of the world.

## "New World" Literature: Early African American Writings

The history of the people of African descent on the shores of the colonies usually begins with the 1619 landing of African indentured servants in Virginia, brought by a Dutch frigate to the shores of the "New World." Historians estimate that more than half the Africans seized in their homeland did not complete the voyage across the Atlantic. The journey aross the Atlantic, known as the Middle Passage, required enduring inhumane treatment, unsanitary living conditions, restraints on hands and feet, near starvation, and an uncertain future in the hands of the captors. Many Africans either died of disease contracted on the slave ships or committed suicide by jumping overboard. Those who did survive the journey were quickly forced into unmerciful working conditions, either on the tobacco (and later sugar cane) plantations on the Caribbean islands or in the fields of the colonies.

Initially, African people were brought to the "New World" as indentured servants, like many European people. The early indentured servants could then work, earn, or purchase their freedom after completing several years of labor. In some instances, African servants who purchased their freedom became voting and landowning members of the colonies (Cowan & Maguire, 1994). Mixed marriages between African and European servants and free people (as well as with Native people) were not uncommon. A sizable mulatto population, however, began to trouble the ruling class of European landowners (Franklin & Moss, 1994). This "problem" was dealt with by laws that required children to assume the birthright of their mothers; thus many mixed-race children—fathered by European or European American landowners—became servants like their mothers.

Along with other scholars interested in contextualizing the history of African American literature, I believe that it is important to acknowledge the circumstances of slavery to understand early African American literature. Barksdale and Kinnamon (1972) suggest that "slavery had the negative effect of divesting Africans of a substantial portion of their own culture," and "slavery by its very nature as an economic institution largely denied Blacks the opportunity and the occasion to create written literature" (p. 2). For example, slave codes were enacted and enforced in the Caribbean islands as early as 1694 to curb the liberties and freedoms of slaves. Soon thereafter, the colonies followed the slave-code patterns of the Caribbean islands and restricted the movement and liberties of slaves. Franklin and Moss (1994) argue that "the docility of slaves, about which masters boasted, was thus achieved through the enactment of a comprehensive code containing provisions for punishment designed to break even the most irascible blacks in the colony" (p. 58). Clearly, the transported Africans were undergoing two acculturative processes. First, they were becoming acculturated with Africans from various geographic and language groups. Second, Africans were attempting to understand and learn Western culture "and reinterpreting it with their own experience" (Franklin & Moss, 1994, p. 26). The result of this dual process was a unique set of customs rooted in African tradition in the colonies.

As Africans adjusted to their new lives in slavery, there was little opportunity to learn to read and write. African slaves had to first master the language of the oppressor before considering the notion of literacy. Slave owners were aware of the liberating effect of literacy acquisition. Therefore, while they insisted that African slaves learn and use English (or the language of the slave owner), they were less willing to have slaves acquire the skills of literacy. In fact, most colonies (and later states) adopted laws forbidding the teaching of reading and writing to slaves.

One of the unique responses to the acculturation process was the early writings of Africans in the colonies and England. The limited writings of several slaves suggest that their acquisition of literacy skills was an exception to the laws and customs of the land. Autobiographies and biographies of early authors indicate that the early authors lived atypical lives under slavery. Often taught to read and write through some fortuitous set of circumstances, the writings of African Americans clearly exhibit the language, style, and genres of their European masters, predominantly the English (Barksdale & Kinnamon, 1972, p. 2). The earliest recorded published writings of Africans in English reveal the conversion of Africans to Christianity, the strong influence of Christianity in their thinking, their ability to reconcile the contradiction of the Christian beliefs of their slaveholding masters and their position as slaves, and their hope for a better life in the hereafter.

Chronologically, the earliest recorded published writing by an African in the colonies is a poem composed by Lucy Terry (1746). Kidnapped as a child from her family and home in Africa and brought to the "New World," the young Lucy Terry learned to read and write. Terry's singular recorded work, "Bar Fight," details a scuffle between colonists and Native Americans. Another example of early writing is also a poem, "An Evening Thought: Salvation by Christ With Penitential Cries," by Jupiter Hammon (1761). Although little is known of him, it is believed that Hammon was born a slave and remained one throughout his life. His poem illustrates the tension that many African and African Americans experienced between the tenets of Christianity and the enslavement of people by Christians. Like so many African American authors that followed him, Jupiter Hammon was able to reconcile the contradiction by relying on salvation and a better afterlife. The idea of an afterlife is in accord with many beliefs in African religions.

The most celebrated and anthologized early African American writer is Phillis Wheatley. Wheatley, like Terry, began her life in Africa. She was captured as a child by slave traders in her native Senegal and brought to the colonies aboard a slave ship. Shortly after her arrival she learned to read and write in English, through informal tutoring sessions given by her master, John Wheatley. Her first published poem, "On the Death of the Rev. Mr. George Whitefield," was written when she was 14. After many unsuccessful attempts at publishing her poetry in the colonies, the Wheatleys manumitted Phillis and sent her to London with their son to publish her writings. In England Phillis was free, for England had freed all slaves in 1772. Phillis's first book of poetry, *Poems on Various Subjects, Religious and Moral, by Phillis Wheatley, Negro Servant to Mr. Wheatley of Boston*, was published in 1773. Given the unusual privileges that Phillis experienced as a manumitted slave, her early writing did little to communicate the evils of slavery. Her poetry was obviously a product of its time, as it emphasized her position as a Christian more than her life as a slave. Her later writings represent a more mature person who is interested in politics and develops a growing sense of nationalism. Wheatley's accomplishments as a young author living under the bondage of slavery and writing in a foreign language cannot be disputed as a great achievement. The writings of Lucy Terry and Phillis Wheatley also helped to establish the dominant role that African American women would take as writers of African American literature.

## Literature Written in the Antebellum Period

The African American literature produced during the antebellum era began to focus more directly on the evils of the institution of slavery and the fate of African Americans who fled slavery for freedom. Slave narratives make up the bulk of the literature written during this period and include strong religious themes.[1] Many slave narratives were written to appeal to and encourage European Americans in the North to join in the antislavery movement. Fugitive slave narratives and first-person accounts of the horrors of slavery drew upon the life experiences of slaves and were instrumental in evoking public outcry for the abolition of slavery. The slave narrative evolved into a unique form of autobiography, one of the most important genres created by people of African descent. Henry Louis Gates (1987), an African American literary critic, argues that these early accounts of human bondage are "the very foundation upon which most subsequent Afro-American fictional and nonfiction narratives are based" (p. xii). Many early slave narratives were written by "house" Negroes, the mulattos, and the privileged slaves who witnessed the physical brutality of slavery while suffering from the psychological and physical pain of slavery.

Slave narratives have been recorded from as early as the 1700s to as late as 1944. Typically, slave narratives chronicle the life of a slave from the perspective of the victim, detailing kidnapping, transport, sale, acculturation, brutality, escape, and life after slavery. The slave narratives, of which more than 6,000 were written, appear to serve two distinct functions. First, slave narratives gave voice to the secrets and horrors of slavery as experienced by slaves of African descent, who were regarded as human merchandise. Until the publication of the slave narratives, slaves were without a voice or the protection of laws from any and all treatment, no matter how inhumane, that was bestowed upon them by their master, his wife, his surrogates, or his relatives. The slave narratives offered slaves an avenue by which to expose the daily physical, psychological, and sexual abuse that they were made to endure. Often purchased for their stature, size, and strength, the physical abuse of African American men was particularly brutal. Slave masters and overseers sought to break the spirit of the men by making them endure gruesome tortures. African American women were often purchased for the master's lusts. The sexual abuse of the African American female slave was given limited exposure in the writings of this period. Slave marriages were not allowed, and marriage between slave owner and slave was unsanctioned, as miscegenation was illegal in most states. The offspring of these unions—the mulattos, quadroons, and octoroons—were often treated more kindly than other slaves. In addition, African American female slaves endured much psychological abuse. As the victims of forced concubinage, the women were often promised the freedom of their children—a promise that was often broken. The wives of the landowners also harassed the mothers of the mixed-race children or had the mother and the children separated and sold. The opportunity to report these abuses, whether written by an amanuensis or a slave, was liberating.

Second, slave narratives were a means by which various abolitionist groups were able to share their support of fugitive slaves, denounce the unjust treatment of slaves with authentic accounts of the brutality experienced by the slaves, and reconcile their Christian self-worth by exposing the "peculiar institution" with firsthand accounts from those who had endured human bondage. Slave narratives were used to graphically detail the treatment of slaves and to compel Euro-

American Christians in the North to oppose the practice. The language and style of the narratives were strongly influenced by the writing conventions, language, and style of their European and Euro-American contemporaries. The writings of African American slaves, to varying degrees, reflected the ways of the European American masters and the growing sense of "Americanness."

One of the general characteristics of early slave narratives was the use of fictional geographical locations, names, or titles. Among these slave-narrative authors, there was always a need to remain anonymous, as the Fugitive Slave Laws (1789 and 1850) required the return of escaped slaves to their "owners." However, the later slave narratives named their owners and tormentors and supplied geographical information as a way of authenticating their stories. Early slave narratives did not reveal the means of escape or the routes to freedom. Again, the protection of the authors and of those who would come after them was of utmost concern. Themes in slave narratives include the challenge of a slave's humanity; his or her ability to forgive the oppressors; living in constant fear of sexual assault; daily life (working from 4:00 a.m. to after dark) under the watchful eye and temperamental care of overseers; and the pain of white men kidnapping children, separating families, and hunting, torturing, maiming, and killing slaves. Clearly, the slave narrative spoke for the millions of slaves who daily endured the brutality of the slave system and were illiterate and could not openly share accounts of their lives.

The first published slave narrative, written by Olaudah Equiano, was *The Interesting Narrative of the Life of Olaudah Equiano, or Gustavus Vassa the African, Written by Himself*. The 400-page narrative was published first in London (1789) and later in the colonies (1791). It has recently been republished (1995). It is believed that Equiano's narrative, a vivid and compelling testimony of the horrors of human enslavement, inspired the abolition of America's sanctioned slave trade. Equiano describes the struggle between his longing to return to the land of his birth and the process of acculturation he underwent as a result of his enslavement. Of the early published slave narratives, Equiano's offers a moderate account of the life and fate of slaves under colonial rule, yet it serves to help readers understand the mistreatment of slaves and their daily experiences under the overseer.

While Equiano's work serves as a first among slave narratives, several other celebrated slave narratives were written early. The authors of these narratives are Briton Hamon, 1760; Frederick Douglass, 1845; William Wells Brown, 1847; James Pennington, 1849; Henry Box Brown, 1849; and Harriet Jacobs, 1861. Their works are among the most celebrated of the slave narratives; they were written by former slaves and authenticated by European Americans who knew the authors to be ex-slaves. For example, Frederick Douglass' *Narrative of the Life of Frederick Douglass, an American Slave, Written by Himself*, published in 1845, and Harriet Jacobs' *Incidents in the Life of a Slave Girl, Written by Herself*, published in 1861, are recognized as authentic and important contributions to American literature.

In *Narrative of the Life of Frederick Douglass, an American Slave, Written by Himself*, Douglass describes his birth as a slave on a Maryland plantation in 1818. His mother, Harriet Bailey, never revealed the identity of his father, although it was believed to have been the master of the plantation on which Douglass was born. Douglass's original version (1845), *Narrative of the Life of Frederick Douglass, an American Slave, Written by Himself*, was revised twice under the titles *My Bondage and My Freedom* (1855) and *Life and Times of Frederick Douglass* (1881). Like the writers before and after him, Douglass wrote about many previously untold horrors of slavery. Although he was not the only slave to face inhumane treatment, his tale explicitly illustrates the never-ending torture and threats of life endured by slaves. His articulation of the treatment of African American male slaves exposes the regularity of the brutality of slavery. Douglass's narrative also portrays him as a man who would not allow himself to be broken by slavery. The humanity of the slaves in the face of inhumane treatment and the inability of slaveholders to break the spirit of the slaves are also consistent themes in slave narratives.

Harriet Jacobs' *Incidents in the Life of a Slave Girl, Written by Herself* (1861), is one of the few slave narratives written by an African American woman that was published. Jacobs describes the harrowing sexual harassment she endured for years in the home of Dr. Flint, where she was a house Negress. Jacobs' narrative was groundbreaking because it was one of the few written by an African American woman that detailed the sexual exploitation of slave women by slave owners. In addition, Jacobs' narrative illustrated how slave families were broken up by slave owners and often at the request of their jealous wives. She also shared the heartbreak of watching one's children be forcibly snatched and given or sold into a life of human bondage at the whim of the owners. Jacobs' narrative offers the reader a glimpse of the courage and strength of the slave women who had to endure these hardships. Jacobs' narrative also articulates a very different view of the life of the "tragic" mulatto slave woman in contrast to the romanticized "slave" novels written by Euro-American women, who tended to sentimentalize the lives of mulattos, the constant fear of rape, and a life of concubinage.

It is important to note that Jacobs' narrative was written and published with the assistance of a European American abolitionist, Lydia M. Child. As editor, Child was careful to steer Jacobs' narrative so that it would appeal to an audience of Euro-American women in the North. Thus, Jacobs used a style that was popular for fiction in the late 1800s and that was meant to elicit sympathy from its readers. Nevertheless, Jacobs tells her story with great passion, for she had escaped the emotional, psychological, physical, and sexual bondage of slavery. The authenticity of her story has been painstakingly researched and the narrative republished as edited by Jean Fagan Yellin (1987).

Ironically, all slave narratives had to be authenticated by Whites in order to prove their truthfulness. Letters of authentication had to be included with each narrative, since the readers of slave narratives were often European American sympathizers in the North. Abolitionists used the slave narratives to garner support for the antislavery movement. However, not all slave narratives were written by African Americans. Since most slaves were illiterate, many would-be African American slave authors had to rely on Euro-American editors to record their life stories. In the hands of the editor, the life story became fodder from which the editors selectively recorded the slaves' firsthand accounts. Euro-American editors seldom recorded everything dictated by the slaves, especially incidents of miscegenation and sexual exploitation, in an effort to appeal to a Northern, Euro-American, Christian, antislavery audience. Editors freely interspersed abolitionist rhetoric throughout the material. Even more disconcerting than the edited versions of slave narratives were the Euro-American impostors. Two examples were written by European Americans posing as slave authors: Richard Hildreth's *The Slave; or, Memories of Archy Moore*

(1836) and the alleged testimonies recorded in Theodore Dwight Weld's *American Slavery as It Is: Testimony of a Thousand Witnesses* (1839). Publishers were concerned about printing the works of impostors, so they often sought verification of the authenticity of slave narratives. The verification came in the form of letters of support written by White abolitionists and African American free men.

Slave narratives were not the only form of literature written by African Americans during this period. Other forms of writings included letters, speeches, autobiographies of free African Americans or manumitted slaves, newspaper and journal articles, songs, poems, essays, and confessions of criminals. Very few novels were actually written during the antebellum period. Two works of fiction, however, were forerunners of later attempts to capture African American life experiences in prose. First, William Wells Brown's novel, *Clotel, or the President's Daughter* (1853), was first published in London. Brown declares that his novel is fiction based on fact. The most salient, though still disputed, fact is that President Thomas Jefferson fathered children by one of his female slaves, Sally Hemings. The second work of fiction was Harriet Wilson's novel, *Our Nig: Or, Sketches From the Life of a Free Black* (1859). Wilson's novel was the first to be published by an African American in the United States and the first to be written by an African American woman. In fact, the novel was printed for Wilson rather than "published" by a commercial press. The customary tale is that Wilson had the novel printed to raise income for her destitute family. From all scholarly accounts, it appears that Wilson's fictional tale is a semiautobiographical portrayal of the life of a slave girl and the lives of all who "own" her. The story of servitude and the emotional, psychological, and physical abuse at the hands of several of her "owners" is followed by the equally depressing events of a failed marriage, abandonment, ill health, the birth of a son, and poverty. The events of the novel closely parallel those of Wilson's own life, as can be seen from the closing pages of the novel.

## Literature of the Late 1800s and Early 1900s

The Civil War brought with it a renewed attempt by African Americans to learn to read and write and to express their ideas in written form. There seem to have been numerous opportunities to learn the skills of literacy in Union camps, but very few copies of the letters, articles, and short stories written by African Americans during this period have been recovered. In the years following the Civil War, the U.S. government sought to improve the education and literacy skills of African Americans. Under the direction of the Freedmen's Bureau, hundreds of schools, known as Freedmen's Schools, were established to educate African American children and adults. The Freedmen's Bureau, with the aid of the American Tract Society, developed specially designed curricula to improve the intellectual abilities of African Americans and acculturate African Americans into Euro-American middle-class values. In addition, the thrust for racial equality found that "the freedmen's educational movement represented a unique opportunity to disprove popular theories of racial inferiority and to prepare the former slaves for full citizenship" (Morris, 1981, p. x). The literature used to teach African Americans in the Freedmen's Schools was new or republished works written by Euro-Americans and published by the American Tract Society of Boston and New York. Special care was taken in the design and content of the materials to reflect the goals of the Bureau. For example, materials were written that would encourage readers to desire and value an education; to adopt Christian values of temperance, morality, and forgiveness; and to acquire the middle-class values of hard work, thrift, and self-improvement (Morris, 1981). The titles of the readers beyond the primary level are quite revealing of their content—for example, *Advice to Freedmen* by Isaac Brinckerhoff, *Friendly Counsels for Freedmen* by Jared Waterbury, *John Freeman and His Family* by Helen Brown, and *Plain Counsels for Freedmen* by Clinto Fisk.

Two publications of the Freedmen's books merit special mention. First, Lydia Maria Child edited volume 6 in the series, and in it she used short stories and biographies written by African Americans, a real break from previous editions. Second, one of the most interesting publications used in the Freedmen's Schools consisted of a newspaper written by an enterprising group of African American men. The newspaper, the *Freedmen's Torchlight*, was instructional for all age levels. Its stated goal was to offer instruction created by African Americans for African Americans. The *Freedmen's Torchlight* followed the style of other African American newspapers and journals by offering helpful hints, news articles, stories, and basic literacy lessons.

The African American church has always been a steady rock for African Americans in the tumultuous seas of life in America. During the post–Civil War years, it played a fundamental role in the lives of the freed men and women by supporting the spiritual, cultural, and literary character of their lives. Many of the African American churches owned their own presses and published materials written by African Americans. Church-related publications were concerned with educational and literary as well as religious matters.

The African American press was pivotal in communicating the concerns and issues most central to the African American community. The first African American newspaper was founded in 1827. Since that time the African American press has played an instrumental role in shaping public opinion and recording daily events and concerns in the African American community. A review of these papers offers an uncommon view into African American literary concerns and the accomplishments of African American writers. The editors of African American presses felt compelled to share the unfolding history of the experiences and lives of African Americans from their own perspective—a viewpoint that often contradicted the representation of the same events in the mainstream press. In general, African American newspapers promoted education and "social uplift." They also provided an important outlet for African American writers of fiction and poetry.

Through the efforts of Henry Louis Gates, Jr., the New York City Library's Schomberg Library of Nineteenth-Century Black Women Writers and Oxford University Press have republished several novels written at the close of the 19th century by African American women. This collection includes Amelia Johnson's two novels, *Clarence and Corinne, or God's Way* (1890) and *The Hazeley Family* (1894); Frances Harper's novel, *Iola Leroy: Or, Shadows Uplifted* (1892); Emma Dunham Kelley-Hawkin's two novels, *Four Girls at Cottage City* (1898) and *Megda* (1891); Mary Seacole's *Wonderful Adventures of Mrs. Seacole in Many Lands* (1857); and Pauline Hopkins' two novels, which were serialized in *Colored American Magazine*, and *Contending Forces: A Romance of Negro Life North and South* (1900). According to Gates (1988), Hopkins' serialized novels appeared in magazines intended for the African American professional class. The characters in each of these novels appeared as "unraced" folks; that is, their racial identities are left to the reader to determine. The female writers wrote in an effort to depict African Americans as "normal" people with desires, hopes, and dreams, but they were aware that the mainstream public was not willing to see African Americans in that light. Thus, they attempted to transcend race by making it a nonissue. For example, their descriptions of the physical qualities of the characters are purposefully left vague, allowing the reader to apply his or her race to the characters. In this way, the books became popular among all races; thus there appears to have been a consciousness in the authors of the buying power of the more prosperous Whites. As literary critic C. Christian (1988) notes in the introduction to the republished *The Hazeley Family*, the characters are "racially indeterminate, which in this country is generally translated as white" (p. xxvii). Like many novels written by women of this period, these novels and short stories center on home, the welfare of children, and Christian values, complete with happy endings that reward virtuous living.

Johnson's novel *Clarence and Corinne, or God's Way* (1890) is most often cited as appropriate for young adults. Many African American churches strongly encouraged its use and suggested that it become part of each church's library. It seems to have been favorably received; it is a story about children who are left destitute by an alcoholic father and an emotionally depressed mother, and it served as a literary example of the effects of alcoholism on the lives of children. Its timely publication articulated the growing national concern for better care of children, the personal and familial damage caused by alcoholism, and the sure reward that accompanies living by Christian values. The desire to instill mainstream middle-class morals and values into African American novels continued through the early years of the 20th century.

The early years of the 20th century evinced a wealth of literature written by and about African Americans. Several interwoven factors appear to have supported this change. First, there were increased educational opportunities during the post–Civil War years that improved the educational level and reading interests of the African American community. Even in the poverty-stricken rural South, African Americans sought educational opportunities, long denied to them in the schools established for them, through the benevolence of Northern churches, philanthropic organizations, and the willpower of African American families.

Second, the Great Migration, or mass exodus of African Americans from the rural agrarian lifestyle of the South, led to African Americans seeking a better life in America. The Great Migration began in 1916 and continued until shortly before the Depression in 1929. It was spurred economically by the boll weevil, floods, low sharecropping wages, agricultural mechanization, and soil exhaustion. It was spurred socially by the repressive Jim Crow laws and customs, as Southern Whites turned to more open and violent means to maintain White supremacy.

Third, there was a nearly insatiable interest in African American folklore by Euro-Americans in the North. The interest was generated by the publication of folktales, spirituals, and work songs of African Americans gathered by Euro-American workers of the North during Reconstruction. The characters of these published works were taken from the oral folktales of Stackalee, John Henry, "Buh Rabbit," Uncle Remus, Tar Baby, Shine, and the Signifying Monkey, among others. The origins of many of these tales, and the way in which they were related, can be traced back to the African oral tradition. The tales often portrayed the desire for freedom, the need to defend oneself, and the use of wisdom to escape from the master (Mullane, 1993). Like their African predecessors, African American folktales were often told to explain natural phenomena, to remember community and familial histories and culture, to educate, and to entertain. Most African American folktales, spirituals, and work songs had not been written down or published, and Euro-American collectors of the North were eager to publish them for Northern audiences.

Finally, there was an increase in the amount of degrading racial stereotyping of African Americans in the literature produced by European Americans. The stereotypes included, but were not limited to, the happy shuffling Negro; the fat, unattractive mammy; the tragic mulatto; the backward, immoral, and primitive Negro; the "aunties" and "uncles"; and the Jezebels and Sapphires. Yet the stereotyping found in literature was only a mirror image of the stereotyping experienced daily by African Americans as they sought employment, education, and entertainment opportunities in a racially divided country. Then, as now, African American writers spoke out strongly against the use of stereotyping in both fiction and nonfiction, attempting to supplant myths, distortions, and misinformation with more factual and representative information. Numerous works published by African Americans in the early decades of the 20th century reflect the opposition they encountered in every walk of life. Perhaps no other work captures the pulse of African American life under the oppressive status of second-class citizens as eloquently as W. E. B. Du Bois' *The Souls of Black Folks* (1903). In this collection of essays, Du Bois offers an introspective look at the experiences of African Americans. He became a spokesman for African Americans of every economic level but especially for an emerging African American intelligentsia. As editor of *The Crisis*, the official magazine of the NAACP (National Association for the Advancement of Colored People), which was founded in 1910, DuBois also helped to launch the literary careers of many young African American authors. He was not alone in his desire to improve the lot of African Americans. Booker T. Washington, another African American leader, also sought to improve life in America for African Americans through self-improvement, economic opportunities, and social separation. His autobiography, *Up From Slavery: The Autobiography of Booker T. Washington* (1901), was an instant best seller, especially among Euro-Americans, who enjoyed his American success story and welcomed its inspirational, nonaccusatory tone.

One of the few works of literature from this period written by an African American that is used in high schools is James Weldon Johnson's *Autobiography of an Ex-Colored Man*. This novel was originally published anonymously in 1912 and republished under Johnson's name in 1927. The novel details the story of an African-American man who passes as White in order to participate in mainstream American life. The book has a well-conceived plot, interesting characters, and a realistic message. It was so realistic that many people believed it was an actual autobiography and not a work of fiction. Johnson was also a poet, essayist, critic, anthropologist, and lyricist. He wrote "Lift Every Voice and Sing," which is commonly referred to as the African American national anthem.

## The Harlem Renaissance

Nearly half a million African Americans migrated from the South to northern and western states between 1916 and 1918. The Great Migration created large Negro communities outside the South, especially in the industrial cities of the North, such as New York and Philadelphia. African Americans moved to the North in the hope of finding greater economic and educational opportunities. Many rural African Americans possessed few job skills and limited educational training, yet both were needed to secure gainful employment in the North. From the years immediately preceding World War I to those directly following its cessation, the United States was fraught with racial tensions between European and African Americans as everyone struggled to better themselves. African American soldiers faced a particularly perplexing time in adjusting to life in the United States upon returning from the war. Unlike many White soldiers, they were not greeted with welcoming parades, although they too had fought in foreign lands for the freedom of all Americans. When they returned "home," they found that they had very little freedom.

The period commonly referred to as the Harlem Renaissance began in 1915 and continued through 1945. The literature written by African Americans at this time is full of racial pride. Collectively, this body of literature eloquently expresses the feelings and desires of African Americans as they struggled to find a place in American society. Most of the writings point to education as a goal and encourage its readers to "social uplift." A review of the writings also suggests a renewed sense of appreciation for the uniqueness of African American folk ways and literature that had been long abandoned for mainstream, middle-class values. African American writers began to incorporate their knowledge and understanding of African American folklore and folk ways into their writings, which reflected both the African roots of literacy and the African American experience (Mullane, 1993). Ann Petry's historical fiction depiction of the Salem witch trials in *Tituba of Salem Village* (1948), serves as an example.

Folk culture is evident in many writings of African Americans during this period, from the poetry of Langston Hughes to the novels of Zora Neale Hurston. Authors sought to capture a range of African American life, from the rhythm of Harlem to the sweltering heat of the South to the beat of the Caribbean islands. The dialect and pulse of African American people took shape in literature. The literature produced by the young writers of the Harlem Renaissance did not always bode well with more established African American writers. The older writers feared that White Americans would find confirmation of racial stereotypes in the literature produced by the young breed of writers, which vividly portrayed the seedier side of African American life in Harlem. The young writers, however, were defiant and viewed the Harlem Renaissance as a time to express their growing self-awareness, emerging voices, and racial pride with youthful enthusiasm. The younger authors did not seek the approval of Euro-American critics, nor did they adhere to their standards. The literature of the Harlem Renaissance is often anthologized in secondary school textbooks, although the selections that are used often reflect adult literature and not the literature written for younger readers.

An example of a publication aimed at young readers is Elizabeth Ross Haynes's *Unsung Heroes* (1921). Her book was a renewal and continuation of a long tradition in African American literature of emphasizing the lives of very accomplished African Americans as examples to future generations. Clearly, the message in such works is that African Americans can make it in the United States despite racism. This book includes biographies of such heroes as Frederick Douglass, Paul Laurence Dunbar, Booker T. Washington, Sojourner Truth, and Toussiant L'Ouverture. In addition, the book includes biographies of some unsung heroes: Alexandre Dumas, Paul Cuffe, Josiah Henson, and John Mercer Langston.

During this period, W. E. B. Du Bois teamed up with the accomplished literary editor, Redmond Fauset, to edit and publish *Opportunity* (1919) and *The Brownies Book* (1920–1922). *Opportunity* was a literary magazine that showcased the talents of aspiring young African American authors, and *The Brownies Book* was a literary magazine for children and young adults. *Opportunity* became an important outlet for many talented writers during the Harlem Renaissance, for it nurtured and published the early writings of young authors. One of the most popular African American publications of the 1920s was *The Brownies Book*, which was created for African American children ages 6 to 16. The editors referred to them as "Children of the Sun." The magazine expressed the views and hopes of racial pride from the perspective of its well-educated publication staff—W. E. B. Du Bois, Jessie Fauset, and Augustus Dill. According to the authors, a major goal of the magazine was to "seek to teach Universal Love and Brotherhood for all little folk—black and brown and yellow and white." Other goals included "making colored children realize that being colored is a natural beautiful thing, to make them familiar with the history and achievements of the Negro race; to make them know that other colored children have grown into beautiful, useful and famous persons" (D. Johnson, 1990, p. 15). The editors stressed racial pride, the history and achievements of African Americans, and words of advice and encouragement. The magazine included stories, games, poems, letters from children and parents, biographies of famous African Americans, reports on international cultures, photographs and artwork of African American artists, and accomplishments of African American young people from all over the country.

While there was a proliferation of published works by African Americans during the Harlem Renaissance, very few books were written for young adults. Some of the major authors of the period were Countee Cullen, Nella Larson, Claude McKay, and Jean Toomer. Several works by Langston Hughes and Arna Bontemps were written for children and young adults and their writings dominated the African American children and young adult market. Their writings include poems, folklore, and novels. Bontemps' career began as a poet in 1924 and expanded to include other genres over the next 50 years. His early novels, *Black Thunder* (1936) and *Drums at Dusk* (1939), helped to establish him as an important author of the Harlem Renaissance. His later two novels are a fictional account of the Gabriel Posser slave rebellion in Virginia in 1800 and the Haitian slave rebellion of 1791–1804, respectively. Bontemps was among the first African American authors to write with the young adult in mind. Bontemps also edited several books for young people, including *Golden Slippers: An Anthology of Negro Poetry for Young Readers* (1941). Hughes and Bontemps combined to edit *Book of Negro Folklore* (1958) and *Great Slave Narratives* (1969).

Arna Bontemp's *We Have Tomorrow* (1945) is an important work that encourages young African Americans not to forsake their dreams, regardless of the obstacles. Using the biographies of African American men and women in the early stages of their careers, Bontemps presents the stories of 12 pioneers. He stresses that they are fulfilling their dreams as Americans, not African Americans, yet they realize that they are blazing trails not traveled by African Americans before. The careers of the biographies include cartoonist, milliner, sociologist, nurse, book publisher, sports star, and pilot. Another of

Bontemps's works for young people was *The Story of the Negro* (1948), an easy-to-read narrative history that chronicles the life of Africans from their kidnapping and enslavement on the shores of the "New World" to policies enacted by President Franklin D. Roosevelt.

Langston Hughes's writings, covering more than three decades, include fiction, drama, history, biography, autobiography, translations, and books for children. He published his first major poem, "The Negro Speaks of Rivers," in *The Crisis* in 1921. In 1926 he published his first book of poetry, *The Weary Blues*, in which he articulates the richness of African American folk culture, blues, and jazz. Hughes became known as the Poet Laureate of Harlem for his many works of poetry. However, beginning in 1930 his work focused on protesting social and political injustice. As an author of more than 50 books, Hughes wrote in a wide variety of genres, including two autobiographies, *The Big Sea* (1940) and *I Wonder as I Wander* (1957). Perhaps his most endearing works, certainly suitable for young adults, are his Jesse B. Semple (Simple) stories: *Simple Speaks His Mind* (1950), *Simple Takes a Wife* (1953), and the *Best of Simple* (1961). Originally the character Jesse B. Semple in a newspaper column written by Hughes, Semple came to represent the Negro everyman in American society. In simple honest speech and dialect, Semple used wisdom and common sense to share his insight on the affairs of the country and the world. The Simple books were widely read and enjoyed by African Americans.

The works of Richard Wright and Zora Neale Hurston have also come to represent the writing of the period for secondary school readers. The works of these writers, though not initially intended for young adults, are now included in many high school literature anthologies and book selections. For example, in the waning years of the Harlem Renaissance, the focus of African American writers turned from racial pride to racial protest after two World Wars and the Great Depression had brought little change in the lives of, and opportunities for, African Americans. The writings of Richard Wright, among others, illustrates the frustration of the second-class-citizen status of African Americans during the postwar period. Wright drew upon his own background in a poverty-stricken, poorly educated, dysfunctional family from the rural South. He fled the injustices of the South and his unfortunate circumstances for Chicago, where he joined the Writers Project of the Works Progress Administration. He won acclaim for his book, *Uncle Tom's Children: Four Novellas* (1938), stories that depict racial conflict and physical violence. His most powerful novel, however, was *Native Son* (1940), later followed by *Black Boy: A Record of Childhood and Youth* (1945). Wright's *Native Son* traces the life of Bigger Thomas, a 20-year-old rebellious African American man shaped and hardened by his life on the South Side of Chicago in the 1930s. As he understands his choices in life, he is either to submit to the oppression of Whites or commit some act of violence that will ultimately land him in jail. From the opening pages of the novel, the reader comes to understand Bigger's sense of despair and resentment as well as his internal demons and environmental realities. He is beset by problems of poverty, racism, and a family that appears to be submissive to a hostile White environment. An obvious theme of the novel is Bigger's sense of fear. He is often portrayed as overwhelmed and fearful of the White world. The novel shares Bigger's innermost thoughts as he unwittingly murders his landlord's daughter and later his girlfriend, in whom he has confided. The remainder of the novel shares Bigger's growing sense of a conscious identity and his eventual trial and failed appeal. The novel ends as Bigger is on death row awaiting execution. Much controversy has surrounded the characters in the novel as stereotypical, from the image of Bigger as a "nigger" to the image of Whites as cold, uncaring, and hostile.

Wright's autobiographical work, *Black Boy*, was actually the first installment of a longer work, *American Hunger*; however, the objections of the publishers caused only the first half of the manuscript to be published. The novel is Wright's story of growing up in the racially divided, hate-filled South (Mississippi, Arkansas, and Tennessee) during the early 1900s. The autobiography, which reads like a novel, describes Wright's struggle to find meaning and a sense of self under the oppressive domination of Southern Whites and an unyielding yet dysfunctional family that insists on unthinking obedience. The inability to control any facet of his life was too much for Wright to bear. He wrote, "Because I had no power to make things happen outside of me in the objective world, I made things happen within." Throughout the novel, at home, at school, or at one of his many jobs, Wright fights for his individualism and self-esteem as he elegantly describes the racial, emotional, and psychological oppression endured by African Americans. One constant message to Wright from the onset of the book is to be silent. As a result, Wright fought to be heard all his life. Now, many years after his death, his work lives on, and his voice continues to be heard.

Like Richard Wright, Zora Neale Hurston's artistry and giftedness as a writer has only been acknowledged long after her death. Hurston published seven novels between 1931 and 1943: *Jonah's Gourd Vine* (1934), *Mules and Men* (1935), *Their Eyes Were Watching God* (1937), *Tell My Horse* (1938), *Moses, Man of the Mountain* (1939), *Dust Tracks on a Road: An Autobiography* (1942), and *Seraph on the Suwanee* (1948). She also has more than 70 other written works. The most widely read and praised of her writings is the novel *Their Eyes Were Watching God.* Hurston was an anthropologist, a folklorist, and a novelist, and she incorporates each talent in her story of Janie and her loves—Logan, Joe, and Vergible "Tea Cake" Woods. Her anthropological training is apparent in her ability to capture the dialect and folk ways of her characters. As a folklorist she weaves a tale of love, humor, mystery, and suspense. The story begins as Janie tells her friend Phoeby how her third husband died during a hurricane, and how she comes to understand the real meaning of the love she has searched for all her life. Hurston often mixes fact with fiction. For example, Eatonville, Florida (her birthplace), is an entirely African American community founded by Joe Starks, Janie's second husband. When first published, the novel was condemned for its use of dialect and an alleged lack of message or theme. However, this novel, along with several other works by Hurston, have been republished and praised in the 1990s for some of the very same reasons that they were criticized in earlier times: the ability to capture the dialect and folk ways of Southern rural African Americans and the universal themes of self-love and the strength of womankind.

During the Harlem Renaissance, the African American press continued to be an important source of information and print media for the African American community. Newspapers, periodicals, and magazines shared the lives of African Americans, their triumphs, accomplishments, and plight. As African American men and women fought on foreign lands for freedoms they were denied at home, the U.S. government, in an effort to officially recognize the African American presence in the armed services, appointed Ted Poston to the position of racial advisor to the Office of War Information. Poston, a seasoned newspaperman, lent his special talents to coverage of African Americans during the war years. He also wrote short stories, and through the efforts of Kathleen Hauke they have been published in a collection entitled *The Dark Side of Hopkinsville* (1991). The collection includes 10 delightfully funny stories of growing up in the African American community of Hopkinsville, Tennessee, as told by Ted Poston. Poston's stories center on his family and its standing in the African American community as well as on other members of the community. He creates several lifelike characters who engage in the kind of shenanigans, adventures, and community rousing found in many small towns.

Despite Poston's lighthearted appeal, life for African Americans in the United States was still fraught with racial and economic discrimination. By midcentury the struggle for equality had arrived at the doors of the federal courts and would not be denied, as African Americans sought to desegregate schools and reverse the *Plessy v. Ferguson* decision (1896), or the "separate but equal" standard. The efforts for equal rights were fought for by both European and African Americans, and they faced fierce resistance. *Brown v. Topeka* (1954) and the Civil Rights Act (1957, 1960), authorized the federal government to force the desegregation of schools and other public facilities. However, the federal government moved slowly to enforce the laws, and African Americans grew impatient for the freedoms that had been denied to them ever since their ancestors' arrival centuries before.

## Literature of the Civil Rights Era

Following the fruitful and productive period of the Harlem Renaissance, publications by African American writers declined dramatically. The already sparse literature written for African American young adults dwindled to almost nothing after 1945. Most notable are Gwendolyn Brooks' books of poetry, *A Street in Bronzeville* (1945), *Annie Allen* (1949), and *The Bean Eaters* (1960), and her novel, *Maude Martha* (1953); James Baldwin's *Go Tell It on the Mountain* (1952) and *Nobody Knows My Name* (1961); Ralph Ellison's *The Invisible Man* (1952); and Paule Marshall's *Brownstones, Brown Girls* (1959).

Gwendolyn Brooks became one of the first African American poets to win the Pulitzer Prize and has led a prolific literary career for more than 50 years. She continues to write and to read from and lecture on her writings today. From the onset, her poetry revealed her commitment to family, community, and race in its descriptions of African American life in the urban cities of the North. Brooks' ability to emulate the sounds and rhythm of African American life can be read in her works, as can her ability to share, in few words, the sights, tastes, and feel of African American life. For example, her novel, *Maude Martha*, is an episodic story of the life of a young African American female from childhood through womanhood. Maude, the main character, is plain-looking, shy, and studious and very unlike her attractive sister Helen, to whom she constantly compares herself. Maude expresses disappointment in her lack of beauty, defined by a White standard that she realizes she will never reach. What appears to be a recurring theme of insecurity is actually a deeper notion of inner strength that Maude has developed over the years. In spite of the oppression and poverty around her and a husband who is self-absorbed and inattentive to her needs, Maude preserves her dignity. Readers come to appreciate her qualities of resistance, hope, and self-love. During the long gray days of her dismal life, she is able to hope for a brighter tomorrow and to see the beauty in her community, her life, and herself. Perhaps Brooks' greatest triumph in this novel is her ability to share the life of the ordinary African American woman, a real departure from earlier novels that have relied on the lives of tragic mulattos, destitute wayward women, or large, nurturing, asexual mammies.

Several novels depict the complexity of the lives of young adults during this period. For example, James Baldwin's *Go Tell It on the Mountain* (1952) is an autobiographical first novel. The narrative was an outlet for the psychological wounds inflicted on Baldwin by his stepfather. As a mirror of his life, the story is about John Grimes, a sensitive 14-year-old boy living under the religious rigidity of a mentally ill stepfather. John, like most teenagers, is in search of himself and his place in the world. The novel attempts to explain John's passage from childhood to manhood. Through a series of flashbacks, readers come to understand the history of the Grimes family through the life stories of Gabriel, Florence, and Elizabeth Grimes. Baldwin's personal relationship with religion, as a teenager preacher at the Fireside Pentecostal Assembly, is clear as he references biblical passages and uses biblical allusions throughout the novel.

One of the most anthologized works from this period is Lorraine Hansberry's play, *A Raisin in the Sun* (1959). In this play, Hansberry described the lives of the Younger family and their desire to take hold of the American dream. Another example of coming-of-age and family struggle is found in Paule Marshall's *Brown Girl, Brownstones* (1959). Marshall, the daughter of Barbadian immigrants, also wrote a collection of stories, *Soul Clap Hands and Sing* (1961), and a second novel, *The Chosen Place, the Timeless People* (1969). Her first novel is a coming-of-age story about Selina Boyce, a teenage girl living in Brooklyn, whose parents are immigrants from Barbados. Selina must deal with her cultural island roots, coming-of-age, her parents' disintegrating marriage, and racial conflict. Much of the novel portrays Selina's love and admiration for her easygoing, idealistic father, who inherits money and wishes to return home to Barbados, and her disdain for her mother's strong-willed determination to purchase a house in the United States. In the end, Selina realizes that she is more like her mother, a relationship that is healed as Selina embarks on her own search for self as she returns to her Caribbean roots.

During this period, African American writers joined others in protesting the barriers to entering mainstream American life. As African Americans became more vocal in their demands for equal rights, African American authors also became more vocal as they produced social protest literature. Writers on the political front eloquently expressed the rising discontent of African Americans with the status quo. Typical of these writings were Baldwin's *Nobody Knows My Name* (1961) and *The Fire Next Time* (1963). The 1960s found many African Americans revolting against racial injustice and discrimination by using various forms of nonviolent protest, including sit-ins, marches, demonstrations, and voter registration. Martin Luther King, Jr., exposed the depth of racial hatred and discrimination, as dramatized nightly in media coverage of demonstrators marching and being repelled by water hoses or gas. King's *Letter From Birmingham Jail* (1963) helped to stir national support for the Civil Rights Movement. King calls for a peaceful solution to racial discrimination in the nation, in his "I have a dream" address and his prophetic "I've been to the mountaintop" speech; both are important readings from this period. In addition, Malcolm X, with Alex Haley, published the *Autobiography of Malcolm X* in 1964. This work captures the life of Malcolm and offers readers a broader understanding of the goals of this African American leader than the radical, violent, sterotypical image publicized by the national media.

## Literature of the Black Arts/ Black Aesthetic Movement

In contrast to King's nonviolent stance, the Black Power Movement began in 1966 as some African Americans grew tired of the snail's pace by which the federal government and the nonviolent forms of protest moved, as well as in response to the Watts race riots of 1965. The Black Panther Party came to symbolize and articulate Black nationalism and revolution. Many African Americans turned their thoughts to their African roots and sought to better understand their African heritage. It was during this period that Kwanza was established by a professor of African American studies, Dr. Maulana Karenga, chairman of the Black Studies Department at the University of California. During Kwanza (December 26 through January 1), people celebrate African American culture and community with feasts, storytelling, and symbolic activities. It was also popular during this period to adopt African names, dress, and cultural ways. The natural hairstyle worn by many African Americans was a sign of pride in their African heritage and a sign of protest of Euro-American culture and notions of beauty.

Black nationalist groups demanded control of schools in the African American community and sought to introduce courses that focused on African and African American history, language, thought, and literature. The Black Arts Movement, a sister movement to the Black Power Movement, fought for liberation through art, music, drama, and literature (see the writings of LeRoi Jones/Amiri Baraka, Don Lee/Haki Madhubuti, Nikki Giovanni, and Sonya Sanchez, among others). The writers of the Black Arts Movement sought to redefine the standards of African American literature; known as the Black Aesthetic Movement, it centered on constructing an African American set of standards by which to evaluate African American writings. The rise of African American female authors was also a result of this movement. The works of African American poets Sonya Sanchez and Nikki Giovanni are a testament to the power of the movement.

If 1920–1960 was a sparse period for African American young adult literature, 1960–1980 more than compensated for it. By the 1960s and 1970s, African Americans had become a visible and vital part of urban life as Euro-Americans fled the cities for the suburbs. In the United States, the rebellious 1960s and early 1970s was a time of open expression of resistance to authority and sexual repression, drug use, and individual freedom. The nation was in the midst of a most unpopular war; it was fought on the battlefields of Vietnam, and resistance to it was fought on college campuses, on city streets, and in government meetings. The media was pivotal in its coverage of the war and the national protests. Every night the war was televised, along with the names of all the soldiers reported missing or dead. The nightly scroll of Americans losing their lives helped to spread despair about the future among young people. Many African Americans managed to maintain their strong religious beliefs, folklore, and sense of community and began to write. For the first time in history a proliferation of young adult African American literature appeared. The literature can be divided into three categories: realistic fiction, historical fiction, and science fiction.

The realistic fiction written during this period dealt with coming-of-age as experienced by teenagers of African descent in urban centers. Collectively, much of the literature reflects life in urban centers, including many of the problems that come from living in poverty. Among the first published writers of young adult literature during this period was Kristen Hunter. Hunter's writings, like those to follow (e.g., Sharon Bell Mathis and Alice Childress) articulate a conscious effort to instill racial pride, affirm cultural beauty, and acknowledge community among African Americans. Their stories are told within and as a part of the communities in which the characters live. There are no excuses or attempts to sanitize the lives of the characters. For example, in Hunter's young adult novel, *Soul Brothers and Sister Lou* (1976), Hunter describes how 14-year-old Louretta Hawkins begins to understand herself and her world through her involvement in a neighborhood musical group. The story is upbeat and at times unrealistic, yet entertaining. By way of contrast, Sharon Bell Mathis depicts some of the harsh realities experienced by children living in urban ghettos and struggling with poverty in her novels *Listen for the Fig Tree* (1974) and *A Teacup Full of Roses* (1972). Mathis's work is like another young adult fiction writer, Alice Childress; they both seek to realistically depict the lives of those living in poverty.

Childress was raised by her grandmother, who insisted that she record her thoughts, and her ability to be reflective resonates in the independence of her characters. In an interview about her work, Childress (1956) states, "I write about characters without condescension, without making them into an image which some may deem more useful, inspirational, profitable, or suitable" (p. xii). Childress further argues that it is important to offer a more humane picture of America's underclass, one that is not used as "source material for derogatory humor and/or condescending clinical, social analysis" (p. xii). Her work describes many forms of destruction in the lives of her characters (self, relationships, families, institutions, and society) while challenging the prevailing images of Black characters. She creates vivid, lifelike characters with striking images and careful words. In her book, *Conversations With a Domestic*, Childress created a female counterpart to Langston Hughes's Jesse B. Semple in Mildred, an "ordinary" African American female domestic worker. Childress's 62 stories of Mildred describe how she sees and interacts with the White world with philosophical insight and humor. Mildred was brave and wise enough to speak out against the exploitive working conditions that many African American female domestic workers faced daily in their efforts to care for their families. Several short stories in the collection have been published in high school literature anthologies, most notably "The Pocketbook Game" and "The Healthcard."

Other features of Childress's writings include her straightforward approach to controversial topics and her use of an omniscient point of view. In her first young adult novel, *A Hero Ain't Nothing But a Sandwich* (1973), the main character is a 13-year-old drug addict named Benjie. Childress helps the reader to understand Benjie by using alternating chapters that show how others in his life view him and his problem. Everyone appears to want Benjie to enter and complete a treatment program; however, as the book ends the reader is not sure of Benjie's decision. In her more recent young adult novels, *Rainbow Jordan* (1981) and *Those Other People* (1989), Childress continues to tackle uncharted areas in young adult literature. Two examples illustrate Childress's willingness to attack contemporary issues such as dysfunctional and changing family relationships, homosexuality, AIDS, and interracial dating. Her novel *Rainbow Jordan* is dedicated to children who are being raised by someone other than their biological parents. Rainbow, the main character, is a physically and emotionally abused teenage girl living in a single-parent home with an adult who is not gainfully employed—not your typical main character but reflective of the life of some children. In *Those Other People* Childress focuses on teenage homosexuality. The novel centers on the life of a gay teenager who hasn't revealed his sexual preference to his parents. Structurally, these two novels follow Childress's pattern of alternating between the points of view of various characters and sharing the innermost thoughts of the main character. *Those Other People* is also unique in that it describes the difficulties endured by a Euro-American gay male teenager—a departure from Childress's previous works, which have focused solely on the relationships in African American families and communities.

Historical fiction also became a very popular genre during this period for writers of African American literature for young adults. One popular writer of historical fiction is Julius Lester, a prolific writer who has been a constant contributor to the body of young adult literature for nearly three decades. His first book for young adults, *To Be a Slave* (1968), a Newberry Honor Book, was the first book written by an African American to receive that award. In 1972 he was a National Book Award finalist for *Long Journey Home: Stories From Black History*.

Lester's early writings reflect his scholarship and interest in African American history and narrative. For example, *To Be a Slave* is a significant book that records the language, rhythm, and voices of former African American slaves. By using transcriptions of interviews, Lester allows former slaves to speak for themselves about the inhumane treatment they endured. The interviews are written in narrative form and collectively become a story of what it was like to be an African American slave. Lester also includes reprints of published slave narratives, which were written to help encourage support for the antislavery movement. Another example of Lester's work in historical fiction is his second award-winning book, *Long Journey Home*. It includes six short stories based on real-life events with some poetic license. The stories describe the lives and experiences of "ordinary people" doing the extraordinary. Lester (1972) states that "these stories comprise the essence of black history, . . . as individuals who embodied in their lives and actions the ethos of their times, and for that reason stand out above the mass" (p. xi).

A decade later, Lester accomplished a similar feat with his book, *This Strange New Feeling* (1982). Again, he retells three historically documented stories of events in the lives of African Americans during slavery. This book is a collection of romantic stories of African Americans. In the first story, based on an account published in *The Anglo African Magazine* (Vol. 1, No. 10, 1859), Lester used historical documents to tell the love story of William and Ellen Craft. He was inspired to collect and publish these stories after his own chance encounter with their great-granddaughter. *This Strange New Feeling* is unique in that tells both sides of slavery, from the viewpoint of the owners and their perceived needs as well as from the viewpoint of the slaves. For the Crafts, freedom comes in the love that is shared between them and in the ability to live as human beings in the United States. This collection of stories differs radically from the Euro-American depictions of love between African American slaves. The collection helps to dispel the myths that are perpetrated in Euro-American novels of the uncontrollable sexual desires and emotional immaturity of African American slaves. Furthermore, this book explores and illustrates the depths of the romantic love, controlled passion, respect, and commitment of African American couples. Lester describes the tender love and affection that oppressed people displayed despite the fact that their conditions denied them the many pleasures and comforts of life. Finally, Lester's mastery of the genre is seen in his beautifully written novel, *Do Lord Remember Me* (1984), which is poetic in its use of word pictures that capture the rhythm and song of the language and the folk ways of African Americans. Following is a short passage that illustrates the richness of the language:

> Charles, I been knowing you since before you knowed yourself. I knowed your daddy be'ore you was a twinkle in his eye, and I remeber ol' Trembel, your granddaddy, too. Didn't think too highly of him, though. He knew that when old folks started off reciting you family history, they hadn't come to pass the time of day. (p. 13)

Lester was not the only African American author to gain popular support for his work in historical fiction during this period. The works of two African American female authors, Mildred Taylor and Virginia Hamilton, are legendary. Taylor's *Roll of Thunder, Hear My Cry* (1976) offered a fresh look at the strength, devotion, and courage of the African American family in her description of the adventures of the Logan family during the Depression in rural Mississippi. Taylor has written two sequels about the Logan family, *Let the Circle Be Unbroken* (1981) and *The Road to Memphis* (1990). All three books are popular choices of teachers and African American young adults.

The works of Virginia Hamilton represent some of the best African American young adult writing available. An award-winning author, Hamilton is beginning her third decade of writing books for children and young adults. Her many awards include being the first author of children's literature to receive the John D. and Catherine T. MacArthur Fellowship and the first African American woman to receive the Newberry Medal (for *M. C. Higgins the Great*, 1974). She also has received Newberry Honor Book awards, the Boston Globe-Horn Book Award for Nonfiction, American Library Association Notable Book awards, and American Library Association Best Book for Young Adults awards, among others. Her works center on the lives of African Americans in the United States and includes historical and realistic fiction. She challenges readers to understand the past, as in *The House of Dries Drear* (1968), and to accept the present, as in *Cousins* (1990). She also writes about the struggles of biracial girls and their coming-of-age in *Arilla Sun Down* (1976), a powerful story of a mixed-race African American and Native American girl, and *Plain City* (1993), the story of a mixed-race African American and Euro-American girl seeking to understand her past.

The third genre which African American authors entered during this period is science fiction. Octavia Butler's creative and unique blend of historical fiction and science fiction offered another means of telling our stories. Butler's *Pattern Master* (1976), *Mind of My Mind* (1977), and *Kindred* (1979) are exemplary of her creative melding as she address historical struggles of race, gender, and power.

Finally, several other novels from this time period have been used in high school literature classes and have caused concern over the suitability of the works for high school students. These include *I Know Why the Caged Bird Sings* (1969) by Maya Angelou, *The Bluest Eye* (1970) and *Sula* (1973) by Toni Morrison, *The Autobiography of Miss Jane Pittman*

(1971) by Ernest Gaines, and *Roots: The Saga of an American Family* (1976) by Alex Haley.

## African American Literature in the 1980s and 1990s

The 1980s and 1990s have been labeled the Second Renaissance of African American literature. Several interwoven factors have contributed to the recognition of the importance of writing and publishing more African American literature, but none has been as influential as the Afrocentrism Movement. The movement began as a response to the demand to include African American history and literature courses in colleges and high schools. In some areas of the country, it has progressed to the point of establishing separate Afrocentric schools in several large cities. Another important factor has been the debate over the place of multicultural literature in the curriculum. The canonical literature taught in high schools has come under attack for its European male-dominated offerings, to the near exclusion of works by people of color and by women. While there has been a renewed interest in African American literature on the whole and a special emphasis on sharing the "classics" in African American literature, its place in the high school curriculum is still uncertain. Finally, the Second Renaissance of African American literature has been "created out of an African American consciousness and experience" (D. Johnson, 1990, p. 81) that does not attempt to compete with or mimic Euro-American experiences.

Today, young adult literature has been positively affected by the greater number and variety of published works that target African American young adults. Themes of African Americanness pervade new novels, prompting D. Johnson (1990) to describe this phenomenon as "telling the stories of Black people as Black people—not the stories of a few representative African Americans depicted in white worlds. In this way, a broader and 'truer,' more inclusive mural of African Americans begins to unfold" (p. 52). Contemporary literature depicts a range of African American life, from urban centers to suburbs to rural settings, that is more representative of life in America for African Americans.

The young adult literature of the Second Renaissance includes re-published slave narratives with introductory scholarly essays; for ex-ample, Henry Louis Gates, Jr.'s, 1983 reprint of Harriet Wilson's, *Our Nig: Or, Sketches From the Life of a Free Black*; Jean Yellin's 1987 reprint of Harriet Jacobs' *Incidents in the Life of a Slave Girl*; Robert Allison's 1995 reprint of *The Interesting Narrative of the Life of Olaudah Equiano*; and Nell Painters' *Soujourner Truth: A Life, a Symbol* (1996). Fictional works of this period can be seen as extensions of an earlier interest in family lineage and generational sagas—for example, *Mama Day* (1988) by Gloria Naylor—and fictional slave narratives—for example, Sherley Williams' *Dessa Rose* (1986).

Autobiographies and biographies remain popular genres for Afri-can American writers. Publications during this period include the re-published Booker T. Washington's *Up From Slavery: The Autobiography of Booker T. Washington* (1993); memories of those who took part in the Civil Rights Movement, such as Septima Clark's *Ready From Within: Septima Clark and the Civil Rights Movement* (Brown, 1986); Yvonne Thornton's *The Ditchdigger's Daughters* (1996), and Melba Pattlio Beals' *Warriors Don't Cry* (1994); memories of strong supportive African American families and communities, such as *Betsey Brown* (1985) by Ntozake Shange and *When We Were Colored* (1995) by Clifton L. Taulbert; and those that deal with social issues like divorce, such as *Sweet Summer: Growing Up With and Without My Dad* (1989) by Bebe Moore Campbell.

Julius Lester's autobiographical *Lovesong: Becoming a Jew* (1988) reveals how he has come to understand himself better since his dis-covery of his mixed racial and religious heritage. In addition, Lester returns to writing historical fiction in his moving novel, *And All Our Wounds Forgiven* (1994).

Contemporary young adult literature focuses on several recurring themes: parental conflict, intergenerational problems, culture, sub-stance use, sexual encounters, and peer pressure. There has been a bountiful crop of literature published during this period, some of which takes a fresh look at African American life. For example, J. Thomas captures the intimate role of religion in the lives, culture, and history of African Americans in her characters in *Marked by Fire* (1982), *Bright Shadow* (1983), and *When the Nightingale Sings* (1992). In the novel

*Marked by Fire*, Thomas emphasizes the role of the Church in helping to solidify community and form identity, themes often missing in much of the young adult literature. Moreover, Thomas articulates a deep understanding of the love and support that are natural and often unspoken aspects of the richness of African American community life. For example, *Marked by Fire* details the life of Abyssinia Jackson, from the events preceding her birth until her teen years, in a small African American community in the rural Oklahoma town of Ponca City with an insider's heart, soul, ear, and eye for detail. In this novel and in all of Thomas's novels, she includes fathers and father figures; an often unstated concern in young adult fiction is the representation of males in African American families. The use of fathers and father figures has varied from saints to demonlike men, as authors and readers struggle to relate the pressures and constraints upon African American men in the roles of father, brother, relative, and friend. Thomas's writings hint to a recent trend in young adult literature that attempts to understand the psychological as well as societal constraints under which African American men must learn to function and survive in the United States. Thomas's novels encapsulate many of these current trends, as they center around cultural and religious aspects of African American community life. Each of Thomas's novels allows young adults to see themselves and their cultural and religious customs as normal and acceptable by highlighting their importance in our daily lives.

The young adult literature of the 1990s reflects the changing nature of life in America for African Americans. Novels now focus on the social challenges of teenage unemployment, school violence, alcohol and drug abuse, sexual harassment, and HIV infection and AIDS. Several recurrent themes in modern young adult literature include self-identity, conflicts with parents, peer pressure, and the role of African American history in shaping the lives of the characters. Impressively, there are more novels that depict a range of African American experiences, from upper and middle class to rural to urban poor; there are more novels that represented ranges in family composition and relationships; and there are more novels that openly address issues long thought taboo for young adults.

## Summary

The history of African American young adult literature is intimately tied to the history of Africa and African American culture, language, and folk ways. African American literature began shortly after African slaves were brought to this country. Early literature resembled the literature of Euro-Americans in style and content; as African Americans became acculturated, they began to venture into their own unique forms of literature, such as slave narratives. The literature by African Americans has survived in spite of limited opportunities to acquire literacy, publish works, and receive recognition for their writing. The literature of the Harlem Renassiance reflected the growth of literacy opportunities for African Americans and an interest in our lives and writing. The publication of literature especially designed to appeal to young adults can be seen in the growing number of publications during this period. Interest in African American young adult literature increased slowly over the years, culminating in a watershed of materials during the Black Arts Movement. Today, there is a plethora of publications aimed at this audience.

Ironically, the literature used in secondary schools seldom incorporates the available young adult literature. As research in young adult literature attests (Applebee, 1989; Graff, 1992), much of the current literature used in secondary classrooms today was considered adult literature in the past. The African American literature typically used in secondary schools is more adult in nature than much of what has been reviewed here. Missing from this review are the writings of several African American authors who have tremendous appeal to young adults: Rosa Guy (*The Friends, Ruby, The Ups and Downs of Carl Davis III*, and *The Music of Summer*); Rita Garcia Williams (*Blue Tights*); and Walter Dean Myers (*Scorpions, Glory Field*). Their writings are not part of the curriculum. The absence of their work in this chapter is not because these authors' voices are unimportant but because their work has yet to enter the mainstream of young adult literature used in schools in grades 9–12.

More than two decades ago, Stanford & Amin (1978) observed that "the old convention of keeping all literature incorporating sex, other adult themes, and street language taboo until college, regardless of the facts of students' real lives, has given way to a tendency to see adult reading as appropriate for high school students" (p. 6). The use of adult fiction in high school literature classes appears more prominent with the work of non–European American authors. The adult African American literature often used in secondary schools is far more complex, sophisticated, and graphic in nature than young adult literature. Educators, parents, and community groups have voiced their concern over a number of African American adult novels used in literature classes at the secondary level, including *The Color Purple* (1982) by Alice Walker, *Beloved* (1987) by Toni Morrison, *Middle Passage* (1990) by Charles Johnson, and *Waiting to Exhale* (1992) by Terri McMillian. These are all wonderfully written books, but they are not young adult literature. Clearly, there is an ample supply of African American young adult literature from which one can select that young people will find challenging and enjoyable.

## Notes

1. The slave narrative was not, however, the most influential form of literacy used by the abolitionists to support their cause. Speeches given by ex-slaves were often used to compel audiences to action. Barksdale and Kinnamon (1972) reveal that "not only did Black autobiographers, polemicists, and poets exercise their pens against slavery, but Black abolitionist lecturers ventured across the North carrying the message of freedom to town, hamlet, and cabin. Oratory, it should be remembered, was a major literary form in nineteenth-century America. . . . The best Black oratory still retains considerable emotive power in printed form." (p. 61)

2. Dianne Johnson (1996), with the assistance of Oxford University Press, has edited and republished selections under the title *The Best of the Brownies' Book*.

## Reading List

Allison, R. (Ed.), (1995). *The interesting narrative of the life of Olaudah Equiano, written by himself.* Boston: St. Martin's Press.

Angelou, M. (1969). *I know why the caged bird sings.* New York: Bantam.

Baldwin, J. (1952). *Go tell it on the mountain.* New York: Bantam.

Baldwin, J. (1961). *Nobody knows my name.* New York: Bantam.

Baldwin, J. (1963). *The fire next time.* New York: Bantam.

Beals, M. (1994). *Warriors don't cry: A searing memoir of the battle to integrate Little Rock's Central High.* New York: Washington Square Press.

Bontemps, A. (1936). *Black thunder.* New York: Macmillan.

Bontemps, A. (1939). *Drums at dusk.* New York: Macmillan.

Bontemps, A. (Ed.). (1941). *Golden slippers: An anthology of Negro poetry for young readers.* New York: Harper & Brothers.

Bontemps, A. (1945). *We have tomorrow.* Boston: Houghton Mifflin.

Bontemps, A. (1948). *The story of the Negro.* New York: Knopf.

Brooks, G. (1945). *A street in Bronzeville.* New York: Harper.

Brooks, G. (1949). *Annie Allen.* New York: Harper Row.

Brooks, G. (1953). *Maude Martha.* New York: Harper Row.

Brooks, G. (1960). *The bean eaters.* New York: Harper Row.

Brown, C. (Ed.).(1986). *Septima Clark and the Civil Rights Movement, ready from within:A first person narrative.* Trenton, NJ: Africa World Press.

Brown, H. (1849). *Narrative of Henry Box Brown.* Boston: Brown & Sterns.

Brown, H. (1864). *John Freeman and his family.* Boston: American Tract Society.

Brown, W. (1847/1970). *Narrative of William W. Brown, a fugitive slave, written by himself.* Boston: Anti-Slavery Office.

Brown, W. (1853/1995). *Clotel, or the president's daughter: A narrative of slave life in the United States.* New York: Carole Books.

Butler, O. (1976). *Pattern master.* New York: Warner Books.

Butler, O. (1977). *Mind of my mind.* New York: Warner Books.

Butler, O. (1979). *Kindred.* Boston: Beacon Press.

Campbell, B. (1989). *Sweet summer: Growing up with and without my dad.* New York: Ballantine Books.

Chase-Riboud, Barbara (1994). *The president's daughter.* New York: Crown.

Childress, A. (1956). *Like one of the family: Conversations from a domestic's life.* Boston: Beacon Press.

Childress, A. (1973). *A hero ain't nothin but a sandwich.* New York: Coward, McCann & Geoghegan.

Childress, A. (1981). *Rainbow Jordan.* New York: Coward-McCann.

Childress, A. (1989). *Those other people.* New York: Putnam.

Douglass, F. (1845/1961). *Narrative of the life of Frederick Douglass, an American slave, written by himself.* New York: Penguin.

Douglass, F. (1855). *My bondage and my freedom*. New York: Miller, Orton, & Mulligan.

Douglass, F. (1881). *Life and times of Frederick Douglass*. Hartford, CT: Park Publishing.

Du Bois, W. E. B. (1903/1989). *The souls of black folks*. New York: Bantam.

Ellison, R. (1952). *The invisible man*. New York: Random House.

Equiano, O. (1789/1995). *The interesting narrative of the life of Olaudah Equiano, or Gustavus Vassa the African, written by himself*. Boston: Bedford Books.

Gaines, E. (1971). *The autobiography of Miss Jane Pittman*. New York: Bantam.

Gaines, E. (1983). *A gathering of old men*. New York: Vintage.

Gaines, E. (1993). *A lesson before dying*. New York: Vintage Contemporaries.

Greene, M. (1991). *Praying for Sheetrock: A work of non-fiction*. New York: Fawcett.

Guy, R. (1973). *The friends*. New York: Holt, Rinehart & Winston.

Guy, R. (1976). *Ruby*. New York: Bantam Doubleday.

Guy, R. (1989). *The ups and downs of Carl Davis III*. New York: Delacorte Press.

Guy, R. (1992). *The music of summer*. New York: Delacorte Press.

Haley, A. (1976). *Roots: The saga of an American family*. Garden City, NJ: Doubleday.

Hamilton, V. (1968). *The house of Dries Drear*. New York: Collier Books.

Hamilton, V. (1974). *M. C. Higgins, the great*. New York: Simon & Schuster.

Hamilton, V. (1976). *Arilla Sun Down*. New York: Scholastic.

Hamilton, V. (1982). *Sweet whispers, Brother Rush*. New York: Avon Books.

Hamilton, V. (1990). *Cousins*. New York: Philomel.

Hamilton, V. (1993). *Plain city*. New York: Scholastic.

Hammon, J. (1761). An evening thought: Salvation by Christ with penitential cries. In D. Mullane (Ed.), (1993). *Crossing the danger water: Three hundred years of African-American writing* (p.27). New York: Doubleday.

Hamon, B. (1760). *Narrative of the uncommon sufferings and surprising deliverance of Brian Hammon, A Negro man*. Boston: Green & Russell.

Hansberry, L. (1959). *A raisin in the sun.* New York: Random House.

Harper, F. (1892/1988). *Iola Leroy: Or, shadows uplifted.* New York: Oxford University Press.

Harris, E. (1993). *South of haunted dreams: A ride through slavery's old backyard.* New York: Simon & Schuster.

Hauke, K. (Ed.). (1991). *The dark side of Hopkinsville: Stories by Ted Poston.* Athens, GA: University of Georgia Press.

Haynes, E. (1921). *Unsung heroes.* New York: Du Bois & Dill.

Hopkins, P. (1900/1988). *Contending forces: A romance of Negro life North and South.* New York: Oxford University Press.

Hughes, L. (1940). *The big sea: An autobiography by Langston Hughes.* New York: Knopf.

Hughes, L. (1950). *Simple speaks his mind.* New York: Simon & Schuster.

Hughes, L. (1953). *Simple takes a wife.* New York: Simon & Schuster.

Hughes, L. (1957). *I wonder as I wander.* New York: Rinehart.

Hughes, L. (1961). *Best of Simple.* New York: Hill & Lang.

Hughes, L., & Bontemps, A. (1958). *Book of Negro folklore.* New York: Dodd, Meade.

Hughes, L., & Bontemps, A. (1969). *Great slave narratives.* Boston: Beacon Press.

Hughes, L., & Hurston, Z. (1931/1990). *Mule bone: A comedy of Negro life.* New York: Lippincott/HarperCollins.

Hunter, K. (1976). *Soul brothers and sister Lou.* New York: Scribner.

Hurston, Z. (1934/1990). *Jonah's gourd vine.* New York: Lippincott/HarperCollins.

Hurston, Z. (1935/1990). *Mules and men.* New York: Lippincott/HarperCollins.

Hurston, Z. (1937/1990). *Their eyes were watching God.* New York: Lippincott/HarperCollins.

Hurston, Z. (1938/1990). *Tell my horse.* New York: Lippincott/HarperCollins.

Hurston, Z. (1939/1990). *Moses, man of the mountain.* New York: Lippincott/HarperCollins.

Hurston, Z. (1942/1991). *Dust tracks on a road: An autobiography.* New York: Lippincott/HarperCollins.

Hurston, Z. (1948/1990). *Seraph on the Suwanee.* New York: Lippincott/HarperCollins.

Jacobs, H. (1861). *Incidents in the life of a slave girl, written by herself.* Boston: Published for the author.

Johnson, A. (1890). *Clarence and Corinne, or God's way.* Philadelphia: American Baptist Publication Society.

Johnson, A. (1894). *The Hazeley Family.* Philadelphia: American Baptist Publication Society.

Johnson, C. (1990). *Middle passage.* New York: Plume.

Johnson, J. (1912/1927). *Autobiography of an Ex-colored man.* New York: Knopf.

Kelley-Hawkins, E. (1891). *Megda.* Boston: Earle.

Kelley-Hawkins, E. (1898). *Four girls at Cottage City.* Boston: Earle.

Lester, J. (1968). *To be a slave.* New York: Scholastic.

Lester, J. (1969). *Black folktales.* New York: Grove Press.

Lester, J. (1969). *Revolutionary notes.* New York: Baron.

Lester, J. (1969). *Search for the new land.* New York: Dial Press.

Lester, J. (1972). *Long journey home: Stories from Black history.* New York: Dial Press.

Lester, J. (1972). *Two love stories.* New York: Dial Press.

Lester, J. (1982). *This strange new feeling.* New York: Dial Press.

Lester, J. (1984). *Do Lord remember me.* New York: Holt, Rinehart & Winston.

Lester, J. (1988). *Lovesong: Becoming a Jew.* New York: Holt.

Lester, J. (1994). *And all our wounds forgiven.* New York: Arcade.

Lester, J. (1995). *Othello: A novel.* New York: Scholastic.

Mandela, N. (1994). *Long walk to freedom: The autobiography of Nelson Mandela.* Boston: Little, Brown.

Marshall, P. (1959). *Brown girl, brownstones.* New York: Feminist Press.

Marshall, P. (1961). *Soul clap hands and sing.* Madison, NJ: Chatham.

Marshall, P. (1969). *The chosen place, the timeless people.* New York: Vintage.

Mathis, S. (1972). *A teacup full of roses.* New York: Viking.

Mathis, S. (1974). *Listen for the fig tree.* New York: Puffin Books.

McMillian, T. (1992). *Waiting to exhale.* New York: Simon & Schuster.

Morrison, T. (1970). *The bluest eye.* New York: Knopf.

Morrison, T. (1973). *Sula.* New York: Plume.

Morrison, T. (1987). *Beloved.* New York: Plume.

Myers, W. (1988). *Scorpions.* New York: HarperCollins.

Myers, W. (1994). *Glory field.* New York: Scholastic.

Naylor, G. (1988). *Mama Day*. New York: Ticknor & Fields.

Njeri, I. (1982). *Every good-bye ain't gone*. New York: Vintage.

Parker, G. (1995). *These same long bones*. New York: Plume.

Pennington, J. (1849/1971). *The fugitive blacksmith; Or, events in the life of James W. C. Pennington*. New York: Westport.

Petry, A. (1948). *Tituba of Salem village*. New York: Crowell.

Phillips, C. (1993). *Crossing the river*. New York: Vintage.

Seacole, M. (1857). *Wonderful adventures of Mrs. Seacole in many lands*. Boston: Earle.

Shange, N. (1975). *For colored girls who considered suicide when the rainbow was enuf*. New York: Collier Books.

Shange, N. (1985). *Betsey Brown*. New York: Picador USA.

Taulbert, C. (1995). *When we were colored*. New York: Penguin.

Taylor, M. (1976). *Roll of thunder, hear my cry*. New York: Penguin.

Taylor, M. (1981). *Let the circle be unbroken*. New York: Penguin.

Taylor, M. (1990). *The road to Memphis*. New York: Penguin.

Terry, L. (1746). Bar Fight. In H. Gates & N. McKay (Eds.), (1997). *The Norton Anthology of African American Literature* (p. 137). New York: Norton.

Thomas, J. (1982). *Marked by fire*. New York: Avon Books.

Thomas, J. (1983). *Bright shadow*. New York: Avon Books.

Thomas, J. (1992). *When the nightingale sings*. New York: HarperTrophy.

Thornton, Y. (1996). *The ditchdigger's daughters: A black family's astonishing success story*. New York: Plume.

Walker, A. (1982). *The color purple*. New York: Washington Square Press.

Washington, B. (1901/1993). *Up from slavery: The autobiography of Booker T. Washington*. New York: Carole.

Washington, M. (Ed.). (1993). *Narrative of Sojourner Truth*. New York: Vintage Books.

Wheatley, P. (1773). *Poems on various subjects, religious and moral, by Phillis Wheatley, Negro servant to Mr. Wheatley of Boston*. In R. Barksdale & K. Kinnamon (Eds.), (1972). *Black writers of America: A comprehensive anthology* (pp. 40–44). Englewood Cliffs, NJ: Prentice-Hall.

Williams, R. G. (1988). *Blue tights*. New York: Bantam Books.

Williams, S. (1986). *Dessa Rose*. New York: Berkley Books.

Wilson, H. (1859/1983). *Our nig: Or, sketches from the life of a free Black*. Boston: Rand & Avery.

Wright, R. (1938). *Uncle Tom's children: Four novellas*. New York: HarperCollins.

Wright, R. (1940). *Native son*. New York: HarperCollins.

Wright, R. (1945). *Black boy: A record of childhood and youth*. New York: Harper & Row.

X, Malcolm. (1964). *Autobiography of Malcolm X* (as told to Alex Haley). New York: Random House.

# References

Allison, R. (Ed.), (1995). *The interesting narrative of the life of Olaudah Equiano, written by himself*. Boston: St. Martin's Press. (originally published in 1789).

Applebee, A. (1989). *A study of book-length works taught in high school English courses* (Report No. 1.2). Albany, NY: Center for the Learning and Teaching of Literature.

Aptheker, H. (Ed.). (1980). *Writings in periodicals edited by W. E. B. Du Bois: Selections from the Brownies' Book*. Millwood, NY: Kraus-Thomson.

Barksdale, R., & Kinnamon, K. (1972). *Black writers of America: A comprehensive anthology*. Englewood Cliffs, NJ: Prentice-Hall.

Bell, B. (1987). *The Afro-American novel and its tradition*. Amherst, MA: University of Massachusetts Press.

Bennett, L. (1982). *Before the Mayflower: A history of Black America*. Chicago: Johnson.

Bloom, H. (1994). *The Western canon: The books and school of the ages*. New York: Riverhead Books.

Brinckerhoff, I. (1864). *Advice to freedmen*. New York: American Tract Society.

Childress, A. (1956). *Converstions from a domestic's life*. Boston: Beacon Press.

Christian, C. (1988). *Black saga: The African American*. Boston: Houghton Mifflin.

Cowan, T., & Maguire, J. (1994). *Timelines of African-American history: 500 years of Black achievement*. New York: Perigee Books.

DuBois, W. E. B. (Ed.), (1920–1921). *The Brownies Book*. New York: DuBois & Dill.

Fisk, C. (1866). *Plain counsels for freedmen*. Boston: American Tract Society.

Franklin, J., & Moss, A. (1994). *From slavery to freedom: A history of African Americans*. New York: McGraw-Hill.

Gates, H. (Ed.), (1987). *Black literature and literary theory*. New York: Routledge.

Gates, H. (Ed.). (1987). *The classic slave narratives*. New York: Penguin.

Gates, H. (1987). *Figures in black: Words, signs, and the "racial" self*. New York: Oxford University Press.

Gates, H. (1988). *The signifying monkey: A theory of African-American literary criticism*. New York: Oxford University Press.

Gates, H. & McKay, N. (Eds.). (1997). *The Norton anthology of African American literature*. New York: Norton.

Goss, L., & Barnes, M. (Eds.). (1989). *Talk that talk: An anthology of African-American storytelling*. New York: Touchstone Books.

Graff, G. (1992). *Beyond the culture wars: How teaching conflicts can revitalize American education*. New York: Norton.

Hildreth, R. (1836) *The slave; Or, memories of Archy Moore* and the alleged testimonies recorded in Theodore Dwight Weld's (1839) *American slavery as it is: Testimony of a thousand witnesses*.

Hildreth, R. (1836/1969).*The slave; Or, memories of Archy Moore*. Negro University Press.

Huggins, N. (Ed.). (1995). *Voices of the Harlem renaissance*. New York: Oxford University Press.

Hughes, L. (1921). The Negro Speaks of Rivers. *The Crisis*, 23. p. 4.

Hughes, L. (1926). *The Weary Blues*. New York: Knopf.

Johnson, D. (1990). *Telling tales: The pedagogy and promise of African American literature for youth*. New York: Greenwood Press.

Johnson-Feelings, D. (1996). *The best of the Brownies' Book*. New York: Oxford University Press.

King, M. (1963). Letter From Birmingham Jail. In, *Why we can't wait*. New York: HarperCollins.

Morris, R. (1981). *Reading, 'riting, and reconstruction: The education of freedmen in the South 1861–1870*. Chicago: University of Chicago Press.

Mullane, D. (Ed.). (1993). *Crossing the danger water: Three hundred years of African-American writing*. New York: Doubleday.

Painter, N. (1996). *Sojourner Truth: A life, a symbol*. New York: Norton.

Rollock, B. (1984). *The Black experience in children's books.* New York: Garland.

Smith, K. (Ed.). (1994). *African-American voices in young adult literature: Tradition, transition, transformation.* Metuchen, NJ: Scarecrow Press.

Smith, V. (1987). *Self-discovery and authority in Afro-American narrative.* Cambridge, MA: Harvard University Press.

Stanford, B., & Amin, K. (1978). *Black literature for high school students.* Urbana, IL: National Council of Teachers of English.

Van Sertima, I. (1976). *They came before Columbus: The African presence in ancient America.* New York: Random House.

Waterbury, J. (1864). *Friendly counsels for freedmen.* New York: American Tract Society.

Weld, T. (1839). *American slavery as it is: testimony of a thousand witnesses.* New York: Anti-Slavery Society.

Yellin, J., (Ed.). (1987). *Incidents in the life of a slave girl, written by herself.* Cambridge, MA: Harvard University Press.

## Chapter 4

# A Continuing Journey:
# The Puerto Rican Reality
# as Viewed From the Narrative

*Antonio Nadal* and *Milga Morales-Nadal*

*My name is Johnny Stranger*
*and I've come across the sea,*
*If you've never seen an immigrant,*
*just take a look at me.*

*Now please don't think I'm different,*
*because I am an immigrant.*
*Remember that you were once an immigrant too . . .*

JHS 50, Brooklyn, New York, 1958

These words, taken from a seventh-grade play performed more than 30 years ago in a New York City public school during the celebration of Pan-American Week, purported to reflect a tolerance for difference and its acceptance as a paradigm for American society. A critical evaluation of these lyrics in hindsight reveals the confusion that has been wittingly and unwittingly generated about the perception and definition of an immigrant in U.S. society. In this particular case, the example is ever more poignant, given the fact that the child chosen to sing these words is Puerto Rican: Puerto Ricans, as we will see in this chapter, are *not* immigrants. Moreover, through the use of creative literature, we will demonstrate that the complex reality of Puerto Ricans residing in the mainland United States and in Puerto Rico, and the islands precarious yet relevant relationship to the United States, might become part of the discourse on multicultural and interdisciplinary teaching and learning.

## Puerto Ricans' Nonimmigrant Status

In *The Ethnic Myth* (1985), Steven Steinberg refers to the United States as "a nation without a people." He suggests that, with the notable exception of Native Americans, the American people are not ethnically rooted in the American soil. He differentiates colonial settlers from immigrants, by inference defining *immigrant* as a person who enters an alien society and is forced to acquire a new national identity. Significantly, the colonists referred to themselves as *emigrants* rather than immigrants—identifying with the country they left behind rather than the country they entered. As transplanted British, they sought to forge a *new* England on the North American continent. Consequently, the apparent acceptance of people outside this group was not characterized by ethnically pluralistic altruism but rather guided by economic necessity and carried out via settlement, expansion, and agricultural and industrial development (Steinberg, 1985, p. 11). In 1751, Benjamin Franklin wrote, "Why should Pennsylvania, founded by the English, become a colony of aliens who will shortly be so numerous as to Germanize us . . ." (p. 11). This suspicion of and hostility toward the non-British is encountered in other writings of the Founding Fathers and has been generalized and extended beyond Europeans to peoples of color who have been made part of this nation through conquest, exploitation, and enslavement.

John Ogbu's frequently cited work (1978) has been summarized effectively by several authors, including Catherine E. Walsh in *Pedagogy and the Struggle for Voice* (1991). Ogbu's contention that Puerto Rican migration to the mainland is more like the migration of West Indians to Britain than the migration of, for example, the Japanese to the United States, suggests degrees of difference in the conception of *migration* versus *immigration*. Ogbu has classified Puerto Ricans, Chicanos, Native Americans, and African Americans within the category of people who have been subjected to conquest, slavery, and colonization. According to Walsh (1991), "Ogbu's distinction between minority groups helps explain why it is that some language minority students have more academic success than others. . . . [T]he impact of being a colonialized minority clearly defines and positions the latter group's [Puerto Ricans] lived reality" (pp. 121–122).

U.S. school curricula often ignore the information that could help educators understand the particularities of the Puerto Rican minority in the United States. While most U.S. schoolchildren are exposed to some notion of the history of Native Americans as the original inhabitants of the North American continent, rarely do they study the aboriginal Taino population of Puerto Rico. Moreover, most Americans do not know that Puerto Rico was a fully autonomous nation before the Spanish-American War in 1898; it was ceded to the United States as war booty by the losing Spanish side in the Treaty of Paris (Olga & Waggenheim, 1973). In an effort to sustain the hard-won autonomy granted prior to the U.S. military invasion, one of Puerto Rico's most renowned scholars, Eugenio Maria de Hostos, sought an audience with President McKinley to ask that Puerto Ricans be allowed to decide their political future by popular vote. In reference to this mission, Hostos stated, "It looks now as if my native land is destined to become American territory, whether the inhabitants desire it or not. . . ." (Olga & Waggenheim, 1973, p. 112).

The ensuing Americanization of Puerto Rico may be characterized as insensitive, arbitrary, and often brutal. From its inception, the economic transformation of the island was predicated on the maximization of profits and the exploitation of cheap labor. The creation of an expendable and seasonal labor force in the oligarchical and largely American-owned sugar industry set the foundation for the "push-out" migrant who now alternates between island and mainland job markets as circulatory and redundant workers (*El Centro*, p. 89). In the latter phase of this process, the "modernization" of Puerto Rico stressed the industrial and commmercial development of the island at the expense of its agricultural production. The massive and unplanned displacement of the Puerto Rican peasantry exacerbated the disruption of social patterns that affected the traditional extended family with its folk ways and mores. This forced urbanization yielded an uprooted and itinerant work force that extended beyond island boundaries to the inner cities of the United States. As the Puerto Rican reality is transformed, so too will be the themes that capture the dynamic essence of the generations to follow.

# From "the Land" to the Cement Jungle

In the song "Lamento Borincano," Puerto Rican composer Rafael Hernandez evokes a narrative style characteristic of the Puerto Rican peasant. Written 31 years after the American military occupation began, the lyrics speak of the lament or deep sorrow of the Puerto Rican *jibaro* (peasant) who works the land but reaps little or no profit with which to feed and provide for his family. In this same decade of the 1930s, an emergent militant response to the broken promises of American capitalist democracy was chronicled and denounced in the music and verse of Rafael Hernandez as well as in popular folklore. While Hernandez's "Preciosa" depicted the United States as a colonial tyrant, an Afro–Puerto Rican dance form known as *plena* revealed the people's cynicism with the "New Deal," which promised a full plate and a new pair of trousers. This critical look at "La PRERA" (Puerto Rican Economic Relief Administration) was surpassed in quantity by poems and songs that focused on the relationships between men and women in Puerto Rican society.

This brief account provides a context for the development of a series of themes that emerge from the sociohistorical, economic, and political evolution of a people who, under earlier Spanish rule, resisted colonization and cultural genocide and still continue to forge an identity outside island borders. The lives of Puerto Ricans outside Puerto Rico are reflected in a body of literature produced by the efforts to find "definition"; to identify cultural moorings; and to critically assess the forces that impact (a) migration, (b) the forging of a national consciousness intersecting issues of race, ethnicity, language and gender, and (c) an emerging dialogue on religion in the Latino context.

# Marques's *La Carreta*:
# An Incomplete Journey

An understanding of Puerto Rican literature within the context of the United States must begin with an examination of the sociohistorical and economic factors that impacted Puerto Rico during the period of the Great Depression in the United States. Images of "Brother, can you spare a dime?" and once-successful Wall Street lawyers and bankers selling apples on the streets of Manhattan have been preserved in the print and visual archives of this country, but images of quaint shacks and picturesque countrysides often belie the story of exploitation of the Puerto Rican peasantry during this era.

Puerto Rico in the 1930s was largely agricultural. Men, women, and children worked the land on a seasonal basis. During the sugar cane harvest, the island's main provider of employment, men labored from dawn to dusk for less than 50 cents a day. Women were often employed in the tobacco industry as *despalilladoras* (separating and cleaning tobacco leaves). Women also worked the *doble jornada* (doubling their day with work in the domestic sphere nurturing, feeding, and clothing their families).

While in 1920 a child labor law provided for the exclusion of children from the workplace, an exception was made for children who resided in communities where there were no schools within a reasonable distance. Technically, however, children were required to attend night school if there was one within a kilometer of their homes. In reality, less than 16 percent of the school-age population was enrolled. A significant factor was the implementation of a language policy instituted in Puerto Rico in 1899 that made English the primary language of instruction, even though the lingua franca of the people was Spanish (M. Rodriguez, 1947). The school-age children of that generation recount the somewhat comical and absurd classroom incidents involving the clash of cultures. Some of these are captured in the stories of Don Peyo Merce, a fictional rural teacher impacted by the law decreeing English as the official language of instruction (Diaz-Alfaro, 1951). Maria Sanchez, Professor Emerita of Brooklyn College and former chairwoman of the Puerto Rican Studies Department, notes that as her elementary school teacher in rural Cayey drilled English sentences such as "I am a boy," students often resisted these repetitive and out-of-context utterances by responding mockingly with "Ay, me voy." ("Oh, I'm leaving"). It was not until 1946 that the folly of the language policy was recognized, and Spanish was restored as the language of instruction. Yet it is clear from the literature produced by Puerto Ricans in the United States and Puerto Rico that the language issue is still not resolved.

Rene Marques's *La Carreta* (*The Oxcart*), a three-act play originally written in a dialect of Spanish characteristic of the Puerto Rican *jibaro* and subsequently translated into English, captures not only the dynamism of language use among Puerto Ricans but is also a historical depiction of the Puerto Rican journey. Written in 1953, during the height of the post–World War II migration of Puerto Ricans to the United States, *The Oxcart* is both a vehicle of transportation and a symbolic bridge between the countryside and the metropolis.

The first act is set in rural San Juan, where generations of the family depicted have lived but are now readying to leave in search of the "progress" of urban San Juan. Luis, son of the matriarch, Dona Gabriela, is convinced that the future of Puerto Rico and of his family is no longer in the cultivation of the land but in the "machines" of industry. His grandfather, Don Chago, is convinced that Luis's head is filled with *musarañah* or confusion. Luis responds:

> 'Grandpa,' I'm thinking of the future. Land is not worth much unless you have a lot of it. More and more there is less work in the countryside and more machines taking over. Only the government and the corporations are benefitting from the land. . . . The future is not in the land but in industry. We have to leave the countryside. (p. 10)

The decline of Puerto Rico's rural economy was motivated by the colonial government's emphasis on modernization and industrialization as the answer to the demise of the sugar cane industry in particular and agricultural production in general. The industrialization plan, initiated in 1948 and known as Operation Bootstrap, resulted in the large-scale displacement of the Puerto Rican peasantry from rural mountain areas to the urban slums of San Juan.

The second act finds the family in La Perla (the Pearl). Ironically, this shantytown, situated at the foot of the majestic El Morro castle, contains no wealth and no opportunities for obtaining it. The illusion of good employment, schools, and social progress is shattered and, in Luis's words, becomes the curse of the poor peasant migrant.

In an attempt to maintain the integrity of the family and rid himself of *la maldicion* or curse of poverty, Luis runs from the reality of La Perla to the slums of New York City. In a small apartment of the Morrisania section of the Bronx, the family confronts the ultimate alienation of the newcomer. Luis loses his life in an industrial accident, leaving his mother and sister to lament their abandonment of the land in search of an illusory progress. The play ends with a recognition by Luis's sister Juanita that "It is we who must forge our own destiny." Juanita and her mother stand together ready to return to what they left behind, a culture and identity that seemed to have been lost in this journey.

More than 30 years later a young "Nuyorican" poet, Abran ("Tato") Laviera, returned to the themes of *La Carreta*. In his view, Marques's idealization of the return to the land belies what in fact really happened to this generation. The land had been appropriated by developers, petrochemical and pharmaceutical companies, and other multinational corporations, including hotel chains. Laviera's *La Carreta Made a U-Turn*, a collection of poetry, acknowledges the disappointment of the Puerto Rican who, facing the conditions on the island, picks up once more and makes his or her way back to the United States.

By 1960, the Puerto Rican population in the United States had grown to more than a million. It was and is characterized by the circulatory migration often referred to as a "revolving door," or commuter migration (Acosta-Belen, 1993). In addition, a sizable population had become permanent residents of the United States while affirming a separate cultural identity and maintaining ties with the island. These efforts gave rise to the formation of Puerto Rican institutions that advocated for community development and educational equity as well as hometown groups organized to foster links to the homeland. Racial and linguistic discrimination were often issues of concern within the community. Non–Puerto Rican scholars would attempt, within the context of the classical "immigrant" experience in the United States, to describe and analyze Puerto Ricans as "newcomers" and "strangers" (Senior, 1959, 1961).

With the first publication of Piri Thomas's *Down These Mean Streets* in 1967, a more authentic description of the Puerto Rican reality in the United States was popularized and made accessible to the American mainstream. A compelling autobiographical work that has been characterized as an example of testimonial literature portraying the Puerto Rican experience in New York, Thomas's book makes poignant references to the issues of race, cultural identity, and class as a backdrop to the searing encounters of his childhood. As is the case with most Puerto Ricans, Thomas is the product of racial mixing: His father is dark-skinned, and his mother is a light-skinned woman who could pass for

White in the United States. Growing up in the racial cauldron of New York's East Harlem during the 1940s, the author vividly describes the racial and ethnic turf battles characteristic of the enclave communities of the newly arrived and settled immigrant groups. In a chapter entitled "Alien Turf," Thomas humorously depicts the encounters between himself and the Italian youths of the neighborhood to which he had just moved. Part of his coming-of-age as a young Black Puerto Rican in New York is defined in these turf clashes. He writes, "Sometimes you don't fit in. Like if you are a Puerto Rican in an Italian block" (Thomas, 1991, p. 33). The obvious understatement of this quote belies the pain and hurt of a young man excluded from participating in the life of a community because of his race. Aware of the duality in his ethnic and racial background, Thomas attempts to define himself to the Italian youths who confront him on it, " 'I'm Puerto Rican,' I said. 'I was born here' " (p. 34).

From the optic of what we now refer to as a multicultural America, which purports to respect difference and diversity as a working paradigm for American society, Thomas's statement in the ethnically and racially pluralistic Harlem of the 1930s and 1940s may appear outdated. Yet then as today, the struggle for identity was framed by an atmosphere of racial bigotry toward those whom we deemed different from and therefore inferior to ourselves. Thomas's work reflects urban America during a world war against the evils of Nazism—Hitler's ideology of White (Aryan) supremacy and anti-Semitism. Internally, the United States was called to conscience for its treatment of African Americans in the socioeconomic sphere. Then as now, worsening economic conditions provided a backdrop for racist acts against African Americans and the scapegoating of recently arrived immigrants. World War II brought economic relief through government involvement in the creation of thousands of factory jobs for the war effort.

However, racial discrimination persisted and African Americans were routinely blocked from employment in the major defense industries. Takaki (1993) observes, "Warplanes—Negro Americans may not build them, repair them or fly them but they must help pay for them." Only after a sustained effort by African American political leaders—including A. Philip Randolph, head of the Brotherhood of Sleeping Car Porters—was U.S. policy clarified concerning discrimination in defense industries or the government. Thomas's allusion to his father's employment in an airplane factory in 1944 is an example of the forced response to previous discriminatory hiring practices. The relative prosperity that such employment brought the Thomas family allowed his father to save enough money for a down payment on a house in the suburban town of Babylon in Long Island, New York. A young Piri Thomas approached this new move with trepidation, sensing that the social atmosphere would not be much different than in his present neighborhood. Thomas articulates these fears by suggesting, "My friend Crutch had told me there were a lot of Paddies [derogatory term for Irish] out there, and they didn't dig Negroes or Puerto Ricans" (Thomas, 1991, p. 86).

Thomas's experience in the suburban context served to remind him of the racial divide. Contrary to the conventional wisdom that living in the suburbs signals the achievement of the American dream, Thomas came head-to-head with the second-generation children of European immigrants whose own families had experienced the shame of rejection by the descendants of the early settlers. For the first 250 years of American history, the vast majority of immigrants came from northern and western Europe. After the Civil War, immigrants from eastern and southern Europe arrived at American shores. By 1900 there were Italian communities in every American city in the Northeast. In the urban ghettos of the United States, the existence of dozens of other ethnic groups reinforced more particularized feelings of community. More conscious of politics and ethnicity than ever before, the eastern and southern European immigrants acquired a strong sense of ethnic nationalism. The Irish Catholics, as well as the Italian Catholics, had large families and often maintained extensive kinship ties in their new communities, "But as soon as they could save enough money, the immigrants purchased homes in the outskirts of the city or in the suburbs . . ." (Olson, 1994, p. 225).

These were the communities that the Thomas family encountered. As indicated by the title of the chapter in which Thomas talks about the suburbs, "Babylon [was] for the Babylonians" (Thomas, 1991, p. 86). In one of the most searing accounts in this chapter, Thomas appears to reluctantly admit that his friend Crutch was right. At a school dance in a conversation with a White girl, he again explains, "I ain't a Spaniard from Spain. . . . I'm a Puerto Rican from Harlem" (p. 88).

When Thomas asks the girl to dance and she coyly refuses, he becomes suspect. He overhears her telling a White boy, "Imagine the nerve of that black thing. . . . He started to talk to me and what could I do except be polite and at the same time not encourage him." To which a voice answered, "We're getting invaded by niggers" (p. 90).

While Thomas's book highlights issues of race in wartime urban communities, Nicholasa Mohr's *Nilda* (1986) provides us with an internal narrative of a Puerto Rican family in New York's Spanish Harlem as seen from the perspective of a young Puerto Rican girl born in Puerto Rico and raised in New York City. Set in the years during the American involvement in World War II, the book is written as a diary of a girl coming of age in a troubled but cohesive extended family. In contrast to Thomas's *Down These Mean Streets*, Mohr writes from a perspective of optimism that stems from her unstinting belief that family relationships can serve as a bulwark from the ignorance and misunderstanding often encountered in societies where pluralism and diversity coexist precariously. Nilda, the main character in Mohr's book, affords us an entry to the social institutions that have molded Puerto Rican communities in the United States. Her observations of the process of assimilation and acculturation include insightful anecdotes about the role of these institutions vis-a-vis the Puerto Rican community. The enclave of Puerto Rican migrants described so vividly by Mohr is a product of an economically displaced peasantry and proletariat from Puerto Rico during the years following World War I and extending through the era of the Great Depression to U.S. involvement in World War II. This was a time of great political turmoil in Puerto Rico's history.

Agitated by the bankruptcy of the U.S.-based economy in the early 1930s, the island's dependent relationship became an issue. The response was an organized militant movement asserting political self-determination for Puerto Rico. Thousands of the island's inhabitants joined in the protest of a colonial relationship that appeared to be temporarily assuaged by the extension of New Deal policies to the island. The growth of a populist movement, led by the man who would become the island's first elected Puerto Rican governor, Luis Munoz Marin, posited an alternative to the militant demands of the Nationalist Party but did not stem the increasing flow of poor families to the large urban centers of the United States, such as New York City. Unlike the southern and eastern European immigrants who arrived at Ellis Island in earlier decades, Puerto Ricans, as U.S. citizens, migrated to urban shores in great numbers with the expectation of returning home once economic conditions improved. These conditions laid the groundwork for what eventually would be called "the aerial bus route" (Gonzalez, 1989).

Spanish Harlem (El Barrio) became the quintessential home of this exiled migrant community. It attempted to recreate the cultural life of the island's barrios and the norms and values of an agrarian-based society deeply grounded in the respect and dignity of the individual. In a telling example from *Nilda*, the cultural conflict comes to the fore when Nilda accompanies her mother to the Welfare Department. Asked to approach the desk, Nilda observes that the social worker, Miss Heinz, does not even visually acknowledge the presence of her mother or herself. When she finally does, she assumes that Nilda's mother is not going to understand her, for she turns to Nilda and says, "My name is Miss Heinz. Does your mother understand or speak English?" (Mohr, 1986, p. 65). As Nilda's mother responds in the affirmative, the social worker proceeds to assert her authority by questioning Nilda's presence as well as the number of baths she takes. The pain of humiliation and condescension becomes exacerbated at the thought that the truth of her mother's statements will be determined through a follow-up visit by a welfare "investigator." Nilda is also surprised at the less-than-truthful responses of her mother to the social worker's questions, and her youthful thoughts do not allow her to understand the bind her mother finds herself in and why she has to respond in that manner.

Language as a determining force in the lives of Puerto Ricans in the United States will continue to play a role in future decades. Mohr's *Nilda* utilizes a first-person narration to effectively portray the young protagonist's extended family through her eyes but also in their own words and their perception of the "Other" society as insensitive and alien. The novel is sprinkled with expressions, aphorisms, and linguistic constructions that meld the English and Spanish languages as a metaphor of the Puerto Rican reality in the United States. Nilda dutifully works on a school writing assignment on the Founding Fathers but has to stop when her mother asks her to join in a spiritualist prayer session to prevent her brother from going to jail. The monotonous litanies in Spanish to various saints and spirits are contrasted with the standard, expository English that Nilda must use in her composition.

The blending of these two worlds is a running leitmotif in *Nilda*. Variations on this theme appear in the works of later writers of short stories, poetry, and essays. Mohr was also among the first authors of Puerto Rican writing in the United States to portray the woman's reality in her role as "materfamilias" as well as mediator and social activist. In the style of Marques's Dona Gabriela and Juanita in *La Carreta*, Mohr depicts the suffering and turmoil of the Puerto Rican woman in an alien environment but also shows her inner strength and resilience when crisis threatens to undo the fabric of the family.

The theme of family also comes to the forefront in Edward Rivera's *Family Installments* (1982). This novel utilizes the vignette to chronicle the ordeal of a migrant Puerto Rican family in the period following World War II. Like the writers previously discussed, Rivera taps his personal reminiscences of his life as a young boy in Puerto Rico. The son of a dirt farmer in tobacco country, he is brought to the United States during the period that Puerto Rican migration peaked and the island was approaching a crossroads in its relationship with the United States.

Beginning in the late 1940s through the early 1970s, colonial leaders and the U.S government embarked upon a plan to modernize the island as a model of democratic, capitalist development in Latin America. The plan would be known as Operation Bootstrap. It involved industrial and commercial development by focusing on depressed urban areas that were a product of the failed economic policies of the colonial government in the early war years. The linchpin of the plan was the attraction of American capital by providing investors with a generous tax exemption that could last from 7 to 30 years and a dirt-cheap labor force that crammed the cities after finding no employment in the depressed agricultural sector.

Operation Bootstrap never lived up to its promise, and the employment it generated was not sufficient to accommodate the tens of thousands of workers displaced in the sugar cane industry. A similar fate awaited the small-scale coffee and tobacco farmers. In many cases, American companies opportunistically used up their tax exemption and then closed plants that were relocated elsewhere on the island under a different name to once more take advantage of the tax exemption. The response of the colonial government to the displacement and chronic unemployment of the peasant population was to force these Puerto Ricans into an involuntary migration to the United States. Most left with the expectation that their lives in U.S. urban jungles would improve economically, so that the odyssey would end with their return to their native land in a state of financial security that was not available to them when they left the newly urbanized Puerto Rico.

Rivera's *Family Installments* picks up where Marques's *La Carreta* leaves off. Whereas Marques sees the future of the involuntary migrant in his or her return to reclaim the patrimony of the land, Rivera is aware that the odyssey is largely one-way. Geran Malanguez's family will never truly feel a part of their adopted country, but they will struggle together to forge a new identity that will retain the most precious elements of their culture while negotiating with the new social environment. The book is replete with tragicomic instances in which Geran's son Santos learns to adapt to the values and mores of a Catholic education dispensed by second-generation Irish nuns and priests who have very little tolerance for the cultural and linguistic diversity of the Puerto Rican children. Geran had enrolled Santos in Catholic school so that he would learn some discipline and not be perverted by those public school kids that the priests and nuns said were so bad. Santos was aware, however, that the public schools were filled with kids like himself whose parents, unlike his own, could not stretch their meager resources to send their children to parochial schools. Early on he experienced the sting of racial discrimination, which exists in American society as well as in Puerto Rican families, where skin color may determine social preference and status. Santos's pale, white skin often led to his being mistaken for an ethnic White. He secretly reveled in this confusion and, recalling a discussion on the American melting pot in his Catholic school, would say the following:

> Nobody had ever taken me for someone whose veins might contain Negro or Arab or Caribbean Indian blood. I was too light-skinned for that. On various occasions I had been mistaken for a Jew, an Italian, a Greek, even a Hungarian; and each time I had come away feeling secretly proud of myself for having disguised my Spik accent and with it my lineage. I could almost feel myself melting smoothly and evenly into the great Pot. (Rivera, 1982, p. 148)

These childhood encounters and his increasing awareness of what it meant to be Puerto Rican in the United States would eventually mold the grown-up Santos to truly appreciate the diversity in his ethnic and racial heritage. But his coming-of-age in the streets and schools of El Barrio would have an indelible impact on his character and personality. Returning to his native Puerto Rico in his last year of college, Santos feels estranged from the village he knew as a boy. He realizes that he no longer belongs there, even if his parents decide to return to the island. At this moment he is painfully aware of how much of his heritage he has lost, but he is also cognizant of how much he has gained in his experience as a Puerto Rican in the United States.

## Summary

We have attempted to portray the sociohistorical and economic reality of Puerto Ricans residing in the United States by examining selected creative works of literature. The focus has been on a play and three novels. The reader has been provided with a discussion of significant events in the social history of Puerto Rico that create a context for the analysis of these works. A conscious decision was made to select novels and a play over other forms of written expression, such as poetry, to enable classroom teachers to present the explicit, concrete, and testimonial accounts of the most accomplished Puerto Rican writers in the United States. This initial exposure to the literature of and about Puerto Ricans in the United States in the novel may serve as a useful starting point for the subsequent examination of more coded texts in the genres of poetry, the short story, and the essay. In addition, the themes of race, class, gender, ethnicity, identity, and language, as well as topics related to migration and immigration, have been uncovered as central and integral to the literature under discussion. Enabling students to understand these texts using the aforementioned themes as lenses may objectify and illuminate their own reality.

# Reading List

The titles that follow are a selection of creative works of recent vintage that may help the English Language Arts or ESL teacher in the secondary school. All may be found in English or in English translation.

Acosta-Belen, E., & Sanchez-Korrol, V. (1993). *The way it was and other writings*. Houston, TX: Arte Publico Press.

> The authors have edited a collection of essays by the legendary Puerto Rican labor activist and journalist, Jesus Colon. The introduction is must reading to fully understand the sociohistorical and cultural context of New York City between the World Wars and the poignant perceptions of a Black Puerto Rican living in two worlds.

*Centro Boletin* of Hunter College's Puerto Rican Studies Research Center (1979–1997).

> The *Boletin* is published once a year by Hunter College's Puerto Rican Research Center and provides a vehicle for Puerto Rican and other Latino academic and community scholars to publish research articles as well as creative literature of different genres.

Gonzalez, J. L. (1989). *La guagua aerea (The aereal bus)*. Rio Piedras, Puerto Rico: Editorial Universitaria.

> Short essays and musings by the illustrious Puerto Rican novelist, essayist, and short story writer that focus on the Puerto Rican reality in the diaspora, which now has a two-way ticket in the island-mainland connection.

Hernandez-Cruz, V. (1990). *Red beans*. Houston, TX: Arte Publico Press.

> A witty collection of poems by the famed Nuyorican poet. Hernandez-Cruz captures the reality of the Puerto Rican in the United States as expressed through a unique, code-switching bilingualism that peppers his poems.

Marques, R. (1961). *Cuentos Puertorriquenos de Hoy (Puerto Rican short stories of today)*. Rio Piedras, Puerto Rico: Editorial Universitaria.

> This classic collection of short stories by the renowned author of *The Oxcart (La Carreta)* renders a somber, existential view of the Puerto Rican reality in the United States and Puerto Rico in the context of the island's colonial status.

Nadal, L. P. (1993). "Suburican." *The Olive Tree*, 40.

> This poem, written by a young, third-generation Puerto Rican, focuses on the issues of language, identity, and class as prisms to understand the Puerto Rican as outsider in both her own community and the broader U.S. society.

Pietri, P. (1973). *The Puerto Rican obituary*. New York: Monthly Review Press.

> The title is the lead poem of this reedited collection by the dean of the Puerto Rican "street poets." Pietri's *Obituary* is both humorous and searing in its portrayal of the Puerto Rican's existence in the urban ghettos of the United States.

Santiago, E. (1994). *When I was Puerto Rican*. New York: Prentice-Hall.

> An insightful collection of autobiographical vignettes that reads as a novel and documents the rites of passage and pains of acculturation of a young Puerto Rican woman and her family.

Santiago, R. (1995). *Boricuas: Influential Puerto Rican writings—an anthology*. New York: Ballantine Books.

> An extensive, broad-based collection of writing in various genres. Fifty pieces by 40 writers run the gamut of urban Puerto Rican life on both shores. Issues of race, identity, class, language, and religion are treated with sensitivity, and the pride of a people in their struggle for self-affirmation is depicted.

Turner, F. (Ed.). (1984). *Puerto Rican writers: At home in the USA*. New York: Scholastic.

An excellent anthology of Puerto Rican writers of the second and third generations in the United States. The author has included some important feminist voices, such as Sandra Esteves, Aurora Levins-Morales, and Judith Ortiz Cofer. Essays and poetry predominate in this valuable yet little-known collection.

# References

Acosta-Belen, E. (1993). Beyond island boundaries: Ethnicity, gender and cultural revitalization in Nuyorican literature. In T. Perry & J. Fraser (Eds.), *Freedom's plow: Teaching in the multicultural classroom* (pp. 121–142) New York: Routledge.

Diaz-Alfaro, A. (1951). *Terrazzo*. Rio Piedras, Puerto Rico: Editorial Universitaria.

History Task Force, El Centro de Estudios Puertorriquenos. (1979). *Labor migration under capitalism*. New York: Monthly Review Press.

Laviera, A. (1984). *La carreta made a u-turn*. Houston, TX: Arte Publico Press.

Marques, R. (1953). *La carreta*. San Juan, Puerto Rico: Plus Ultra.

Mohr, N. (1986). *Nilda*. Houston, TX: Arte Publico Press.

Ogbu, J. (1978). *Minority education and caste*. New York: Academic Press.

Olga, J., & Waggenheim, K. (1973). *Puerto Ricans: A documentary history*. Princeton, NJ: Marcus-Weiner.

Olson, J. S. (1994). *The ethnic dimension in American History*. New York: St. Martin's Press.

Rivera, E. (1982). *Family installments*. New York: Prentice-Hall.

Rodriguez, M. (1947). *Osuna*. Madrid, Spain: Prensa-Española.

Senior, C. (1959). *The newcomers: Negroes and Puerto Ricans in a changing metropolis*. Cambridge, MA: Harvard University Press.

Senior, C. (1961). *Strangers then neighbors*. New York: Freedom Books.

Steinberg, S. (1985). *The ethnic myth*. New York: Scholastic.

Takaki, R. (1993). *A different mirror: A history of multicultural America*. Boston: Little, Brown.

Thomas, P. (1967/1991). *Down these mean streets*. New York: Vintage Books.

Walsh, C. (1991). *Pedagogy and the struggle for voice*. New York: Bergin & Garvey.

**Chapter 5**

# Asian/Pacific American Literature: The Battle Over Authenticity

*Sandra S. Yamate*

Timing is everything, goes the old adage. Nowhere is that more true than in the context of literature, especially Asian/Pacific American literature. To truly appreciate literature, one needs to understand not only the time period of the setting but also the time period in which it was written and the contemporary issues and concerns, as well as societal norms and values, that may have influenced the author. The logic by which historiography reminds students of history—that a description of events and an analysis of the impact or ramifications of those events can differ dramatically, depending on whether the historian is a contemporary or not—is just as true for an analysis of literature. It is particularly true in the case of Asian/Pacific American literature, which continues to grapple with its own history and its perceptions of Asian/Pacific Americans' place in the United States. Indeed, Asian/Pacific American history is so intertwined with its literature that it is almost impossible to discuss the literature without the history.

## Asian/Pacific American Beginnings

Any discussion about Asian/Pacific American literature in its historical context would logically begin at the beginning of that history. This is easier said than done, however. Even if we exclude from consideration the theories of prehistoric Asian nomadic tribes crossing to the Americas by way of a land mass spanning the Bering Strait, or of Pacific Islander peoples who traveled in rafts to the coasts of Central and South America, it is not clear just how, when, or where we should identify the beginning of Asian/Pacific American history in the Americas, much less the United States. Asian/Pacific Americans are an ethnically diverse group. Some of these ethnic groups have been in the Americas for centuries, such as the Chinese, who settled in Mexico and Central America as early as the 17th century. This was a consequence of trade with Spain and its colonies, and the Chinese became indentured or contract laborers—commonly referred to as "coolies"—imported by the Spanish into Cuba to supplement the African slave labor force on the sugar plantations. Some have been in the United States for more than a century, with families whose roots as Americans stretch back five or six generations to times when those of Asian ancestry were denied the opportunity to become naturalized American citizens. Other ethnic groups are more recent arrivals, immigrants or refugees with strong emotional and psychological ties to their countries of origin, who may not yet view themselves as Americans, much less Asian/Pacific Americans. Can Asian/Pacific American history begin before everyone was present? Do all the members of the group have to accept the label before it is legitimate?

Even if we try to arbitrarily choose a beginning point—the first documented arrival in the United States of an Asian or Pacific Islander, the first American born of Asian or Pacific Islander ancestry, or the first citizen of Asian or Pacific Islander ancestry—other issues remain to be considered. As alluded to earlier, for many Asians and Pacific Islanders, their arrival in the United States does not translate into immediate self-identification as an American or even an Asian/Pacific American.

Furthermore, the very concept of a Pan–Asian/Pacific American identity is relatively new and remains controversial, particularly among those who are newer to the United States and those who already have been acculturated into "American culture." Even among those who have banded together under the banner "Asian/Pacific American," the concept is not always an easy one to accept. For some, the overriding concern is their own ethnic group's representation within a multitude of ethnic groups, frequently for the sake of advancing the preeminence or superiority of their own ethnic group rather than promoting truly Pan–Asian/Pacific American ideals and goals for the benefit of Asian/Pacific Americans regardless of ethnicity. Consequently, what is Chinese American, for example, may not be accepted as Asian/Pacific American by a Filipino American or an Indian American. Many whose ancestors arrived from China, Japan, and Korea are reluctant to recognize a common racial or political bond with those of South Asian ancestry whose families arrived from India, Pakistan, and Bangladesh. Something Pan–Asian/Pacific American may also not be accepted by someone to whom ethnicity is all important, or who perhaps rejects the idea as an invention of European Americans to neatly pigeonhole those who for so many years have been labeled neither White nor Black but "Other." Therefore, is the beginning of Pan–Asian/Pacific American history the time at which the concept first evolved? Or is it when it became (or becomes) the politically correct label for the majority of Americans of Asian and Pacific Islander ancestry? Will it be when the concept is more uniformly accepted and realized by Asian/Pacific Americans themselves? Or is there some other triggering mechanism?

In the interest of promoting Pan–Asian/Pacific American identity, despite the risk of offending or alienating those for whom an Asian/Pacific American context cannot possibly exist prior to the arrival of significant numbers of individuals from their own particular ethnic group, and without trying to emphasize one ethnic group over another, for our purposes the beginning will be defined as the mid-19th-century arrival of sojourners and immigrants from Asia and the Pacific to the United States. Their writings about their lives in, their thoughts and perceptions about, and their hopes for America provide the first body of literature of Asians and Pacific Islanders in this country.

# A New Source of Labor: Asian/Pacific Americans in the 19th and Early 20th Centuries

In the aftermath of the War of 1812, as industrialization was revolutionizing the United States, and Americans were looking westward toward their Manifest Destiny, American business found itself in need of cheap labor. Consequently, as Irish immigrants, followed by central and southern European immigrants, were used to operate the sweatshop factories of the East Coast, Chinese and other Asian laborers were brought in to provide labor for agriculture and industry in Hawaii and on the West Coast. Yet while the European immigrants gradually assimilated into the dominant American culture, their Asian counterparts had a far different experience. Indeed, as Professor Evelyn Hu-DeHart (1992) points out, of all the non-European groups in the United States, those of Asian ancestry come closest to conforming to the notion of being immigrants like the Europeans. The Africans who were brought to this country as slaves certainly came in a most involuntary fashion. Native Americans and Spanish-speaking peoples were already living in the West and Southwest. And although the Asians who migrated across the Pacific may not have all come voluntarily, they did not come as slaves and so their arrival most closely approximates the circumstances of immigrant Europeans.

Nevertheless, the reception and subsequent treatment of immigrants from Asia was grossly disparate from that received by European immigrants. Most European immigrants, within a generation or so, were able to physically blend into American society and assimilate. Asian immigrants had no such opportunity and could not obtain American citizenship. Alien land laws passed at various times prevented them from owning real estate. They were restricted in the types of occupations they could pursue. They were unwelcome, even if their labor was not unwanted.

> American opinion makers of the time—missionaries, diplomats, employers of Chinese workers—invariably portrayed them [Asian immigrants] as idolatrous and godless, politically servile, morally depraved, physically degenerate, loathsomely disease-ridden, savage, childlike, lustful, sensual, and, in sum, irredeemably backwards. Thus, Asians were judged ineligible for citizenship in this country. They were viewed as incapable of assimilating into an American society devoted to freedom and a cohesive nationalism. Indeed, seen in this context, the yellow masses were considered a peril to progress and the unity of this still young nation. (Hu-DeHart, 1992, p. 8)

Nevertheless, the mid-19th century saw a worldwide decline in the African slave trade. Labor was crucial to support the growing American economy. To satisfy the demand for labor, American business ransacked the world, particularly China, in a search for laborers. When gold was discovered in California in 1849, the United States stepped up its introduction of successive waves of mostly Chinese men as a cheap and docile labor force for the Western mines and railroads.

European immigrants came to resent the Chinese as unwelcome competitors. That was not surprising. Racial and ethnic intolerance and prejudice were quickly recognized as an effective means of controlling, manipulating, and subjugating laborers. In Hawaii, for example, where the Native Hawaiians were declining in number and even those willing to work were considered lazy and undisciplined, Chinese laborers were brought in to set an "example." Sugar plantation managers hoped the Hawaiians would be "naturally jealous" of the foreigners and "ambitious" to outdo them. They encouraged the Chinese to call the native workers "Wahine, wahine!" or "Woman, woman!" in Hawaiian (Takaki, 1989, p. 25). In this fashion an ethnically diverse work force was used by American business as a mechanism of control. Diversity was deliberately designed to break strikes and repress unions.

The growing Chinese labor force, however, made many European Americans uneasy. Consequently, in 1882, the Chinese Exclusion Act prohibited the entry of any more Chinese laborers into the United States. This law was also interpreted to prohibit the entry of the wives of Chinese laborers who were already here. In 1888, the restriction was further tightened to prohibit a Chinese laborer in the United States from leaving and then returning to the United States and to make it unlawful for any Chinese person, except a merchant, to enter the country.

In the 1880s and 1890s, the United States initiated the importation of Japanese laborers. The Japanese labor force was intended to serve as a check upon the Chinese. By 1900, however, Japanese labor was perceived as growing too numerous, and this perception resulted in the 1908 Gentlemen's Agreement restricting Japanese immigration. Businesses scrambled for a new source of labor and looked to Korea. The Korean labor supply, however, was cut off in 1905, when the Korean government prohibited further emigration. In 1906, Filipino labor began to be imported. Unlike the Chinese, Japanese, and Koreans, the Filipinos came from a United States territory and had the benefits of citizenship. Around 1909, Asian Indian laborers were introduced into the United States when a small colony of Sikhs began working in the vineyards around Fresno, California. By 1917, Congress had prohibited any further immigration from India, and Indian immigrants soon found themselves subjected to many of the same restrictions and prohibitions as Japanese Americans. In 1924, the National Origins Act was passed; this was designed to prohibit any further Japanese immigration, and, to prevent the development of families and communities of Asians in the midst of European America, it barred the entry of women from China, Japan, Korea, and India. Even Asian wives of United States citizens could not be brought into the country because they were classified as "aliens ineligible for citizenship." While the law did not apply to Filipino migration (since the Philippines were a U.S. territory), the 1934 Tydings-McDuffie Act addressed this "oversight" by establishing Philippine independence and then limiting Filipino immigration to 50 persons a year. As long as they were cheap laborers, and in the absence of alternative labor sources, Asians were tolerated. But by the 1920s, when Mexico became the newest source of labor, Asians had become the first people to be specifically barred by law from entering the United States because of their race.

The lives of these early Asian immigrants was not easy. Whether they worked on the sugar plantations of Hawaii or the railroads, mines, farms, or factories of the West Coast, they toiled for long hours and little pay. Consequently, if they did find time to pursue literary interests, their literature has generally not survived.[1] Still, by the first part of the 20th century, a rich and vibrant literature written by Asian/ Pacific Americans was coming into existence, and modern students can rejoice over its survival.

One such cause for celebration is the work of Edith Maud Eaton. Eaton, who wrote under the pseudonym Sui Sin Far ("Water Lily" in Cantonese), was born in 1867 to a Chinese mother and an English father. Although she could pass for White, she chose to live and write as a Chinese American. She traveled back and forth across North America and produced a series of stories (1909) that give us the only contemporary view into the lives of late 19th-century Chinese Americans in the United States and Canada. For instance, her two-part short story, "The Story of One White Woman Who Married a Chinese" and "Her Chinese Husband," is a compelling and poignant tale about an early interracial marriage, told with a matter-of-fact honesty, sensitivity, and calmness that make its ending all the more tragic. Another story, "Leaves From the Mental Portfolio of an Eurasian" is an insightful and candid examination of social mores and attitudes about race in turn-of-the-century America.

Less sophisticated, perhaps, but no less telling than Sui Sin Far's stories, are the anonymous poems of Angel Island. Angel Island, which lies in the middle of the San Francisco Bay, has sometimes been called the Ellis Island of the West. Between 1910 and 1940, when Chinese exclusion laws required immigrants to prove themselves to be related by blood to a current U.S. resident in order to gain entry, Chinese immigrants were detained at Angel Island and subjected to repeated interrogations by immigration officials—for periods that could stretch from a few weeks into months or even more than a year. Passing the grueling examinations meant taking a ferry ride to San Francisco to begin a new life. Failure meant permanent deportation back to China. The facilities were primitive at best, with little or no privacy and plenty of despair and frustration. On the walls of the wooden barracks where the detainees were held, these Chinese immigrants wrote poems and rhymes expressing their anger, frustration, despair, and fear; capturing their dreams, ambitions, and hopes; and preserving their views and impressions of this first taste of life in America. The poems show that Angel Island was not a euphoric gateway to Utopia for these Chinese immigrants, but

> a contradiction of the principles of liberty that testified to injustice ... [and] reveals an appreciation of the American principles of justice and democracy. They expected to be treated on that level and they believed that they should be accorded such rights. This was ... the first crude sign of their Americanization. (Chan, Chin, Inada, & Wong, 1991, p. 141)

Although the poems are written in colloquial Cantonese, Marlon K. Hom has translated many of them in "Immigration Blues" and "Lamentations of Stranded Sojourners" in *Songs of Gold Mountain* (1987). With great integrity and eloquence, Hom's translations capture the spirit of the poems as anonymous, and therefore more revealing, messages from the souls of the authors. They display the simplicity, earthiness, and humanity of those faceless voices as they first encounter the racism, prejudice, and biases that will influence their Americanization and their lives as Americans.

Americanization is further explored and articulated in a brilliant autobiographical novel, *America Is in the Heart* (1946) by Carlos Bulosan. Bulosan was a self-taught writer and union activist who was born in the Philippines in 1913 and immigrated to Seattle in 1930. *America Is in the Heart* tells the story of a young boy growing up in the Philippines, his immigration to the United States, and his experiences there. With fine brush strokes, Bulosan paints a picture of an America that many Americans never saw acknowledged but that nevertheless existed. His is one of the few detailed accounts of life in the United States during the 1930s and 1940s from an Asian immigrant's perspective. Bulosan's writing is unsympathetic, not sparing his reader any horror, outrage, or tragedy; it is also amazingly nonjudgmental, making for a compelling tale that carries the reader along. Bulosan wrote in a variety of literary genres, and much of his fiction was published during the 1940s in magazines like *The New Yorker* and *Harper's Bazaar*. Unfortunately, he died young, but despite his early death in 1956, his extraordinary talent guarantees his place in American literature.

## American Citizens (Second Class): Asian/Pacific Americans, 1942–1965

On the eve of World War II, the children and grandchildren of the Asian immigrants who had managed to reach the United States despite exclusion laws and other restrictions upon Asian immigration were growing up as "typical" Americans. American-born citizens, they were educated as Americans, recited the Pledge of Allegiance in fluent English, and prepared to grow up and take their place among their fellow Americans. That their immigrant parents or grandparents were ineligible for American citizenship[2] and were "viewed as inherently incapable of Americanization" (Hu-DeHart, 1992, p. 8) was unfortunate, but surely no one would question the citizenship of a generation born on American soil. They would soon discover otherwise.

On February 19, 1942, came one of the defining moments in Asian/ Pacific American history. On that date, after decades of rampant anti-

Asian sentiment in the United States, President Franklin Delano Roosevelt issued Executive Order 9066, which opened the way for the evacuation of approximately 120,000 Japanese Americans from the West Coast and their forced internment in 10 concentration camps. Almost three months earlier, the United States had suffered the bombing of Pearl Harbor and was now at war with Japan. Japanese Americans living on the West Coast—regardless of their citizenship, length of time in the United States, age, education, employment, political ideology, or infirmity—were forcibly evacuated from their homes and sent to live in isolated "camps," located in desolate areas of the country, behind barbed wire and under the watch of armed guards.

The reasons given for the internment ostensibly were military necessity and national security against the possibilities of sabotage. That these reasons were nothing more than contrivances becomes clear upon closer inspection. Japanese Americans were interned without any finding of guilt by any court and, like many Asian Americans before them, they found themselves subjected to grossly disparate treatment compared to their European Axis counterparts. German Americans and Italian Americans were not subjected to the same sort of wholesale imprisonment, even though the United States was also at war with Germany and Italy. The few German Americans and Italian Americans who were imprisoned had at least had the benefit of an administrative hearing on their internment. Furthermore, if the internment of Japanese Americans was truly to prevent the possibility of sabotage, there can still be no justification for interning the bedridden, the children, and the menial laborers who would have little or no opportunity to create sabotage, while not interning the much larger Japanese American population in Hawaii.

The history of the internment, however, goes beyond the imprisonment of American citizens who were denied the due process of law guaranteed by the Constitution. It also includes forcing internees to complete a poorly worded, insulting document called a "loyalty questionnaire," of which two questions required either a "yes-yes" or a "no-no" answer. "Yes-yes" meant that the person answering was agreeing to serve military combat duty and, without any insurance of postwar citizenship, would forswear any allegiance to a foreign country. There was no middle ground, no way to protest the internment while affirming loyalty, and no way to challenge their treatment as citizens while protecting themselves from being countryless.

The loyalty questionnaire paved the way for the creation of an entirely Japanese American regiment. The 100th Battalion/442nd Regimental Combat Team, the most highly decorated unit in U.S. military history, was known as the "Purple Heart Battalion" because of the overwhelmingly high number of members who were killed or injured. In light of the number of casualties, the injustices endured by families and friends who were still interned, and the racist treatment to which the soldiers and their families had been subjected, the history of the 442nd RCT and its military successes in the face of almost insurmountable odds is particularly poignant.

The internment stands as a major scar on the collective psyche of Asian/Pacific Americans. It serves as a reminder that no matter how hard Asian/Pacific Americans may try to acculturate themselves and assimilate into American society, European American society has not been especially accepting or welcoming and may not ever be. Generations later, writers continue to grapple with it as a subject, as a setting, and as an influence upon contemporary Asian/Pacific America. It is no wonder that the internment was and continues to be frequently revisited in Asian/Pacific American literature.

*Nisei Daughter* (1979), Monica Sone's autobiographical novel, examines the state of the Japanese American community in prewar Seattle, the impact of the internment, and its ramifications for Seattle's Japanese American community. By describing her family's history from her father's arrival through her parents' marriage and her own and her siblings' births, from her childhood and adolescence through her family's internment at Minidoka, Idaho, Sone offers the reader a chance to stand in the place of a young Japanese American, to experience the schizophrenia of living a Japanese identity at home and an American identity outside while struggling to develop a unified and consistent self-view, and to begin to understand the internment and America's treatment of Japanese Americans from the perspective of someone who experienced it firsthand. Although the book is sometimes a bit chauvinist, that is more a reflection of the norms of the time in which Sone grew up than any intentional denigration of the roles and value of women. Nevertheless, for young adults, *Nisei Daughter* provides some thought-provoking insight into race relations during that era.

Better known—but lacking the degree of insight, introspection, and historical perspective of *Nisei Daughter*—is James and Jeanne

Wakatsuki Houston's *Farewell to Manzanar* (1973). *Farewell to Manzanar* follows its protagonist as she and her family try to adjust to life after the war outside their internment camp. In an effort to illustrate the confusion the young girl faces as she tries to reconcile her new all-American life with her family's experience, there is, at times, too much focus on the petty and mundane and not enough on the emotional upheaval of the girl and her family.

Perhaps the most straightforward accounts of prewar life and the internment by someone who lived through it are those written by the prolific Yoshiko Uchida. Her books, such as *Journey to Topaz* (1971) and *Journey Home* (1978), are simple, straightforward accounts of Japanese American life during the mid-20th century. At times they are a trifle dry and reserved—perhaps in part because she based much of her writing on her own and her family's experiences, and perhaps because, like many Japanese Americans during that era, she may have unwittingly adopted some of the Japanese American community's own stereotypes of itself, such as uncomplaining strength, limitless patience, and steadfast self-reliance. Her chronological accounts, without the compelling narrative or psychological insight of storytellers like Monica Sone or Jade Snow Wong (see below), may lack somewhat in inspiration, but they nevertheless serve as an excellent introduction to the history of Japanese Americans for preteens and young adults.

Another author, Hisaye Yamamoto, published seven short stories between 1948 and 1961, and

> her modest body of fiction is remarkable for its range and gut understanding of Japanese America. The questions and themes of Asian American life are fresh. Growing up with foreign-born parents, mixing with white and non-white races, racial discrimination, growing old, the question of dual personality—all were explored in the seven stories of Hisaye Yamamoto. (Chan et al., 1991, p. 339)

Her writing is particularly noteworthy because it is the only known description of prewar rural Japanese American life in existence. Fortunately, her stories, poems, and essays have been collected and published in a single volume, *Seventeen Syllables and Other Stories* (1988).

Japanese Canadians were also subjected to internment and Shizuye Takashima's book, *A Child in Prison Camp* (1991), written in diary form, is a moving and masterful recounting of her and her family's life during the war that makes excellent reading for preteens and young adults. Unlike Yoshiko Uchida, Takashima seems more willing to delve into the "less-flattering" emotions of her family and the other internees, allowing them to express anger, frustration, despair, and fear and to be more three-dimensional.

In order to truly grasp the depth of emotion and conflict tapped by *No-No Boy* (1988), the landmark novel by John Okada—particularly the controversial loyalty questionnaire and the inner conflicts of the Japanese American community concerning it—a greater knowledge of Japanese American history is required than is commonly taught in American schools. Yet even for those who are not familiar with the history, Okada's moving tale about a young man who answered the crucial questions on the loyalty questionnaire with "no-no" is brilliant, tragic, and heroic. Okada and his hero, Ichiro, explore the internment of Seattle's Japanese American community and their pain, anger, guilt, bitterness, and depression in the aftermath of the war. Many contemporary Japanese Americans rejected this portrayal, however, and, consequently, the book. It very nearly became doomed to be forgotten but for its reprinting by an Asian American community resource project in 1971.

Anti-Asian sentiment and the resulting limited ethnic labor market was not the sole province of Japanese Americans; it was directed toward anyone of Asian ancestry. Although they did not suffer internment, Chinese Americans were also subjected to limitations based upon race. In Jade Snow Wong's autobiographical novel, *Fifth Chinese Daughter* (1945), one of the earliest books to explore the tensions faced by young Asian/Pacific Americans as they struggle between an Asian or Pacific Islander identity and an American identity, the author describes growing up as a Chinese American before and during World War II. Although the life she describes is somewhat atypical for girls of the time, *Fifth Chinese Daughter* nevertheless provides a fascinating glimpse into the values and social mores of the Chinese community at that time. Jade Snow Wong had educational and employment opportunities unusual for a Chinese American girl or for any young woman from such a socioeconomic background at that time. Modern-day readers may find her pride in her accomplishments and the importance she attaches to them to be somewhat modest and quaint compared to the opportunities now afforded women, but it is important to bear in mind that even the gains that women have now achieved may seem rather limited someday in hindsight.

Another glimpse into Asian/Pacific American life was preserved by Louis Chu in *Eat a Bowl of Tea* (1986). In it, Chu examines Chinatown's bachelor society, which was the result of the exclusion laws that prevented the immigration of Chinese women and the establishment of Chinese American families. With affection and humor, *Eat a Bowl of Tea* is a somewhat satirical tale of adultery and retribution set in a Chinese American community close to the end of World War II. Chu captures the local community politics, its rivalries and repartee, and allows a modern reader to feel, however briefly, that he or she is sharing that life.

# The Growth of an Asian/Pacific American Identity, 1965– the 1990s

The year 1965 was a significant turning point for Asian/Pacific Americans. The U.S. Supreme Court struck down the immigration quotas that were based on national origin. This opened the way for renewed immigration from Asia and the Pacific and led to a burgeoning Asian/Pacific American population. Indeed, in 1965, the population of Asian Americans was about one million, or less than 1% of the U.S. population. By 1985, it had grown to five million, or 2% of the population, making Asian/Pacific Americans the fastest growing minority group (percentage wise) in the United States.

The Vietnam War and subsequent conflicts in Southeast Asia created an added impetus to Asian immigration. With the fall of Saigon in 1975, the United States saw the beginning of an influx of refugee immigrants from many diverse backgrounds that continues to this day. There were Vietnamese, some well-educated and even moderately fluent in English, who were used to urban life and able to travel as a family unit, whereas others made up the hundreds of thousands of "boat people" who risked their lives in barely seaworthy boats against the threat of high seas, inadequate or no provisions, pirates, illness, and an uncertain future, and who, if they survived, were subjected to months or even years in squalid refugee camps before resettling in countries like Australia, Canada, France, and the United States. There were refugees from Laos, some of whom were ethnic Lao, whereas others were Mien and Hmong, rural peoples from the highlands of Laos. The Hmong in particular have had to face enormous adjustments in the United States. Coming from a preliterate, agricultural society, few Hmong arrived in the United States with the skills to accept anything beyond the most menial work to begin building a new life. There were refugees from Cambodia, survivors of genocidal killings, mass starvation, and disease. Many of the Cambodian refugees are women rearing children alone; their husbands, fathers, brothers, and even older sons were killed by the Khmer Rouge. These refugees are a diverse group, but they have one thing in common: They had little or no time to psychologically or emotionally prepare to leave their homelands, and they are now seeking to build a new life because they cannot go home.

The late 1960s through the 1970s also saw the development of a Pan–Asian American, later Pan–Asian/Pacific American, identity among some second-, third-, and fourth-generation Americans of Asian and Pacific Islander ancestry. In some ways part of the Civil Rights Movement that shaped the United States of this era, and in other ways a logical stage in the growth of Asian and Pacific Islander communities in America, this identity manifested itself in the development of Asian American Studies programs at a growing number of colleges and universities across the country and related scholarly research into the many facets of the Asian/Pacific American community. It saw the establishment of a Pan–Asian/Pacific American media that offered newspapers and magazines with a multi-Asian and Pacific Islander ethnic focus rather than the single ethnic focus of earlier publications and community vernaculars. It spurred the creation of Pan–Asian/ Pacific ethnic groups who joined together to promote political empowerment, professional support, social objectives, and educational goals.

Although pride in individual ethnicity was still encouraged and embraced, the reality of what was necessary to achieve political empowerment, survive increasing anti-Asian violence, and guarantee a place in American society—that is, an active, informed, and committed Pan–Asian/Pacific American community—allowed the different Asian and Pacific Islander ethnic groups to begin to share their histories and experiences with each other and the rest of the United States. In this fashion, the growing Pan–Asian/Pacific American movement underscored a renewed vigor in Asian/Pacific American literature. Whereas most earlier Asian/Pacific American writing had been autobiographical in nature, a number of second-, third-, and fourth-generation Asian/Pacific Americans were beginning not only to write about their own lives and experiences but also to revisit and reexamine the experiences of their parents and grandparents. They then coupled these experiences with imagination to create beautiful, magnificent stories, plays, poems, and essays that speak from the heart of Asian/Pacific America.

If the writings of authors like Carlos Bulosan, Louis Chu, John Okada, and Jade Wong can be considered the first flowering of Asian/Pacific American literature, then the mid-1970s surely saw Asian/Pacific American literature begin to take root and blossom. The year 1974 saw the publication of *Aiiieeeee!: An Anthology of Asian American Writers*, truly a momentous occasion in the history of Asian/Pacific American literature. Republished in 1991 as *The Big Aiiieeeee!: An Anthology of Chinese American and Japanese American Literature*, the book takes its name from the sound that European American culture had for so long presented as some all-purpose whine, shout, or scream by Asians. Editors Jeffery Paul Chan, Frank Chin, Lawson Fusao Inada, and Shawn Wong (1991) began to reclaim Asian America's portrayal and assert its legitimate presentation in American culture. Thus, Aiiieeeee! "is more than a whine, shout, or scream. It is fifty years of our whole voice" (Chan et al., 1991, p. x). *The Big Aiiieeeee!* was intended as an anthology of Asian American writers, and although it focused primarily upon American-born and -raised Chinese and Japanese Americans, who had grown up under the influence of an American culture that perpetuated and reinforced European and Christian prejudicial attitudes about people of Asian ancestry, it was nevertheless very Pan–Asian/American in its efforts to encourage readers to reexamine their attitudes, feelings, and beliefs about Asian Americans and their portrayal and place in American society. In other words, the editors of *The Big Aiiieeeee!* asked their readers to historiographically analyze Asian American literature—to question who was writing it, the societal influences upon the authors' reasoning, their analysis, and ultimately the stories they chose to write. This was a significant first in

Asian/Pacific American literature and has guaranteed *The Big Aiiieeeee!* a prominent place in the history of Asian/Pacific American literature.

Indeed, the impact of *Aiiieeeee!* cannot be overstated. As poet, novelist, and editor Jessica Hagedorn (1993) points out:

> The energy and interest sparked by *Aiiieeeee!* in the Seventies was essential to Asian American writers because it gave us visibility and credibility as creators of our own specific literature. We could not be ignored; suddenly, we were no longer silent. Like other writers of color in America, we were beginning to challenge the long-cherished concepts of a xenophobic literary canon dominated by white heterosexual males. Obviously, there was room for more than one voice and one vision in this ever-expanding arena. (p. xxvii)

*The Big Aiiieeeee!* may not be suitable for all preteens or even many young adults without adequate preparatory material or an introduction to Asian/Pacific American history. Most selections will be appropriate for high school students. In any event, teachers who wish to include Asian/Pacific American literature in their classes ought to consider this as a good grounding, particularly if they are unfamiliar with the Asian/Pacific American community and its history and literature.

An excerpt from *The Big Aiiieeeee!* was published as a novel by one of the editors, Shawn Wong. *Homebase* (1990), the story of a Chinese American boy struggling to grow up without a father and to define and accept an identity for himself, has become a landmark novel in Asian/Pacific American literature. With true insight into and familiarity with his subject matter, Wong leads his reader through the history—personal, familial, and communal—that has shaped each of us in a way that makes it new yet familiar, comfortable yet surprising, and simple yet complex. A young reader will not likely appreciate it and may even find it boring and cumbersome. But for a more mature reader—one who has left the shelter of childhood with its easier acceptance of authority figures and the direction they provide, one who is coming to terms with his or her own place in the world as a self-directed adult—*Homebase* speaks to the soul. It offers no easy solutions and does not claim to try. Instead, it serves to validate a quest for self and place and the serenity presumed to accompany the accomplishment of the quest.

The 1970s also saw the publication of Maxine Hong Kingston's highly acclaimed book, *The Woman Warrior: Memoirs of a Girlhood Among Ghosts* (1975), and the beginning of a controversy that continues to challenge anyone studying Asian/Pacific American literature. The book takes its name from the subject of a Chinese childhood chant, "The Ballad of Mulan," which is based upon the legend of a woman named Fa Mulan. Her aged father was too infirm to answer the Khan's call to mount and lead his estate's army into a great war, and so Fa Mulan took her father's place. In *The Woman Warrior*, Kingston weaves a series of tales about her childhood with stories about her mother, fables, and mysticism from the China of her mother's youth. Her writing is clear and sharp. She tells her stories with touches of humor and plenty of drama, and she tells them well. High school students will find themselves carried along by Kingston's prose; if they reread it later in life, they will no doubt find deeper layers of meaning to fascinate them. It is no wonder that *The Woman Warrior* has become one of the pivotal books in Asian/Pacific American literature.

Not everyone, however, is enamored by *The Woman Warrior*. Author Frank Chin (Chan et al., 1991, pp. 2–6) claims that the Fa Mulan legend told by Kingston is a "fake." According to Chin, Kingston—as well as popular playwright David Henry Hwang and celebrated novelist Amy Tan—is faking Chinese literature by coloring it with modern-day sexism, injecting it with Christianity, and infusing it with a feminist spirit that distorts the underlying themes and messages of the tale so that it no longer resembles its original, authentic version. Instead it becomes a tool that reinforces both overt and subliminal European American racism toward those of Asian ancestry in everyone who reads it, including Asian Americans, and justifies this by suggesting that Chinese American immigrants lost touch with Chinese culture and that a faulty memory, combined with a new experience, produced new versions of these traditional stories.

For instance, Chin protests Kingston's version of Fa Mulan being painfully tattooed all over her back. According to Chin, the tattoos actually belong to a hero named Yue Fei, but Kingston has appropriated them for her version of Fa Mulan's tale to give credence to the European American image of Chinese culture as cruel to women. Chin argues that Kingston has deliberately set out to create an unjustifiably misogynist tale that is better suited to the sexism of the West. In his view it has no reality in China.

Some, however, think that Chin's criticism is misplaced at best and misogynist at worst. Elaine Kim, a professor of Asian American Studies at the University of California at Berkeley, and one of the leading lights in the field, comments:

> I read Asian American literature as a literature of protest and exile, a literature about place and displacement, a literature concerned with psychic and physical "home" or longing for a final "homecoming." I looked for unifying thematic threads and tidy resolutions that might ease the pain of displacement and heal the exile, heedless of what might be missing from this homogenizing approach and oblivious to the parallels between what I was doing and dominant culture attempts to reduce Asian American experiences to developmental narratives about the movement from "primitive," "Eastern," and foreign immigrant to "civilized," "Western," and "Americanized loyal citizen."
>
> The cultural nationalist defenses we constructed were anti-assimilationist. But while they opposed official nationalisms, the Asian American identity they allowed for was fixed, closed, and narrowly defined, dividing "Asian American" from "Asian" as sharply as possible, privileging race over gender and class, accepting compulsory heterosexuality as "natural," and constructing a hierarchy of authenticity to separate the "real" from the "fake." According to this definition, there were not many ways of being Asian American. (Hagedorn, 1993, p. ix)

Kim raises some interesting points. When does Asian become Asian American? Who is and is not qualified to write it and critique it? This raises a fundamental question of authenticity. The extreme examples of what Chin labels "fake" are easy to spot, like the children's "classics," *Five Chinese Brothers* and *Tikki Tikki Tembo*. In books like these there is little appreciation or understanding of people of Asian ancestry and their culture or heritage. But if, as Chin implies, it is important to accurately represent a culture and its heritage, is it possible to draw a line where the "fake" ends and creative license, individual experience, and subjective perception begin? The discussion that questions like these stimulate suggests that perhaps in the case of Chin and Kingston—like the loyalty questionnaire administered to the Japanese

Americans interned during World War II—there can be no "right" answer. All we can do is try to choose "better" over "worse." So while Chin is understandably irritated by the misunderstanding and misrepresentation of the roots of Chinese American literature, Kingston as a writer must certainly be allowed a broad literary license to exercise her creativity to the fullest. The conflict comes from the lack of legitimate knowledge of, understanding of, insight into, and familiarity with the history, culture, and literary tradition of Asian/Pacific America. As a result most Americans, including Asian/Pacific Americans, are unable to recognize the liberties that an Amy Tan or Maxine Hong Kingston may choose to take with an old story or the influence that American education, values, or Christianity have had on these writers.

Another literary highpoint of the 1970s was an excerpt from *Aiiieeeee!* about the search for identity by a young Japanese American girl. In 1977, Wakako Yamauchi's "And the Soul Shall Dance" was developed into and presented as a play. With passion and precision, Yamauchi crafted one of the great works in Asian American theater. She delicately explores the tragedy of a couple trapped in an arranged marriage and the American-born generation's feelings of attraction, revulsion, and mystery for the immigrant generation. Set during the Great Depression, it offers an intriguing view of life through the eyes of two Japanese American families, which junior high and high school students alike should find easy to understand.

Mainland Asian/Pacific Americans were not the only writers emerging during the 1970s. Milton Murayama's *All I Asking for Is My Body* (1988) was first published in 1975. Set in Hawaii, where Murayama grew up, the book captures the unique pidgin dialect of the islands in a way that reveals yet another facet of the Asian/Pacific American experience. It is the Hawaii of an earlier day, with a different lifestyle and old-fashioned values, but the reader can already glimpse what will give way to modern Hawaii. Murayama's story successfully weaves a spell that for a little while allows us to nostalgically experience life in a less sophisticated Hawaii. The pidgin may not be easy for younger readers to grasp, but Murayama's talent makes it probable that most teens should be able to understand it.

*Years of Infamy: The Untold Story of America's Concentration Camps* by Michi Weglyn was published in 1976, and it is significant not only for its depth of research, textual clarity, and remarkable perception and analysis but also because it shaped history. Using primary documents to reconstruct the history that led to the internment, Weglyn was the first to grasp and explain the meaning of the Munson Report, a 25-page document by a special representative of the State Department, Curtis B. Munson, analyzing the degree of loyalty to be found among residents of Japanese descent on the West Coast and in Hawaii. Munson conducted his investigation during the fall of 1941 and corroborated almost a decade of U.S. intelligence work, when he determined that there was "a remarkable, even extraordinary degree of loyalty among this generally suspect group" (p. 34). Weglyn's research led her to enunciate the hostage-reprisal theory: Assuming that President Roosevelt accepted the Munson Report but perceived the racist character of the American public at the time, the internment of Japanese Americans was not merely a punitive action but one intended to create hostages, whose existence would ensure better treatment of American captives in the Pacific and who would be the subject of reprisals should America's fortunes at war suffer. Thanks to Weglyn's book, the Japanese American redress movement was launched, a milestone in Asian/Pacific American history.

Asian/Pacific American poetry began to bloom in the 1970s. Lawson Fusao Inada's *Before the War: Poems as They Happened* (1971) was the first book of poetry written by an Asian American to be published by a major publishing company. What makes this particularly remarkable is that Inada's poetry embraces his Japanese American heritage with a dignity and poignancy so honest that at times it is almost sublime. His later books, *Legends From Camp* (1993) and *drawing the line* (1997), continue to follow his life from Fresno, California, to Oregon and provide an insightful look into one man's life and his musings upon it. In *Camp Notes and Other Poems* (1976) by Mitsuye Yamada and *Dreams in Harrison Railroad Park* (1977) by Nellie Wong, both poets reflect on the past with an eye toward the future. Yamada in particular writes simply yet evokes an emotional response that reminds us what poetry really is.

*Thousand Pieces of Gold* (1981) by Ruthanne Lum McCunn marked the advent of the Asian/Pacific American biographical novel. In it McCunn tells the story of Lalu Nathoy, later called Polly Bemis, a Chinese pioneer woman in the American West. The story is fascinating, all the more so because the reader is aware that it is about an actual person. Yet McCunn's writing is uneven, sometimes smoothly flowing and tightly written and sometimes dull and cumbersome. For the most part, however, McCunn does a creditable job telling Lalu's story in a simple and straightforward fashion that most high school students can appreciate.

Certainly no discussion of Asian American literature for preteens, teens, and young adults would be complete without mentioning at least a few of the works of one of the most exceptional and perhaps undervalued Asian/Pacific American authors, Laurence Yep. Yep has extraordinary talent and deserves a special place in Asian/Pacific American literature. He writes for a variety of ages, from children's picture books to young adult novels, and in a variety of genres, from autobiography to historical fiction and science fiction. His works delve into so many facets of Asian/Pacific American life that it is clear he has moved beyond his thinly disguised autobiography to a level of creativity that is a joy to read. In *Dragonwings* (1975), Yep weaves a sensitive and inspirational tale about a turn-of-the-century Chinese immigrant who created a flying machine. In *Sweetwater* (1983), Yep demonstrates his talents with science fiction in a thought-provoking story about the balance between progress and tradition. In *Dragon's Gate* (1993), Yep displays a deft and sure touch with historical fiction as he creates a memorable story about a 19th-century Chinese immigrant who helps to build the transcontinental railroad. Yep puts himself into his mother's shoes in The *Star Fisher* (1991), a story about a Chinese girl growing up in rural West Virginia. In *Shadowlord* (1985), Yep tackles the *Star Trek* universe with a wonderful adventure story featuring Sulu, the character portrayed by George Takei, and Spock, Leonard Nimoy's character. In these and so many of his books, Yep consistently displays an uncanny ability to create complex and interesting characters, and he sets a standard of excellence for anyone writing about Asian/Pacific Americans.

Also notable is Joy Kogawa's *Obasan* (1982), the story of a Japanese Canadian girl and her family, their evacuation from British Columbia, and their internment in Alberta during World War II. A poet, Kogawa writes in a lyrical fashion that captures the depth of emotion and the complexity of the relationships between Asian immigrants and their children. *Obasan* is engaging reading, but it also marks the beginning of Asian/Pacific America's reexamination of its own history. Kogawa was only a child when she was interned, so her perceptions differ from those who experienced internment as adults, such as Monica Sone and Yoshiko Uchida. *Obasan* is part of the continued attempt to understand the impact that internment had upon the Asian/Pacific American community.

With the influx of refugees from Southeast Asia that began during the 1970s, there was also a rise in what might be described as a subgenre of Asian/Pacific American literature: the refugee immigrant's tale of escape from Asia and resettlement in the United States. Among the best are Sook Nyul Choi's *Year of Impossible Goodbyes* (1991), Nina Vida's *Goodbye, Saigon* (1994), and *Eighth Moon* (1983) by Sansan as told to Bette Bao Lord. Perhaps worthy of special note is *Children of the River* (1989) by Linda Crew. Crew tells the story of Sundara, her escape from the Khmer Rouge in Cambodia, and her adjustment to life in the United States. While most books in this subgenre hold the reader's attention through the adventurous nature of the escape and the desire to see the protagonist survive, *Children of the River* is compelling because of its realistic portrayal of the Cambodian refugee community and the struggles its members face in adjusting to life in the United States. Teens in particular will enjoy reading about Sundara. As the book ends, the reader cannot help but wish that the story went on a little longer.

Asian American drama has also blossomed since the 1970s. David Henry Hwang, best known perhaps for *M. Butterfly*, offered America a variety of provocative and insightful views of Asian/Pacific Americans in such plays as *F.O.B.* and *Family Devotions* (1990). Ping Chong's *Nuit Blanche: A Select View of Earthlings* (1986) probes feelings of isolation, alienation, and the progression of human history. Then there is the brilliant Philip Kan Gotanda, among whose works are the poignant exploration of relationships in *The Wash* (1984) and the masterful classic, *Yankee Dawg You Die* (1991). His most recent work, *The Ballad of Yachiyo* (1996), is about a Japanese American woman living on the island of Kauai in 1919. Gotanda's plays are richly layered stories that introduce realistic and fascinating characters and situations that can provide the basis for a stimulating class discussion.

South Asian Americans also began to make their presence felt in literature during this era. One of the most exciting South Asian American writers is Bharati Mukherjee, whose writing is quite elegant and eloquent. Each and every character is multifaceted and unique without being bizarre. She is a true Pan–Asian/Pacific American writer, introducing characters from a variety of Asian and Pacific backgrounds, yet developing each so as to be true to his or her ethnic heritage. Her collection of short stories, *The Middleman and Other Stories* (1988), is a wonderfully rich combination of imagination and realism. Her novels are passionate and powerful, especially *Jasmine* (1991), in which a young woman from India builds a life in the United States, and *The Tiger's Daughter* (1996), in which an Indian woman who has been living in the United States returns to India and begins to see her family, friends, and culture in a different light. Mukherjee has the uncanny ability to write about the mundane and make it magnificent.

Assimilation and acculturation became very popular topics in Asian/Pacific American literature during the 1970s and 1980s. Bette Bao Lord addressed it in her middle readers' book, *In the Year of the Boar and Jackie Robinson* (1984), which is about a young Chinese girl who immigrates to the United States in 1947 and her first year of life in New York. Although it occasionally relies on stereotypes, it is nevertheless a charming story that some junior high school students might enjoy.

## The Next Generation of Asian/Pacific American Writers

Some might groan, moan, or worse. Yet to be fair, in any discussion of Asian/Pacific American literature, there is "pre–Amy Tan" and "post–Amy Tan." With the phenomenal success of her first novel, *The Joy Luck Club* (1989), and on its heels, her second novel, *The Kitchen God's Wife* (1992), Tan forever changed the way that we think, write, and read about Asian/Pacific Americans. She is certainly not without her detractors. Frank Chin (Chan et al., 1991) criticizes her for opening *The Joy Luck Club* with a fake Chinese fairy tale about:

> a duck that wants to be a swan and a mother who dreams of her daughter being born in America, where she'll grow up speaking perfect English and no one will laugh at her and where a "woman's worth is [not] measured by the loudness of her husband's belch." . . . Ducks in the barnyard are not the subject of Chinese

> fairy tales except as food. Swans are not the symbols of physical female beauty, vanity, and promiscuity that they are in the West. . . . There is nothing in Chinese fairy tales to justify characterizing the Chinese as measuring a woman's worth by the loudness of her husband's belch. (pp. 2–3)

Chin pursues his crusade against the "fake" with the fervor of a religious zealot. It seems unfortunate that this campaign sometimes overshadows the fact that Chin himself is a gifted writer with a keen sense of who and what the Asian/Pacific American community is. His novels, such as *Donald Duk* (1991), are complex and clever commentaries on the Asian/Pacific American man. His works are at times thrilling and painful but never boring and never ordinary. They are certainly never fake. Fake or not, we must give credit where credit is due. Tan is an exceptional storyteller. She captures her reader's interest and sweeps them along right from the first paragraph, and one doesn't feel shortchanged at the end of the ride. And, fake or not, the success of *The Joy Luck Club* created an unprecedented interest in Asian/Pacific American writing.

Unfortunately, this increased interest has created a few blockbuster titles but ignores other excellent writers and their work. One of the more significant works that Tan's success may have overshadowed was Jessica Hagedorn's comprehensive anthology of Asian/Pacific American fiction, *Charlie Chan Is Dead* (1993). The collection compiled by Hagedorn is impressive for the diversity of its contributors and the wide-ranging perspectives they offer. At times it is uneven in terms of the quality of the selections, and it lacks background material on each piece and its author that *The Big Aiiieeeee!* provides, which allows the reader to better understand the context of the story. As a result, even older readers might find some pieces difficult. Nevertheless, *Charlie Chan Is Dead* stands as a milepost in Asian/Pacific American literature.

Another collection worthy of merit is *Into the Fire: Asian American Prose* (1996), edited by Sylvia Watanabe and Carol Bruchac. This is an exciting collection of contemporary writings that begins to illustrate the depth, breadth, and range of talent in Asian America. A nice photography and biographical section on each contributing author enhances the reader's ability to glean greater insights from each selection.

*Returning a Borrowed Tongue* (1995), edited by Nick Carbo, is an anthology of Filipino and Filipino American poetry. An impressive collection, it is a wonderful example of the blossoming talent of Asian/Pacific American writers.

Russell Leong's fiction and poetry also merits more attention. His book of poems, *In the Country of Dreams and Dust* (1993), is a magnificent testament to an appreciation of the human condition. Poet and playwright Dwight Okita is another Asian/Pacific American talent whose work is not yet as appreciated as it should be. His book of poetry, *Crossing Against the Light* (1992), is a wonderful collection displaying wit, humor, and warmth as Okita dissects the Asian/Pacific American experience. His plays—particularly *Hiroshima: The Light of 10,000 Suns* (1996), is a compelling discussion of the dropping of the first atomic bomb, and *The Salad Bowl Dance* (1993), an examination of the resettlement of Japanese Americans in Chicago after World War II—remind us that there are always new ways to look at "traditional" Asian/Pacific American subjects. *The Salad Bowl Dance* is particularly unusual because it deals with the Japanese American community's eastward expansion rather than its return to the West Coast.

*From a Three-Cornered World* (1997) is a collection of poems by James Masao Mitsui that span childhood in an internment camp through life as an adult with elderly parents. His poems are brief but delicately honed reflections of the small things that make life significant. David Mura is another talent whose work may have been eclipsed, at least in part, by Tan. His book, *Turning Japanese: Memoirs of a Sansei* (1991), about his first trip to Japan, spoke to the hearts of many third-generation Japanese American men. It provides an interesting glimpse into the psyche of a Japanese American man as he comes into contact with the country of his forebears. Mura's critical essays are lucid and convincing. His poetry, however, leaves something to be desired; he seems to spend an inordinate amount of time grappling with interracial sexual relationships.

Gish Jen's *Typical American* (1991) is yet another wonderful example of modern Asian/Pacific American literature. Jen's writing is a joy to read; it is lucid and lyrical with a well-constructed plot. Cynthia Kadohata's *The Floating World* (1989) is somewhat darker but no less fascinating. Here, Grandmother is not a kindly old lady but a sometimes (through her granddaughter's eyes) mean-spirited, manipulative old woman. Kadohata's story is nevertheless a refreshing look at the grandmother-granddaughter relationship.

*Bone* (1993) by Fae Myenne Ng is another exceptional example of Asian/Pacific American literature for adults and older teens that may have been overshadowed by the commercial success of *The Joy Luck Club*. In her tightly written book, Ng shows the reader new aspects of Asian American relationships and raises issues that existing stereotypes would deny Asian/Pacific Americans much opportunity to confront in public.

Julie Shigekuni and Holly Uyemoto are two gifted, newer writers who do not yet have a huge body of published works, but they will certainly remedy that in time. Shigekuni's *A Bridge Between Us* (1995) follows four generations of Japanese American women and explores the ties that bind them together: love, tradition, and obligation. Shigekuni shatters some of the stereotypes about Japanese American women. Even though she creates what at times seems an atypical situation, the book never ceases to be an intriguing and multifaceted look at an Asian/Pacific American family.

*Go* (1995) by Holly Uyemoto delves into the life of Wil, a woman about to turn 21. Wil is in emotional and psychological turmoil as she tries to take stock of her life and her family, searching for truth and reality amid her family's personalities, mythology, and conflicts. While it may sound heavy or depressing, Uyemoto's writing lifts her story well above the predictable. Her writing is deftly woven with humor, the absurd, and a lucidity that makes every page enjoyable.

*What the Scarecrow Said* (1996) by Stewart David Ikeda is another first novel that showcases a bright and promising talent. Ikeda traces five generations of a Japanese American family from the immigrant Issei's arrival in the United States through pre–World War II promises, the devastation of the internment, and the rebuilding of lives in the aftermath of the war on the East Coast (a nice twist). Ikeda's writing is multifaceted. It is alternately humorous, tragic, surprising, and inspirational; throughout it is eloquent, passionate, and a joy to read. The description of the Japanese Americans being searched prior to their internment seems quite matter-of-fact until the unexpected and eye-opening punchline. As Ikeda tells us about the protagonist's mishaps during a visit by Eleanor Roosevelt, he is witty and hilarious. Truly this book is enjoyable to read.

*Monkey Bridge* (1997) by Lan Cao represents an exciting new voice in Asian/Pacific American literature. The protagonist, Mai Nguyen, is 13 years old when she and her mother are airlifted from Saigon just before that city's fall in 1975. The book traces Mai's attempts to adjust to life in "Little Saigon" in Virginia as she cares for her ailing mother. Cao beautifully depicts the evolving relationship between mother and daughter and deftly explores their feelings of guilt from having survived the war. This book moves beyond the refugee-escape-from-a-foreign-country mold into a genuine exploration of the conflicts and concerns in rebuilding a life.

Even if a reader is not well-versed in reading and understanding Hawaiian pidgin English, Lois-Ann Yamanaka's stories, written in Hawaiian and pidgin English, are occasionally sharp and biting but always original and honest. Yamanaka gives readers a glimpse of the people of Hawaii—their lives, their personalities, and their culture—from an insider's point of view. Pieces like *Empty Heart* (1993) evoke a Hawaii that few tourists will ever see but that residents will immediately recognize and appreciate.

*Tropic of Orange* (1997) by Karen Tei Yamashita is a compelling tale of avant-garde life and relationships in Los Angeles. With a remarkable sure-handedness, Yamashita probes the diversity of Los Angeles and the absurdity of the human condition. Younger students may not appreciate this book, but older readers will certainly find it thought-provoking.

M. Evelina Galang's *Her Wild American Self* (1996), a collection of short stories, is a captivating work. Galang writes with humorous insight and thought-provoking honesty about the experience of being a Filipina American. Older teens and adults will enjoy her commentaries on family, friends, and her own sense of identity as a young woman. Galang has a nice talent for dialogue and her writing conveys a wonderful sense of the joy in life.

Wang Ping's short stories in *American Visa* (1994) are fascinating and highly enjoyable. Using the first-person voice of a woman named Seaweed, Ping tells her tales with a compelling honesty, gracefulness, and insight that make her stories of life during China's Cultural Revolution and immigration to New York particularly expressive.

For young high school readers, Lensey Namioka has created some wonderful stories, such as *Yang the Youngest and His Terrible Ear* (1992), about a young Chinese American boy who lacks the musical talent possessed by the rest of his family, and *Yang the Third and Her Impossible Family* (1995), about a Chinese American girl dealing with her family's Chinese customs. *April and the Dragon Lady* (1994) explores a young Chinese American girl's relationship with her manipulative grandmother, ringing true page after page. Again, though not as well known as Amy Tan, Namioka tells enjoyable stories that young high school students will enjoy reading.

Lauren Lee's *Stella: On the Edge of Popularity* (1994) is well-suited for junior high and high school students. She explores the tensions that many second-generation Asian/Pacific Americans face between cultural preservation and acculturation. At home, Stella's parents and grandmother expect her to conform to life as a good Korean girl, but at school Stella is wholly American, trying desperately to be herself, whoever that might be. The *Korean Central Daily News* proclaimed this to be *the* book that Korean American parents need to read to better understand their children. College-age readers of both sexes have been able to relate to this book.

Teens will particularly enjoy Marie G. Lee's writing. *If It Hadn't Been for Yoon Jun* (1993), which is about a Korean adoptee coming to terms with her identity as a Korean American, and *Finding My Voice* (1992), which is about a Korean American teen struggling to live up to her parents' expectations, are wonderful stories about Asian American girls coming-of-age. In her early 30s, Lee nevertheless clearly remains in touch with the feelings and concerns of 17- and 18-year-olds.

*Children of Asian America* (1996), edited by the Asian American Coalition, defies classification in terms of age appropriateness. A collection of original, contemporary Asian/Pacific American children's stories from 12 Asian ethnic communities, there are layers to each story and its insights that make the book suitable for preteens, teens, and young adults. Funny and poignant, its stories come straight from the heart of the Asian/Pacific American community. It is proving especially valuable in adult ESL classes for teachers looking for short, interesting children's stories that will not insult an adult's intelligence.

## Teaching Strategies

The teacher who attempts to introduce Asian/Pacific American literature into his or her classroom should be prepared from the outset to address the issues of the great diversity within this community. The U.S. Census Bureau has identified more than 50 different Asian and Pacific Islander ethnic groups within the United States. It is not possible, even in a class devoted solely to Asian/Pacific American literature, to present them all. It should also be explained that more writers are of Chinese and Japanese ancestry because these groups have had somewhat longer histories in the United States. As a result, we are just beginning to see a growth in the number of authors of Korean, Filipino, and Indian ancestry, and some of the newest groups, such as the Southeast Asian refugees, are still developing as writers, so their stories may currently be written by authors from other backgrounds.

Teachers also need to avoid falling into the trap of offering literature only from those Asian ethnic groups that are represented in their class, school, or school district. Such offerings may satisfy immediate interest, but this presents a grossly distorted view of Asian/Pacific American identity. It may be interesting, for instance, to discuss the diversity of this group and then read several stories sharing a common theme—such as escape from the home country and resettlement in the United States using books such as *The Year of Impossible Goodbyes* (Choi, 1991); *Goodbye, Saigon* (Vida, 1994); *Eighth Moon* (Lord, 1983); and *Children of the River* (Crew, 1989)—followed by a discussion about the similarities and differences based on time, contemporary politics, and world events.

Another possible theme might center on the tension between Asian identity and American identity. Discussions can focus on generational differences (immigrant versus American-born) and acculturation and assimilation of minority groups in this country, as well as contemporary social values, using books such as *Stella: On the Edge of Popularity* (Lee, 1994); *Yang the Third and Her Impossible Family* (Namioka, 1995); *Finding My Voice* (Lee, 1992); *In the Year of the Boar and Jackie Robinson* (Lord, 1984); *Jasmine* (Mukherjee, 1991); and *No-No Boy* (Okada, 1988).

Gotanda's play, *Yankee Dawg You Die* (1991), is a wonderfully thought-provoking piece that can stimulate great discussion. It raises issues about how minorities are portrayed in the media and the arts, the lack of control that they have over these portrayals, their frustration over the situation, and the options open to them. The concept of stereotypes is a challenging theme to use to explore Asian/Pacific American literature. Older books like *Nisei Daughter* (Sone, 1979) and

*Fifth Chinese Daughter* (Wong, 1945) can be contrasted with *Bone* (Ng, 1993), *A Bridge Between Us* (Shigekuni, 1995), and *Go* (Uyemoto, 1995).

The controversy between the "real" and the "fake" can also be examined. The conflicting arguments of Frank Chin, Maxine Hong Kingston, and Amy Tan can be used to show the diversity of opinions and philosophies within the Asian/Pacific American community and to combat the habit of treating minority groups as monolithic entities.

Effective teaching of Asian/Pacific American literature requires a historical context within which to understand it. This means that, as discomforting as it may be, racism toward Asians and Pacific Islanders in the United States needs to be addressed with the class. Some individuals may want to deny that it exists or has ever existed, but underlying much of Asian/Pacific American literature is a feeling, or even a certainty, that it has existed and continues to exist. American society may find it more familiar and therefore more comfortable to discuss racism in terms of anti-Black sentiment or anti-Semitism, but to truly appreciate Asian/Pacific American literature and to understand it in its rightful context, students must be aware of the way that racism has shaped Asian/Pacific American history. Toward this end, subjects like the Japanese American internment should be discussed in the context of its complete and utter disregard for the civil rights of American citizens of Japanese ancestry and the racist attitudes from which it arose. It must be made clear to students that Pearl Harbor had nothing to do with it—these were, after all, Americans of Japanese ancestry, not Japanese; that national security could not possibly have been threatened by infants, children, the infirm, or the elderly, yet they too were interned; and that no comparison is being made with either the death camps of Nazi Germany or the enslavement of Africans. Each was wrong, and we accomplish nothing debating which was worse. All were evil, and it makes it no better that someone else suffered more, worse, or even the same. Wrong is wrong.

Any teacher planning to include Asian/Pacific American literature in his or her classroom should read a book like *Strangers From a Different Shore* (1989) by Ronald Takaki in order to give themselves greater familiarity with Asian/Pacific American history. *The Big Aiiieeeee!* (Chan et al., 1991), *Children of Asian America* (Asian American Coalition, 1996), and *Charlie Chan Is Dead* (Hagedorn, 1993) are other good background sources.

# Summary

The literature of the Asian/Pacific American community has been greatly influenced by its history. Immigration restrictions and other manifestations of anti–Asian/Pacific Islander attitudes resulted in that history not only influencing how the literature was written but also sparking intense debate about who could or should write that literature, what was actually written, and why. The bulk of the literature was written in the last 25 to 50 years. Although Asian/Pacific American history has left us with a fairly condensed period of time during which this community has produced its own literature, the passions of a Frank Chin, the poise and elegance of a Bharati Mukherjee, the poignancy of a Philip Kan Gotanda, the inventiveness of a Laurence Yep, the popularity of an Amy Tan, and the promise of a Marie G. Lee give us reason for great optimism about the future of Asian/Pacific American literature.

Standard themes will continue to inspire. The immigrant experience will continue to be explored. Assimilation and acculturation versus the preservation of culture will still resurface throughout Asian/Pacific American literature. The significance and consequences of the internment will persist as a commentary on what many Asian/Pacific Americans fear may be reality; it will linger as proof that for those of Asian and Pacific Islander ethnicity, no matter what degree to which they acculturate, it may never be enough.

As these traditional themes continue to evolve, there is every indication that established writers—as well as newer or younger writers like Julie Shigekuni, Holly Uyemoto, Marie G. Lee, and Lan Cao—will offer new but still authentic perspectives on Asian/Pacific Americans. So, too, as Asian/Pacific American history progresses, it will continue to inspire these writers. Let us hope that more Americans will familiarize themselves with that history so that they can better appreciate the talents of these writers and the stories they tell.

# Notes

1. One of the earliest examples of Asian/Pacific American literature is *An English-Chinese Phrase Book* by Wong Sam and Assistants. Published by Wells, Fargo in 1875, with a revised edition published

in 1887, there is no record of who Wong Sam was or who his assistants were. Although designed as a means of teaching useful English phrases, they are literary in their ability to create a picture of what life for an early Chinese American must have been like. *Phrase Book* offers more than just the phrases it teaches. Through these phrases, a reader can glean strategy and tactics for business, criminal law, and dealing with people of European ancestry and their sometimes subjective application of the law. Interestingly, the tactics and strategies offered do not include submission, acculturation, or assimilation.

2. This did not change until the 1952 passage of the McCarran-Walter Act, which nullified the 1790 naturalization law that prevented immigrant Asians from becoming United States citizens.

## Reading List

Asian American Coalition. (Ed.). (1996). *Children of Asian America.* Chicago: Polychrome.

> A thought-provoking and compelling anthology of original, contemporary short stories and poems about the experience of growing up as an Asian American from the Bangladeshi, Cambodian, Chinese, Filipino, Indian, Japanese, Korean, Laotian, Pakistani, Thai, Vietnamese, biracial, and Pan–Asian American communities.

Berson, M. (Ed.). (1990). *Between worlds: Contemporary Asian American plays.* New York: Theatre Communications Group.

> A nice collection of classic Asian American plays.

Bulosan, C. (1946). *America is in the heart.* Seattle, WA: University of Washington Press.

> This autobiographical novel by a Filipino immigrant is a masterful account of life as an Asian American in pre–World War II America. At times painfully brutal and tragic, it transcends mere storytelling with its unflinching honesty, directness, and insight into the condition of Asian Americans. A very special book.

Cao, L. (1997). *Monkey bridge*. New York: Viking.

> A marvelously well-written story about rebuilding a life in America after the fall of Saigon.

Carbo, N. (Ed.). (1995). *Returning a borrowed tongue: An anthology of Filipino and Filipino American poetry*. Minneapolis, MN: Coffee House Press.

> An inspiring collection of poetry that only begins to tap the talent in the Filipino American community.

Cha, T. H. K. (1982). *Dictee*. New York: Tanam Press.

> Sometimes fragmented and disjointed, it is no less powerful in its examination of a Korean immigrant's pain and frustration as she attempts to build an American life.

Chin, F. (1991). *Donald Duk*. Minneapolis: Coffee House Press.

Choi, S. N. (1991). *The year of impossible goodbyes*. Boston: Houghton Mifflin.

> This story follows a Korean girl's life in post–World War II Korea and her escape from North Korea to Seoul. It has all the makings of a good story except that the most intriguing and exciting aspects about which the reader may be curious seem to have happened to older members of the girl's family or community, and it's not clear whether they simply didn't tell her the details of their experiences or if she chose not to relate them; in any event, they're not in the book.

Crew, L. (1989). *Children of the river*. New York: Dell.

> This is one of the better tales of escape from an Asian country and the rebuilding of a life in the United States. In this tale, the heroine, Sundara, is a Cambodian refugee, and author Crew does an excellent job detailing the schizophrenic life of a refugee struggling to hold onto (and perhaps reclaim) something of the life from which she's been abruptly torn while also building a life in the United States. A really well-done story.

Far, S. S. (1912). *Mrs. Spring Fragrance*. New York: A.C. McClurg.

> At times humorous, at times wretched, but always compelling. Although written at a time of different mores and values, contemporary readers will not have any difficulty appreciating this author's work.

Galang, E. (1996). *Her wild American self*. Minneapolis, MN: Coffee House Press.

> A wonderfully witty collection of short stories and personal accounts about life as a contemporary Filipina American. Thoroughly enjoyable reading.

Gotanda, P. K. (1984). *The wash*. New York: Dramatists Play Service.

Gotanda, P. K. (1991). *Yankee dawg you die*. New York: Dramatists Play Service.

> Although *The Wash* is better-known, *Yankee Dawg You Die* is truly brilliant. Two Asian American actors from different generations trade barbs, impart criticisms of each other's choices and careers, offer justifications and rationalizations for those choices and their resultant careers, and rail against and celebrate the opportunities for Asian Americans in the performing arts. At times poignant, hilarious, and uplifting, this is a wonderful piece to stimulate classroom discussion about opportunities for minorities to succeed in the United States.

Hagedorn, J. (Ed.). (1993). *Charlie Chan is dead: An anthology of contemporary Asian American fiction*. New York: Penguin Books.

> An eclectic collection of Asian American writing, it provides a wonderful overview of Asian American literature. More background about the authors and their writings might have made it a somewhat better tool for classroom use, but it is still an exciting and inspiring collection.

Houston, J. D. & Houston, J. W. (1973). *Farewell to Manzanar*. Boston: Houghton Mifflin.

> One of the better known Japanese American internment stories, perhaps because it was one of the first published.

Hwang, H. D. (1990). *FOB and other plays*. New York: Plume.

Ikeda, S. D. (1996). *What the scarecrow said*. New York: HarperCollins.

> This tale follows five generations of a Japanese American family. It is alternately witty and humorous and painful and poignant. The characters are exquisitely drawn and their experiences and perspectives honest and human. This is a three-dimensional look at the internment and is definitely one of the best.

Inada, L. (1971). *Before the War*. New York: Morrow.

Inada, L. F. (1993). *Legends from camp*. Minneapolis, MN: Coffee House Press.

Inada, L. F. (1997). *drawing the line*. Minneapolis, MN: Coffee House Press.

Kadohata, C. (1989). *The floating world*. New York: Viking Penguin.

Kingston, M. H. (1975). *The woman warrior*. New York: Knopf.

> Frank Chin's criticisms aside, Kingston writes beautiful prose and tells an engaging and interesting story that is a pleasure to read.

Kogawa, J. (1982). *Obasan*. Boston: David R. Godine.

Lee, L. (1994). *Stella: On the edge of popularity*. Chicago: Polychrome.

> Protagonist Stella Kim struggles to reconcile her family's pressure and expectation that she be a good traditional Korean girl with her classmates' expectations that she conform to and adopt American values. A sensitive and insightful story that delves into a conflict faced by many Asian American adolescents.

Lee, M. G. (1992). *Finding my voice*. Boston: Houghton Mifflin.

>   Korean American Lee must surely be one of the most promising young Asian American writers. All her books present an honest look at the complexity of life for Asian American young adults. *Finding My Voice*, about a Korean American girl's senior year in high school, offers a glimpse into subjects like Asian parental pressures and expectations that may conflict with a teen's own dreams and ambitions.

Leong, R. (1993). *In the country of dreams and dust*. Albuquerque, NM: West End Press.

Lord, B. B. (1984). *In the year of the boar and Jackie Robinson*. New York: HarperTrophy.

>   Written for younger children, it's an interesting example of the values and messages stressed to an immigrant Chinese girl growing up in New York in the late 1940s.

Lord, B. B. (as told by Sansan). (1983). *Eighth moon*. New York: HarperCollins.

>   This is Lord's story of her younger sister's life in China during the Cultural Revolution and her subsequent escape to America.

McCunn, R. L. (1981). *Thousand pieces of gold*. Boston: Beacon Press.

>   This biographical novel about an early Chinese American pioneer woman, eventually known as Polly Bemis, illustrates how remarkable a woman Bemis was and recounts her fascinating life in a rather dry manner that does not do justice to Mrs. Bemis. The film (1991) is better.

Mitsui, J. M. (1997). *From a three-cornered world*. Seattle, WA: University of Washington Press.

Mukherjee, B. (1988). *The middleman and other stories*. New York: Grove Press.

> This collection of short stories clearly demonstrates why Mukherjee is one of the most celebrated Asian American authors. Her prose is beautiful. Her characters are each unique individuals. Each story is well-crafted and easily grabs and holds the reader's interest.

Mukherjee, B. (1991). *Jasmine*. New York: Fawcett.

Mukherjee, B. (1996). *The tiger's daughter*. New York: Fawcett.

Mura, D. (1991). *Turning Japanese: Memoirs of a Sansei*. New York: Atlantic Monthly Press.

> While many third-generation Japanese Americans say they could really relate to this book, others find it puerile and self-obsessed. Better than Mura's poetry, but not as good as some of his critical essays.

Murayama, M. (1988). *All I asking for is my body*. Honolulu, HI: University of Hawaii Press.

Namioka, L. (1992). *Yang the youngest and his terrible ear*. Boston: Little Brown.

Namioka, L. (1994). *April and the dragon lady*. New York: Harcourt Brace Jovanovich.

> This book didn't garner as much attention as Namioka's *Yang the Youngest and His Terrible Ear* or its companion book, *Yang the Third and Her Impossible Family*, but it is every bit as good, if not better. An interesting look at gender roles and expectations within a Chinese American family.

Namioka, L. (1995). *Yang the third and her impossible family*. Boston: Little, Brown.

Ng, F. M. (1993). *Bone*. New York: Hyperion.

Okada, J. (1988). *No-no boy*. Seattle, WA: University of Washington Press.

> To really appreciate this book, one needs an under-standing of the history of the Japanese American intern-ment, the loyalty questionnaire, and the subsequent controversy over those who answered "no-no" that has yet to be completely resolved by the Japanese American community more than 50 years later. This is a painful, powerful, but ultimately liberating book that should not be overlooked.

Okita, D. (1992). *Crossing against the light*. Chicago, IL: Tia Chucha Press.

Ping, W. (1994). *American visa*. Minneapolis, MN: Coffee House Press.

> A beautifully written collection of short stories about a woman living in China during the Cultural Revolution and her eventual immigration to and attempt to build a life in New York.

Shigekuni, J. (1995). *A bridge between us*. New York: Doubleday.

> A story following four generations of women in a Japa-nese American family, it is beautifully written although the characters are, at times, somewhat two-dimensional.

Sone, M. (1979). *Nisei daughter*. Seattle, WA: University of Washington Press.

> This classic lacks the depth and complexity of more contemporary examinations of Japanese American fam-ily life and Japanese American young women, but it is interesting for its sheer sense of "normalcy." Compared to the troubled young women and the dysfunctional fami-lies presented in other books, *Nisei Daughter* is at times naive, ordinary, or old-fashioned, but it still manages to hold its own.

Tan, A. (1989). *The joy luck club*. New York: Putnam.

Takashima, S. (1991). *A child in prison camp.* Canada: Tundra Books.

Uchida, Y. (1971). *Journey to Topaz.* New York: Scribners.

Uchida, Y. (1978). *Journey home.* New York: Atheneum.

Uyemoto, H. *Go.* (1995). New York: Dutton.

> Protagonist Wil is turning 21 and has already had a break-down. It sounds depressing, and although one may sometimes wish that Wil would just take control of her own life, Uyemoto has such a gift with words that this book is still fascinating reading.

Vida, N. (1994). *Goodbye, Saigon.* New York: Crown.

> A well-written and intriguing look into the Vietnamese American community as it rebuilds itself.

Watanabe, S., & Bruchac, C. (Eds.). (1996). *Into the fire: Asian American prose.* Greenfield Center, NY: Greenfield Review Press.

> This is a wonderful collection of writing from contemporary Asian American authors.

Wong, Jade S. (1945). *Fifth Chinese daughter.* Seattle, WA: University of Washington Press.

> Some of the values and attitudes seem rather too self-deprecating and self-sacrificing, but it is nevertheless an interesting look at life in a Chinese American family during the first half of the 20th century.

Wong, Janet S. (1994). *Good luck gold and other poems.* New York: Simon & Schuster.

> Korean/Chinese American poet Wong has a deft touch with words. Her poems are charming capsules of Asian American attitudes, values, and experiences.

Wong, Janet S. (1996). *A suitcase of seaweed.* New York: Simon & Schuster.

Wong, N. (1977). *Dreams in Harrison Railroad Park*. Berkeley, CA: Kelsey Street Press.

Wong, S. (1995). *American knees*. New York: Simon & Schuster.

Wong looks at Asian American sexuality and relationships in this realistic examination of a love affair.

Wong, S. (1990). *Homebase*. New York: Plume.

Yamada, M. (1976). *Camp notes and other poems*. San Francisco, CA: Shameless Hussy Press.

Yamada, M. (1988). *Desert run: Poems and stories*. Latham, NY: Kitchen Table: Women of Color Press.

Yamamoto, H. (1988). *Seventeen syllables and other stories*. Latham, NY: Kitchen Table: Women of Color Press.

Yamanaka, L. (1993). Empty heart. In J. Hagedorn (Ed.). *Charlie Chan is dead: An anthology of Contemporary Asian American Fiction*. New York: Penguin Books.

Yamashita, K. T. (1992). *Brazil-Maru*. Minneapolis, MN: Coffee House Press.

Not all Asian American immigrants came to North America. In this captivating tale, Yamashita looks at the lives of Japanese Brazilians and their relationships.

Yamashita, K. T. (1990). *Through the arc of the rain forest*. Minneapolis, MN: Coffee House Press.

Yamashita, K. T. (1997). *Tropic of orange*. Minneapolis, MN: Coffee House Press.

Yamauchi, W. (1976). And the soul shall dance. In O. Guernesy (Ed.). *Burn Matel Theater Yearbook 1976–1977*. New York: Dodd Mead.

Yep, L. (1975). *Dragonwings*. New York: HarperCollins.

Yep, L. (1983). *Sweetwater*. New York: HarperTrophy.

Yep, L. (1985). *Shadowlord*. New York: Pocket.

> Even if you're not a fan of *Star Trek*, Yep's foray into the *Star Trek* universe is a thoroughly enjoyable read. When the life of an alien prince is threatened, it's Sulu to the rescue!

Yep, L. (1991). *The star fisher*. New York: Morrow.

Yep, L. (1993). *Dragon's gate*. New York: HarperCollins.

> A brilliant look at the life of a Chinese American immigrant working on the railroad during the 19th century.

Yep, L. (1994). *Child of the owl*. New York: HarperCollins.

> Life in San Francisco's Chinatown through the eyes of a young girl.

Yep, L. (1995). *Thief of hearts*. New York: HarperCollins.

> The sequel to *Child of the Owl*, a biracial Asian American girl and a Chinese immigrant girl come to terms with their Chinese American identities.

Parents and teachers often complain about how difficult it is to find Asian American titles beyond those most commercially successful. The following are wonderful resources from which to order these and other Asian American titles, and each offers a free and very comprehensive catalog:

Asia for Kids
4480 Lake Forest Drive, Suite 302
Cincinnati, OH 45242
(800) 765-5885
(513) 563-3100
Fax: (513) 563-3105

Multicultural Distributing Center
9440 Telstar Avenue, Unit #2
El Monte, CA 91731
(818) 859-3133
Fax: (818) 859-3136

Asian American Bookseller
37 St. Marks Place
New York, NY 10003
(212) 228-6718
Fax: (212) 228-7718

Shen's Books & Supplies
821 South First Avenue
Arcadia, CA 91006
(818) 445-6958
(800) 456-6660

# References

Chan, J. P., Chin, F., Inada, L. F., & Wong, S. (Eds.). (1991). *The big aiiieeeee!* New York: Meridian.

Hom, M. (1987). *Songs of Gold Mountain*. Berkeley, CA: University of California.

Hu-DeHart, E. (1992). From Yellow peril to model minority: The Columbus legacy and Asians in America. *The New World*. Washington, DC: Smithsonian Institute.

Takaki, R. (1989). *Strangers from a different shore*. Boston: Little, Brown.

Weglyn, M. (1976). *Years of infamy: The untold story of America's concentration camps*. New York: Morrow.

A Young adult novel about growing up Korean American. (1994, November 14). *Korean Central Daily News*.

# Chapter 6

# Contextualizing Native American Literature

*Anna Lee Walters* with *Debbie Reese*

*Native American Literature is not a subfield literature.*
*It is not confined to the English language.*
*It is hemispheric in dimension.*

J. Forbes, 1987

## The Cultural Roots

The study of Native American literature begins with an introduction to the extinct and living cultures from which indigenous literatures derive and in which these literatures still most animately reveal themselves. In the United States today, these cultures comprise approximately two million people and are reflected in about 750 related and diverse tribal groups and communities that are now bound together by recent federal-tribal events and relations.[1]

To accept the above population figures, and to consider only tribal nations in the United States as having "Native American literature," is to ignore the hemispheric presence and network of indigenous literatures, which have a long and stable history that has not yet been established in the modern developing nations of the Americas. The pre-Columbian oral roots of indigenous literatures are in Alaska, Canada, Mexico, and South America, as is the future.

The present national boundaries of the modern countries of the Americas separate the extant tribes and have very effectively resulted in the appearance of nonexistent, isolated, and fragmented literatures, disconnected from each other and unintelligible and insignificant to societies and cultural groups other than their own. As a result, students think that Native American literature is recent, shaped largely or solely by the dominant language and society in each modern country. Such thinking frames the study of indigenous literatures in most schools. As long as indigenous literatures are introduced and studied from within national boundaries, a distorted view of them will prevail.

Although members of tribal nations became American citizens only in 1924 and were given the right to vote even more recently, they have been on this continent for thousands of years. When indigenous literatures are permitted to unfold on their own terms, they show not only the knowledge of peoples in the near and distant past but also the long relationships of peace or conflict that they have had with others.

Indigenous literatures generate practical thinking and problem solving about how their societies and cultures have communicated and coexisted with each other in the Americas over long periods. They encourage knowledge of the earth and sky that has always been necessary human survival. The long-term existence of indigenous cultures in the Americas that make indigenous literatures what they are: bodies of knowledge that can serve all humanity. Native people are storytellers with stories passed on from generation to generation. Although effectively capturing the oral tradition can be difficult, many Native authors are successful at conveying the necessary nuances to make the story live in the reader's mind. Paula Gunn Allen's collection, *Spider Woman's Granddaughters* (1989), includes traditional tales and contemporary writing by Native American women. Allen's introduction to the book also discusses Native literature in the oral tradition and what she calls "told-on-the-page" stories that are included in her collection. An excellent example of the ability to capture the oral tradition on the page can be seen in Athabascan author Velma Wallis's *Two Old Women* (1993). Wallis retells a story, told to her by her mother as they gathered wood for the winter, about two old Athabascan women who were abandoned by their tribe during a winter of poverty and extreme hardship. Rather than give up and accept death, the two old women decide to fight for their survival alone in the Alaskan wilderness. The women's courage and determination to survive parallels the history of Native American people as a whole, whose resistance in the face of persecution has prevented them from becoming the vanishing race they were often described as being.

The ability of indigenous peoples to map their physical and spiritual relationships non-geographical boundaries in old and new generations is a distinctive feature of indigenous life through all periods of time. Of the hundreds of unrelated indigenous groups in the United States alone, all express intimate and specialized knowledge of the continent. This is mirrored in indigenous languages and is evident in English indigenous literatures as well.

Indigenous groups are still inclined to view the land from perspectives other than those of modern political nation-states, or falling or rising countries inclined toward war or peace in particular eras as well as in the future. They demonstrate perceptions of this continent that have troubled modern American governments, as well as foreign governments in the Americas, since European contact.

In indigenous experiences and literatures, the continent is more than the old and modern nations that have been formed on them. The continent cannot be contained in political blocs or territories or in time; it is experienced as vibrantly alive and under no human or societal control. This view of a timeless animated cosmos has always been disconcerting and threatening to outsiders, who have tried to change or eradicate it since it was first expressed by indigenous peoples. Wars have been fought because indigenous peoples would not let that perception go; they have therefore suffered for it greatly.

Indigenous expressions of an animated land have led to ideas about the development of human consciousness, human existence, and human rights upon the continent. These ideas, which became fundamental indigenous teachings, were set in motion long before indigenous peoples met Europeans. Indigenous philosophies, laws, and sciences sprouted in this soil. Furthermore, the behaviors of these indigenous groups were consistent with their beliefs about their connection to the land. This was repeatedly witnessed by the early European colonialists.

These continued teachings about the land in indigenous literatures still mark indigenous peoples as they move in modern American society and the other countries of the Americas. The teachings are the basis for their ideas of beauty, ideal human behavior, humor, and health.

These perspectives of the relationship between the land and the existence and welfare of indigenous peoples have been literal and spiritual for many generations. They show that indigenous peoples have been taking longer and broader views of human and nonhuman life, as they observed them in the Americas, long before what is often taught as the "beginning" of civilization here. This was "global awareness" before the term was coined and it became trendy.

The visions of a whole, timeless land had integrity even during periods of war and after boundaries were drawn. The strength and truth of this vision remained while many political states rose and fell. Using this storehouse of information enabled indigenous groups to survive the onslaught of human destruction over the millennia.

The natural world is considered to be the best teacher in indigenous literatures, because all species of life have an order and a pattern of behavior that express wisdom and purpose simply by their fulfillment. The unique species of plants and animals, some of which are now extinct, represents libraries of information held by indigenous peoples. All nonhuman life was a source of knowledge for indigenous peoples. Their ideas about the natural world are complicated and serious, not the silly caricatures in many books where animals mimic human beings and are depicted without divine dignity or grace. This is what happens when indigenous literatures are interpreted in another cultural framework.

Today all the dimensions of indigenous literatures are not realized or are missed because they are approached in a very Westernized way of thinking and constructing meaning. Not only have the bodies of indigenous literatures been given their momentum only recently in American society—as seen in best-selling novels by Native authors, such as Susan Powers' *Grass Dancer* (1994), a multigenerational story of life on the Sioux reservation in North Dakota—but being indigenous and communal are presented solely within the cultural framework of American society and its European antecedents. This does not serve deep thinkers or human society, now or in a thousand years.

Indigenous perspectives on this continent have always been accessible to modern Americans, for many scholars have devoted much time to collecting them. The irony of having collected all these materials is that this storehouse of knowledge has never been used by modern American society (or other countries in the Americas) as credible ways of learning how to live throughout all nation-states, time periods, and crises.

The credibility and integrity of indigenous literatures in American society are now influenced by the small number of indigenous peoples and the historical image of them as opponents of American advancement. *Small* is not beautiful or valued in American society, and a historical foe is difficult to trust.

Throughout the Americas, however, indigenous tribal literatures are the foundation upon which modern nations stand, whether or not this is acknowledged. The legacy of indigenous literatures for modern countries is large and immeasurable. They remain a force in American history and society whether they are wanted or not. This legacy has often been transformed in American society and has become covertly mainstreamed along the way. Perhaps this is easier to see with a critical eye in a neighboring country rather than one's own. That modern nations in the Americas stand upon indigenous literatures is a given. The English language as it is used on this continent contains indigenous words, place names, and regional historical terms. American society was built on this framework, yet the influence of indigenous knowledge on American culture is minimized in texts and curricula. Teachers can infuse existing curricula with little-known details from reference materials such as Weatherford's *Indian Givers: How the Indians of the Americans Transformed the World* (1988), which informs readers about the social, cultural, and political contributions of Native Americans to contemporary society.

Indigenous peoples have undergone transformations but have yet to become full, mainstream American citizens. Although they represent only a fraction of the entire American population, these tribal groups reside within U.S. borders and participate in the American educational system. Extremely cognizant of modern times and trends, indigenous nations have pertinent ideas about issues now engaging American society. Any action taken by the American government affects them too, for better or worse.

The continuation of indigenous peoples in the Americas is a given, no matter how small their population. This thinking is expressed in their literatures: Indigenous continuity does not depend upon external societies or agencies but upon their own resources. The extent of the inclusion and participation of indigenous peoples as citizens in modern countries is not so clear.

School texts do not show the network of indigenous peoples, with their ancient ties to one another, or the range and scope of their literatures beneath the surface of the "New World." How can this be so in the United States, the most highly educated country in the world? Indigenous peoples themselves know their links under the surface of modern countries in the Americas. They often consider themselves members of multiple communities, in and out of American society. In the past, they interacted very openly with the world to teach about human survival and the land as they know it. Interacting with different cultures before and after becoming American citizens gave them a voice and information in affairs that would eventually affect them.

It may come as a shock to most modern Americans that any people, indigenous or not, who reside here would want to interact with the larger world as anything but American citizens—especially people who appear to have no sociopolitical power among themselves. What could possibly be the source of the grandiose idea that indigenous peoples in the United States could meet citizens of the world as equals and that any other community in which indigenous people hold membership could be more powerful than the United States?

The answer is indigenous sovereignty. Before the creation of modern American society and the disenfranchisement of tribal nations, these nations were fully sovereign. New governments never dispelled the tribal memory of it even as they acknowledged it and expressed the right to destroy it.

The visibility of indigenous peoples in the Americas is influenced by both their low numbers and the modern attitude that indigenous groups function in their societies in a static manner. These two factors have joined together to dismiss indigenous literatures or transform them into mainstream experiences in the other countries of the Americas.

As indigenous literatures are taken into the classroom, educators should consider all these points. They must look outside the academic setting and try to see indigenous literatures in the context of the entire hemisphere, the indigenous communities themselves, and the ways in which indigenous literatures can influence modern American society now and in the future.

Anything less than this will not do.

## Legal Cultural Features in the United States

> Contemporary Indian communities, both reservation and urban, represent the continuing existence of a particular group of people who have traditionally had a moral and legal claim against the United States. The fact that many Indian tribes continue to exist unassimilated is not due to the practice of traditional ceremonies as much as it testifies [to] the complex of legal and political ideas that have surrounded Indians for two centuries and made them understand the world in much different terms [than] any other group of American citizens. (Deloria & Lytle, 1984, p. 102)

Indigenous nations are uniquely themselves within American society. Members of indigenous nations hold a dual legal identity that has been quite evident throughout American history. Individuals usually hold a legal membership in an indigenous group that has centuries-old ties to the modern American government, and these individuals are also American citizens. Through these legalities, tribes govern themselves, determine their own membership rolls and criteria, and often interact with representatives of state and federal governments in the interest of their tribal members. These sociopolitical and legal relationships of indigenous peoples arise from the concept of tribal sovereignty, a complex idea in Indian law stemming from the fact that indigenous groups have held certain rights on this continent for centuries, long before the building of modern American society. This is why the newly formed American government entered into treaties with them. From the time of contact, indigenous nations began to assume a single "Indian" identity in the eyes of the federal government has that spread to society as a whole.

In relation to each other, however, tribal groups continue to be autonomous, just as they were in the distant past. Some tribes are related, but many are not. Most often they are classified according to linguistic families or assigned to specific geographical areas by outsiders. In a few cases, some tribes have lived in proximity to each other for centuries but have retained very different cultures and languages, which exist to the present day. Although individuals and groups do join current international and national organizations, these affiliations are of a different nature and duration.

Most tribes have very different histories from each other, from pre-Columbian times to the unique steps taken toward living in modern American society. The profusion of various tribal languages, and dialects within those languages, supports the idea that many developments overlapped with each other. Native American literature springs from this storehouse of peoples' visions of themselves and their place on this continent and in the universe. Thus, indigenous literatures reflect distinctive individual group values and experiences. These languages continue to be principally oral 500 years after European contact.

Modern tribal nations in the United States are united by their long, documented existence on this continent, their extended relationships with hostile and friendly groups, some parallel sociopolitical developments from paleolithic to preindustrial times; and a shared historical experience of European colonization.

A single "Indian" identity was reinforced in American consciousness by federal policies that addressed the legal relationship of the indigenous peoples with the federal government. However, there is probably not just one cause for that mistaken identity.

## Defining Native American Literature

> The image we have of ourselves as Indian people is crucial to who we will be in the future. Who we have been determined to be, according to Euro-American culture and thought, has often been the wrongest [sic] idea of who we are, simply to serve a purpose not our own, a purpose that's external or outside of ourselves. Most times that image has served them, the proponents of Euro-American culture, and it has not served us at all. (Ortiz, 1993b, p. 38)

The term "Native American literature" is a legal fiction. For the purposes of this chapter, it is used to refer to a base of indigenous literatures from North America in indigenous and English languages and to modern literary developments that extend those collective tribal aesthetics and values more fully into American society. This chapter refers only to literary traditions and their modern adaptations as they are treated by indigenous peoples now. Thousands of manuscripts have been written from *external* viewpoints about indigenous peoples in the United States alone, and this is a significant body of work that has had a great impact on American society and has found a lasting, cherished place in American history and experience. This chapter focuses on teaching issues surrounding a more unfamiliar and frequently more inaccessible body of literary traditions that describe *internal* viewpoints of indigenous peoples in the Americas, from ancient times to the present. Lastly, "literature" is used more inclusively here than "Native American."

## Multicultural Issues

> The battle for inclusion in the canon of World Literature has to do with more than having your writing sandwiched between Norman Mailer and Joan Didion in some publisher's collection. If Indian literature is not included in the canon of American letters, if it is not studied in our colleges as legitimate literature, then Native peoples remain invisible in society, and the teaching in our grade schools and high schools will not improve.
>
> Just making requirements, however, does not seem to me to be the answer. Having a cultural diversity requirement does not mean good material will be taught. Indeed, ill informed teachers, perhaps with the best intentions, may simply perpetuate stereotypes. So we don't want a niche, a token work, or class separated from the core of the curriculum. We don't want mere inclusion and we don't want marginal status. Instead we want the influences of tribal literatures on the general categories of American literature and world literature recognized. (Blaeser, 1993, p. 36)

When indigenous peoples of the Americas do not appear in classroom texts *in their own words* concerning their lives in the modern countries of the Americas, something is deeply wrong in the schools and the democracies of those countries. When the ancient living literatures of an entire hemisphere are omitted in modern schools—even though they are a legitimate body of knowledge with value and relevance for the future well-being of all humanity—it becomes very clear that indigenous populations are not considered part of those modern societies. The absence of indigenous literatures in modern schools ensures that a cycle of ignorance about indigenous peoples in the Americas will be perpetuated from generation to generation.

Knowledge of indigenous peoples in the Americas by modern European Americans is no greater than that of their great-great grandparents. This is the heart of the matter. Indigenous peoples have an obscure and ambiguous place in American society; consequently, Native American literature is ambiguous, at best, in the educational system.

Americans simply do not know about indigenous peoples in the United States. They are therefore unable to make simple connections between themselves and indigenous peoples, as American citizens or as human beings, because these possibilities are not taught in our schools, either as real behavior or as scholarship. Most Americans consider themselves well educated even though they lack any knowledge of indigenous peoples or exposure to indigenous literatures. They credit American schools for their education, their ideas of citizenship, leadership, community and global awareness, and their identity. Some Americans have even indicated, in print and other media, that indigenous peoples do not have literature because there is no evidence of intellectual and literary forms that qualify as literature, as it is produced by other civilizations. Some of these people don't know that they have *seen* the evidence.

Others do think that the literature exists, but only in English. Because English is external to indigenous peoples, these forms of literature must also be external to them. Therefore, out of necessity, so called "Native American literature" has been and will continue to be produced best—or even only—by everybody *but* indigenous peoples. Such people point to regions and marketplaces that specialize in this. Historically, there have been periods when *no* contemporary indigenous writers at all were included in the genre, which consisted mainly of imagined views of indigenous life and experience. Indigenous writers were conscientiously excluded from producing Native American literature for mainstream society. This is still happening, especially in some regions and marketplaces.

Schools play a major role in shaping and fostering these perceptions by building curricular units solely from that body of external material about indigenous peoples and not teaching the literatures of indigenous peoples themselves. Most information about indigenous peoples used in all the educational institutions of American society comes from "experts" and authority figures who claim "objectivity" and have academic credentials. These "experts" then become role models for students on how to think about and transmit information on Native Americans. Such teaching styles, ideals, and practices profoundly affect human relations for many generations. They are counterproductive to all peoples on this planet, who have to coexist as equals in any truly democratic society.

Integrating Native American literature thoughtfully and constructively into curricula is one way to address these issues. On a national scale, however, this has yet to happen. There are strong reasons for the way schools are in this country. Native American literature might dilute a curriculum that is already too full, and it might also weaken core American values and chip away at the one large "American" identity that schools have worked so hard to forge.

In *The Owl's Song* (1974) Janet Campbell Hale reveals how misinformation can lead children to hold inaccurate ideas about the lives of contemporary Native people. In her novel, Billy leaves the Benewah reservation in Idaho. His experiences in a public high school are filled with taunts from students who want to know where his teepee is and why he was allowed to leave the reservation. They want him to do a rain dance and make whooping sounds as he passes them in the halls. Hale's novel captures the pain that Billy feels as he struggles to develop his sense of identity.

Native American literature that comes from indigenous peoples themselves often presents views of this country that are alien to American values and experience. It seems to reach out to "bite the hand that feeds it" in its commentary on specific events and values at the very core of modern society. Why should educators want to bring that into school curricula, especially when the integration of indigenous literatures requires a lot of work and appears to have little gain for American society?

All the diverse groups that are represented in Native American literature present another hurdle. They seem to go against the grain of the "melting pot" envisioned by the Founding Fathers of this country. Besides the fact that the cultures are not well known, the argument is that the groups seem unmanageable because they are "too many." Perhaps the solution is, they could all be put into one bag and managed that way?

This is not a new idea: Remove the tribal base or community of each indigenous group and encourage a purely academic approach. This has possibilities, and it is the way that "Indians" and "Native American literature" has been studied up to now, when they *have* been studied.

As if all this were not enough to consider, there is also the commotion from indigenous peoples about the term "Native American literature" having the connotation of English-only usage and being too restrictive for all indigenous literatures. Don't literate societies and their intellectuals know what *really* constitutes literature?

All these points have a bearing on the inclusion of indigenous literatures in American schools. Such a bold step requires more time to ponder everything. In the meantime, those who claim to know about indigenous peoples in the Americas are taking care of everything, they say. Isn't that enough?

## Bridging the Gaps

> The educator who sees education as culturally neutral is similar to the spouse of an alcoholic who denies the alcoholism. There are implications for the practice, self-concept, and feelings that both are unable to face. Perverse ignorance is a particular form of the defense mechanism of denial. . . . It is understandable that the educator with a self-concept bound to the ideal of helping children, with a preparation that does not include multicultural education competence, a curriculum that ignores or systematically distorts the culture of his or her students, and unresolved personal issues of racism and ethnocentrism would be unable to face the extent to which education is not only culturally bound but actively hostile to children. (Hampton, 1993, p. 264)

The climate in American schools is now transitional and requires educators to be more responsive and accountable to the various groups that they serve. This means making Native American literature a part of curricula in a way that will inspire positive multicultural communication among all students and provide practical opportunities to demonstrate more harmonious means of coexistence.

Developing or augmenting the curriculum to include Native American literature involves deciding how and when to integrate it so that the curriculum is seamless, substantive, and constructive. This step requires trained educators who know the literatures and the peoples and who are committed to quality teaching.

To make informed and effective selections of material for classroom use, teachers must know the characteristics of individual indigenous groups as well as their literary styles and aesthetics. Educators may decide to seek more formal training if they become overwhelmed by the volume and diversity of indigenous literatures.

## Teaching Strategies

> The United Nations International School has about 1,400 students, ranging from kindergarten through twelfth grade, from countries all over the world. Approximately half of them are from families affiliated with the United Nations, while the others come from local families in New York. From the earliest grades, the school cultivates a global perspective among students. One of the school's goals is to provide an educational experience that reflects the values and perspectives of those cultures.
> Native American cultures embody traditions that emphasize balance and harmony, and the interrelationship of living things rather than acquisitiveness and the exploitation of resources. With this in mind, in 1984, I began a project to collect Native American stories and poetry for integration into the already existing literature, social studies, and environmental studies programs in the elementary schools. (Cutforth, 1993, p. 38)

Fortunately, there is no one right way to teach Native American literature. The purpose of education is to teach all students to read, write, and think about what it means to be human in any place or at any time and to demonstrate the personal development of knowledge and skills in successful relationships. Native American literature poses the same challenges.

Some schools have integrated Native American literature into their curricula in a number of creative and stimulating ways, depending upon their educational philosophies and the structure of their curricula, but English and Social Studies are probably the most common routes. Thematic study units are also a doorway. Creative and well-trained teachers are critical to the successful integration of all multicultural literature. Native American literature is not often an area in which secondary teachers have been trained, and so they must either train themselves or get help from others. Native American literature is becoming a more frequent component of teacher training, especially for teachers going to reservation settings.

Where Native American literature is not included in teacher training, it must now become a focus area, and schools must commit the resources to train teachers when necessary. Teachers, like anyone else, are products of their times, and it should now be clear that teacher training programs did not foresee a time or place in which indigenous literatures would fit into American schools. Some teachers do not teach Native American literature of their own volition. They take on the assignment unfamiliar with the field and try to make the best of the situation. In general, few teachers think that there is enough time to do well all that is asked of them. Whether writing a lesson plan or guiding a discussion on the most recent reading assignment, teachers need adequate time to give full attention to the task at hand. Teaching Native American literature, even when the job is loved, suffers from teacher workloads. Native American literature in particular requires teachers to be attentive and familiar with communities and cultures that are reflected in various literary forms.

Ideally, the curriculum ought to include credible first-person accounts and perspectives of indigenous peoples in their cultures, within American society, and in the modern world. A fine example is the autobiography of Polingaysi Quoyawayma, a Hopi woman born in 1892. In her autobiography, *No Turning Back: A Hopi Indian Woman's Struggle to Live in Two Worlds* (1964), Quoyawayma recounts her life, from her childhood in old Oraibi to her return to the abandoned village as an adult. Along the way, she describes encounters with "Bahana" (the White man) and eloquently describes the rituals and daily activities of Hopi life. Curious about the White man's ways, she willingly leaves her village to attend school. She eventually becomes a teacher, struggling to provide Indian children with an education that honored their identities while providing them with the necessary skills to excel in the White man's world. Throughout her travels, Quoyawayma returns home and describes the tremendous conflicts between her culture and the White culture. Another fine addition to personal accounts is Patricia Riley's collection, *Growing Up Native American: Stories of Oppression & Survival of Heritage, Denied & Reclaimed: 22 American Writers* (1995). In this volume, 22 Native American writers recall their childhoods in their native lands. Such authenticity is critical because anything less dismisses and minimizes the actual experiences of indigenous peoples.

Classrooms are constructed; in many ways, they are not natural settings for learning. They are often the first meeting place for students of diverse interests and backgrounds. Similarly, most students will have their first exposure to indigenous peoples and literatures there. Students from indigenous cultures must make adjustments to teachers who are not from the same economic, social, or political backgrounds. They must also adjust to Native American literature in the classroom, where it is studied rather than lived. The parameters of knowledge surrounding Native American literature in this environment suddenly shift away from them and into another domain.

Native American literature must not become equated with the formal classroom. It does not always have to be taught and appreciated in a mainstream way. The classroom setting and mainstream teaching strategies leave little room for other ways of interacting with the indigenous knowledge contained in the literature. Some critics call this trend "colonization." It is important to remember that Native American literature is linked to indigenous ideas of education and many other things. Indigenous societies in everyday situations operate very differently than a formal classroom does. Their use of and relationship to literature is not academic; it is functional and integrated into their collective and individual experiences in nonacademic ways.

Teachers will have to do some research to prepare themselves to teach the materials they have selected. How indigenous peoples express their identities and lifestyles goes beyond pseudo-anthropological research. The process of selecting teaching materials often causes good teachers to be introspective. They are concerned with standards of literary merit and genius and often scrutinize their own subjectivity and knowledge of indigenous cultures when making these selections.

When presenting material in the classroom, most teachers find it helpful to frame the selection with an introduction. The origin of the material, the historical and social influences on the literary style or form, and the relationship of the work to the students are possible places to start. It is better to avoid an "anthropological" stance here.

Unwritten as well as written forms may be used, depending on the focus of the class and the level of skill development of the students. For example, in a reading class teachers may select stories or essays to help students practice their reading skills. As the level of student abilities increases or expands, so should the complexity of the selections. Teacher selections should also strive to include more balanced views of key events in American history—views that present Native people as people and not as the savages they are most often depicted as being. In the context of war, for example, both sides commit cruel and inhumane acts. In *James Printer: A Novel of Rebellion* (1997), Jacobs presents a well-balanced historical account of King Philip's (the British name for the Wampanoag leader, Metacom) War. Through the eyes of Bartholomew, a young boy whose family operates a printing press at Harvard College, Jacobs cleverly tells the story of James Printer of the Nipmuck tribe and his role in King Philip's War. The courage, pain, and horrors of cultural conflict and warfare as experienced by both the Native people in New England and the colonists are skillfully presented. The early American printing press figures prominently throughout the story. An Afterword also provides readers with details about Jacobs' research of Printer's life.

Native American literature must be shown to have its own standards, merit, forms, and aesthetics. Teaching Native American literature requires teachers to be able to identify material that is not stereotypical. Teachers can develop a sense of discernment regarding authenticity by immersing themselves in material about a specific tribe and reading in depth about that tribe. Volumes such as Sando's *Pueblo Nations: Eight Centuries of Pueblo Indian History* (1992) provide rich background information that can inform a teacher's selections of literature about Pueblo Indians. The work of Alvin M. Josephy, Jr., *The Indian Heritage in America* (1968) is broad in scope but a worthwhile reference. So too is Ruoff's *Literatures of the American Indian* (1991), which can be used in the classroom as an introductory overview of the many forms of Native American literature. When Native American literature is taught as a body of skills and aesthetics that serves a purpose other than what it serves in indigenous societies, its nature will be misunderstood.

There is always a connection to a core of tribal teachings in Native American literature, even when it expresses distance or alienation from that core. In the academic setting, Native American literature is studied more for the craft of writing and for the intellectual truths it reveals. This way of knowing stresses "objective" reflection on the meaning of writing and indigenous experience. In indigenous settings, older forms of indigenous literatures are actively involved in the creative, critical, and subjective thinking and being of the people on a daily basis.

Because much of what Native American literature contains will be new to most students, teachers must devise ways to get early feedback on student understanding and processing of information. If the student has a problem comprehending the material, this can be more easily remedied the sooner it is realized. When different ideas about the universe or human experience are introduced to anyone, a moment of pause is required to let those new ideas sink in. Most of the suggestions here are simply sound and productive teaching practices that depend on teacher and student rapport. Native American literature can be taught in more lively and interesting ways from what is usually planned. Drama and video productions, for example, can move the study of Native American literature beyond reading and written responses. A word of caution, however: At no time in the study of indigenous peoples or their literatures should students be encouraged to "play Indian" or to create their own "ceremonies" as part of their study. That would seem to be obvious, but it happens often in schools.

It should also be emphasized that half of all Native American literature expresses humor and humorous situations. Very few people in modern American society know this trait of indigenous peoples. Native Americans should also be understood within contemporary settings. Frosch's edited volume, *Coming of Age in America: A Multicultural Anthology* (1994), includes a short story by Creek author Durango Mendoza and D'Arcy McNickle, a member of the Confederated Salish and Kootenai tribes of Montana. Mendoza's short story, "Summer Water and Shirley," concerns siblings, illness, and the prospect of death. McNickle's piece is a delightful story of friendship and conversations shared among young people who ride to school each morning in a buggy. It offers an introspective look into how a teenage boy comes to understand the love of his parents and his first crush. Another excellent anthology with a blend of short stories and poems is *Multicultural Voices: Literature From the United States* (1995).

Native American literature should be taught with consistent formality and attention in schools. A one-hour class on one day is not enough. When the proper effort is initiated, educators will become increasingly aware of their curricula. Strategies that undermine Native American literature include superficial attention, misrepresentation, and framing it in the values of Europe or mainstream U.S. culture. Its purpose in the classroom is not to conform to English language conventions or American perspectives of who "Indians" are. Its purpose in the classroom is to open up a portal through which indigenous peoples speak for themselves without censorship about life in the Americas in the past, present, and future.

Some educators have already considered all these suggestions. They have felt the presence of indigenous peoples in the United States and the other countries of the Americas and have responded in the classroom by quietly teaching Native American literature for some time. They have developed curriculum materials, invited writers and other speakers into the classroom, evaluated and selected teaching texts, and shared teaching strategies, triumphs, and disappointments with others engaged in these activities.

Their accomplishments are a beginning. After 500 years, perhaps the work has begun in earnest. Now we must ask, how soon will we see the quality and effects of this expansive movement?

## The Texts

> More than 30,000 manuscripts have been published about American Indians, and more than 90 percent of that literature has been written by non-Indians. (Fixico, 1996, p. 30)

The texts that are available may present a confusing mass of information to the already overwhelmed teacher. Teachers should look for texts in which indigenous peoples appear in all walks of life and speak, without a middle person to interpret or "help" the speakers, on what it means to live in all their communities. Teachers must be well informed about the strengths and weaknesses of texts and consider other options when texts are nonexistent or inaccessible. Speeches, biographies, histories, indigenous language texts and tapes, autobiographies, photojournalism texts, myths, legends, folktales, interviews, and essays have all been produced, along with novels, poetry, short fiction, and literary criticism. Numerous anthologies of modern forms, several of which specialize in selections from oral traditions, translated into English, are also available.

Indigenous language texts are usually published by tribal entities or institutions, such as the Navajo Nation. There are some exciting developments in the production of these texts, but not enough. Yet what has been done and what is now underway in recording languages and creating new material is inspiring. While large publishers still do not publish manuscripts in indigenous languages, a handful of small presses, regional presses, university presses, and academic presses do. A few English-speaking writers of indigenous backgrounds speak and write fluent indigenous languages, and more writing in indigenous languages is forthcoming. An example is the Princeton Collection of Western Americana publication, *saad* (1995) by Rex Lee Jim, written entirely in Navajo.[2]

Texts are also accessible on the Internet, as well as other kinds of teaching support and information.

## The Forms

### Washington

Oh, how do I long for my native woods.
This place has no charms for me;
the choicest wisdom of this great
American republic gathers here,
around the great National Council fire,
but what I care for that?

This is a city which shines like the ice
which covers rivers in the Long Night's Moon.
Great steps lead up to the Capital,
but my feet hesitate to make the climb.

It is from this place
the decrees have emanated
dooming my hapless race to the grave.
There are markers here for the white
honored dead, but my people are to become extinct
without even leaving a monument
that they once existed a happy race . . .

Ely Parker, February 1846,
after first visit to Washington, D.C.[3]
(Brochac, 1985)

All elements of indigenous literatures cohere within literary forms, which are shaped by indigenous aesthetics and cultural chronologies that vary from tribe to tribe. Acculturation and colonization may also show up in the forms, which have been ordered and arranged by chants, prayers, songs, stories, poetry, and so on for scholarly study. Explaining the forms often becomes pedantic and tiresome, and the categories themselves get in the way when they are put before the expressed form. This activity misleads students into thinking they are studying indigenous literatures when they are actually reproducing a way of knowing that has little if anything to do with indigenous peoples or literatures.

A more useful approach to both oral and written forms is to place them within the cultural chronologies of individual indigenous groups. Only after European contact did some indigenous experiences and literary developments converge in English thought and construction.

The diversity of indigenous communities and groups in the Americas, and the hundreds of tribal languages spoken here in addition to Spanish, French, and English, present literally thousands of forms and innumerable teaching possibilities. Deciding what to select from this vast body of literature may be intimidating.

The parameters of oral traditions are different from those of written texts. They require the active and reciprocal involvement of all participants, and sometimes they appear to be "loose" or "uncontrolled." Although participatory control shifts, there is a definite structure, which might even be quite rigid according to the people's standards. These forms challenge the senses and the intellect in other ways as well. They are often more difficult to access logistically across cultures. Modern written forms tend to gain more acceptance in schools because they are more recognizable and less distant from the norms of American society. These bodies of record have therefore gained more renown, credibility, and authority, especially since they are in English.

# Resources

*The Canadian Journal of Native Studies* is an international Native studies periodical published twice a year in Brandon, Manitoba, Canada. The journal publishes articles and reviews concerning indigenous people and indigenous affairs in Canada, the United States, and other countries of the world.

Indigenous communities are the best resources. Teachers would help themselves by finding out where these are and what is happening there. Tribal peoples are often willing to visit classrooms. Schools and teachers in reservation settings are usually very attuned to how literatures manifest themselves in and sustain the local communities, but this is not always true. Tribal schools and organizations also produce and publish some helpful guides and materials. A handful of colleges and universities publish pertinent information on Native American literature and teaching through their Native American Studies departments. The Newberry Library has offered a very comprehensive summer institute on Native American literature, directed by Dr. Lawana Trout. These teachers know the works of noted Native American authors, such as Leslie Marmon Silko's critically acclaimed *Ceremony* (1977) or the poetry of Joey Harjo. They are also able to share cultural insights about the work of Sherman Alexie, Louise Erdirch, Linda Hogan, Thomas King, D'Arcy McNickle, N. Scott Momaday, Simon Ortiz, Gerald Vizenor, and James Welch (his work is more appropriate for adult readers). Periodically, a university with a large enrollment of indigenous students will offer training on a one-time basis. Indigenous organizations in urban centers are also good resources.

In the long run, most teachers will have to compile materials themselves, according to their own teaching styles and idiosyncrasies, and keep communication flowing in regard to training opportunities, new materials, and strategies. Some textbook publishers have also published teaching units, such as *Plains Native American Literature* (1993) by the Globe Book Company, which teachers should examine.

Teachers are also encouraged to look beyond their country's borders and discover that other nations are wrestling with the same issues in teaching multicultural literature. American educators and education don't have all the answers.

## Summary

At the initial point of contact, we were on the eastern shore of North America. Since then, there has been a great decimation of our numbers, language, and culture. In the average American citizen's mind, there is no Indian existence on the eastern shore any longer, which is sad, because once people get out and find the reality of our existence and see that it is there, they are amazed at the durability, survivability, and sustainability of people who have been able to continue after so many hundreds of years and after so many attempts at devastation. They are amazed at the adaptation that occurred under all those conditions, even to the point of our being written out of history. It is really a great statement to the spirit of the people that we have been able to survive at all. (Chavis, 1993, cited in Farlay, p. 104)

The study of multicultural literature is the study of paradox—the whole human community and its parts. It is the one voice speaking through the many. The very presence of indigenous peoples in the Americas is a study in paradox, reflects several kinds of "Native American" identities that do and don't exist. Native American literature is both old and new, ever changing and ever stable. It is part of many modern nations, although its life flow does not depend upon the continuity of those modern nations; rather, it depends upon the survival of the land and the indigenous peoples and their languages. This literature precedes modern American literature by centuries or even millennia; it is founded in tribal languages and expresses intimate and specialized knowledge of the land. It not clearly and openly part of modern national American literature. Its history is extensive—too extensive to be written in detail, if indeed it can be written at all, given its nature. That task is, however, beyond the scope of this chapter.

Studies of oral traditions and modern literary adaptations of in-digenous peoples have been produced and reproduced in American society and universities, but they have brought indigenous peoples no closer to other Americans and have done very little to affect the sociopolitical status of indigenous peoples in any modern countries of the Americas—except maybe to reinforce the status quo.

The survival of indigenous peoples in the modern countries of the Americas has been gauged in many ways by themselves and by the larger, newer societies in which they reside. In American society, in-digenous peoples have been asked for more than 500 years to tran-scend themselves and become "Americans." Now America must do what it has asked each of its ethnic groups to do: transcend itself and become all its peoples.

Native American literature is not the study of "Indians." If it is a study at all, it is a study of the Americas and the forces in the land that have brought forth human subsistence and history. Nor is the study of indigenous literatures the study of "Indians." It consists of human beings looking both outward and inward for truths about themselves and the universe.

Volumes of scholarly works analyzing Native American literature for academia should not be the end result of teaching it or integrating it into school curricula; that is not the reason indigenous peoples want it included in curricula. Native American literature is larger than that. Some new thinking, some new behavior must come out of the teach-ing and integration that will benefit this continent and all the societ-ies that dwell here.

Mainstream American education faces many crises today. It has not solved the problems of the world or even of its own society. In some ways it has created as many problems as it has solved. Perhaps no one educational system will meet with everyone's satisfaction; perhaps it will take many systems, working cooperatively and in col-laboration with one another, to do this. Yet schools continue to teach the same content in the same way and expect American society to be okay, fully aware that its shortcomings and failures are as numerous as its "successes."

One culture is not more appropriate for a particular time period than another. Cultures exist because they are viable and stand the test of trials and time. The study of all the literatures in the world, "civilized" and not, will only benefit humanity if it moves the learner to become self-educating and critically thinking and acting in a community other than the modern nation-state. It must be lived, not merely theorized.

## Notes

1. The 1990 census gives American Indians a population figure of just under two million. Depending upon the sources of information, the number of tribal groups vary. Some sources identify only tribes that have legal recognition. There are others that have functioned as tribal groups for a long time but have lost legal status in America. There are also tribes that were never legally recognized or did not seek legal recognition.

2. Many tribes are producing writers who use tribal languages, but the Navajo Tribe is most conspicuous because of its size and its use of the Navajo language in most of its agencies and schools. As a result, Navajo writers such as Luci Tapahonso and Irvin Morris appear to be very comfortable with both English and Navajo.

3. Ely Parker was a Seneca, born in 1928. He was highly educated and became General Ulysses S. Grant's military secretary. He also recorded the surrender terms at Appamattox.

## References

Allen, P. G. (Ed.). (1983). *Studies in American Indian literature: Critical essays and course designs.* New York: Modern Language Association.

Allen, P. G. (1989). *Spider Woman's granddaughters.* New York: Ballentine.

Allen, P. G. (1990). Special problems in teaching Leslie Marmon Silko's ceremony. *American Indian Quarterly, 14*(4), 379–387.

Ballinger, F. (1984). A matter of emphasis: Teaching the "literature" in Native American literature courses. *American Indian Culture and Research Journal, 8*(2), 1–12.

Bindler, P. (1995). First death in the fourth world: Teaching the emergence myth of the Hopi Indians. *American Indian Quarterly, 19*(2), 75–89.

Blaesar, K. M. (1993, Spring). Entering the canons: Our place in world literature. *Akwe:kon Journal, 10*(1), 35–37.

Bruchac, J. III. (1985, Spring). The broken rainbow. *North Dakota Quarterly, 53*, 138–159.

Champagne, D. (1996). American Indian studies is for everyone. *American Indian Quarterly, 20*(1), 77–82.

Cook-Lynn, E. (1996). American Indian intellectualism and the new Indian story. *American Indian Quarterly, 20*(1), 57–76.

Cutforth, R. (1993, Spring). Integrating Native American studies into the school curriculum. *Northeast Indian Quarterly, 8*(1), 37–41.

Deloria, V., Jr. & Lytle, C. (1984). *The nations within: The past and future of American Indian sovereignty.* New York: Random House.

Farley, R. (1993). *Women of the Native struggle: Portraits and testimony of Native American women.* New York: Orion Books.

Fixico, D. L. (1996). Ethics and responsibilities in writing American Indian history. *American Indian Quarterly, 20*, 29–37.

Forbes, J. (1987, Fall). Colonialism and Native American literature: analysis. *The Wicazo Sa Review, 3*(2),17–33.

Frosch, M. (Ed.). (1994). *Coming of age in America: A multicultural anthology.* New York: New Press.

Hale, J. (1974). *The owl's song.* New York: Bantam Books.

Hampton, E. (1993). Toward a redefinition of American Indian/Alaska Native education. *Canadian Journal of Native Studies, 20*(2), 261–309.

Hobson, G. (1979). *The remembered earth; An anthology of Native American literature.* Albuquerque, NM: Red Earth Press.

Jacobs, P. (1997). *James Printer: A novel of rebellion.* New York: Scholastic Press.

Jim, R. (1995). *saad.* Princeton, NJ: Princeton Collection of Western Americans.

Josephy, A. M., Jr. (1968). *The Indian heritage of America.* New York: Bantam Books.

Krupat, A. (1989a). *For those who came after: A study of Native American autobiography.* Berkeley, CA: University of California Press.

Krupat, A. (1989b). *Voices in the margin: Native American literature and the canon.* Berkeley, CA: University of California.

Macaruso, V. (1984). Cowboys and Indians: The image of the American Indian in American literature. *American Indian Culture and Research Journal, 8*(2), 13–21.

Mintz, S. (Ed.). (1993a). *Native American voices: A history and anthology.* New York: Brandywine Press.

*Multicultural Voices: Literature from the United States.* Glenview, IL: Scott Foresman.

Ortiz, S. (1993a). Our image of ourselves. *Akwe:kon Journal, 10,* 38–39.

Ortiz, S. (Ed.). (1993b). *Earth power coming: Short fiction in Native American literature.* Tsaile, AZ: Navajo Community College Press.

Penny, D. (1993). Indians and children: A critique of educational objectives. *Akwe:kon Journal, 10,* 12–18.

*Plains Native American literature* (1993). Englewood Cliffs, NJ: Globe.

Power, S. (1994). *The grass dancer.* New York: Putnam.

Quoyawayma, P., & Carlson, F. (1964). *No turning back: A Hopi Indian woman's struggle to live in two worlds.* Albuquerque, NM: University of New Mexico Press.

Riley, P. (Ed.) (1995). *Growing up Native American: Stories of oppression & survival of heritage, denied & reclaimed: 22 American writers.* New York: Morrow.

Ruoff, A. (1990). *American Indian literatures: An introduction, bibliographic review, and selected bibliography.* New York: Modern Language Association.

Ruoff, A. (1991). *Literature of the American Indian.* New York: Chelsea House.

Sando, J. (1992). *Pueblo Nations: Eight centuries of Pueblo Indian history.* Santa Fe, NM: Clear Light.

Shanley, K. (1994). The lived experience: American Indian literature after Alcatraz. *Akwe:kon Journal, 11*(3–4), 118–127.

Sheridan, J. (1991). The silence before drowning in alphabet soup. *Canadian Journal of Native Education, 18*(1), 23–31.

Silko, L. (1977). *Ceremony.* New York: Penguin Books.

Sneve, V. (1993). Something to be proud of. *Akwe:kon Journal, 10,* 40–41.

Wallis, V. (1993). *Two old women.* New York: HarperCollins.

Weatherford, J. (1988). *Indian givers: How the Indians of the Americas transformed the world.* New York: Fawcett Columbine.

Witalec, J. (ed.). (1995). *Smoke rising: The Native North American literary companion.* Detroit, MI: Visible Ink Press.

## Chapter 7

# Storying in the Mexican American Community: Understanding the Story Behind the Stories and the Cultural Themes Shared in Chicano Novels

*Sylvia Y. Sánchez*

The legacy of Mexican American novels and short stories can be traced to the ancestral Mexican oral tradition. Storytelling predates the arrival of the Spaniards to the shores of the New World. Before the printed word came to the region we now call Mexico, the Aztecs, Mayans, Toltecas, and other indigenous groups used the oral tradition to pass on the stories that chronicled the groups' histories and helped to emphasize their communities' values and beliefs. Similar to the quest of those ancient ones, the Mexican American community has used storytelling to ensure that the younger generation remembers the past, continues its traditions, and shares its world view. By remembering its heritage, the younger generation can claim its cultural identity. The individual and community stories told by Mexican American authors help the group understand itself and identify as belonging to the uniquely Mexican American culture.

Mexican American literature also has a legacy tied to language. Language has played a significant role in defining the distinctive Mexican American culture. The community's sociohistorical experience has brought them in contact with two influential cultures: the Mexican heritage and the United States context. The use of both the English and Spanish languages has affected how these experiences have been viewed by the community. Although in many Mexican

American homes the language of birth continues to be Spanish, and many favorite stories continue to be told in Spanish, the English language has also helped define the particular story of the Mexican community residing in the United States. Laws prohibiting the use of languages other than English, especially the value of promoting monolingualism in schools, have served to emphasize the acquisition of English over Spanish in the Mexican American community. Today in most homes, especially among second- and third-generation Mexican Americans, the use of both English and Spanish is commonplace. Both languages are consequently essential in telling the real story of the Mexican American experience in the United States.

Mexican American authors often can be identified by their usage of both English and Spanish to tell the stories of the distinctive Mexican American experience in the United States. Although most of the literature is primarily written in English, authors sometimes use Spanish words for effect or clarification, and sometimes one finds a direct translation of a story in a novel. Most of the time, however, authors use codeswitching in dialogues as evidence of the language usage common in the Mexican American community. *Codeswitching*, the shifting between English and Spanish when interacting with another Mexican American, is a dialect that follows set rules and is not confusing to the community but rather reflects their particular cultural story. When one listens to or reads the individual and shared stories of the Mexican American people, one must expect to encounter both languages. Mexican American authors were initially criticized by both monolingual Spanish language and English language literary critics for using both languages simultaneously; however, this distinctive ethnic and cultural language style in novels has persevered as an authentic and integral aspect of the Mexican American experience.

## The Early Stories

The early experiences of the Mexican American community in the United States were often recorded only in Spanish. At the turn of the century, many Spanish-language newspapers existed throughout the Southwest. These newspapers served not only as an alternative to the English-language reporting of news but also as a significant literary channel for the authors of short stories, poetry, essays, and serialized novels (Kanellos, 1995). It is not surprising that the foundation of the written literature of the Mexican American community can be traced to the Southwest, and to the Spanish-language newspapers in particular.

Many community stories, however, never made it to the newspapers but were passed on through ballads and the oral tradition. At the turn-of-the-century the border ballad, or *corrido*, a form of storytelling, proliferated throughout the Southwest (Kanellos, 1995). The folk ballad, or Mexican *corrido*, used music and song to tell a story. This form of storytelling was not original to Mexico but was introduced to the New World by the Spanish colonizers and the missionaries. The narrative folk songs were a means for disseminating the information and events of the Mexican American community that the English-language, or Anglo, newspapers did not consider significant or were biased when reporting. Although the Spanish-language newspapers provided more accurate information to the Mexican American community as well as cultural enrichment and entertainment opportunities, they were primarily available only in the larger cities with a significant population of Mexicans. Many Mexican Americans during that time period lived in rural or isolated areas, where accessibility to Spanish-language newspapers was not possible. Additionally many of those who lived in cities that supported Spanish-language newspapers possessed limited literacy skills and were unable to benefit from the written reports found in newspapers. The *corrido* filled this vacuum. There is currently a great deal of interest in understanding the impact of the *corrido* on the Mexican American community, and Herrera-Sobek, in her scholarly work *The Mexican Corrido: A Feminist Analysis* (1990), examines the *corrido* from a unique perspective.

After a disaster or an event of particular interest to the Mexican American community, a ballad or *corrido* was composed to tell the story. *Corrido* comes from the Spanish word that means "to run" or "to flow." The *corrido* is designed to tell a story simply and quickly, without the need to elaborate. The ballads were sung by musical groups performing at local dances throughout the Southwest. This popular format reached a wider spectrum of the community than did the other traditional forms of communication, such as the Spanish-language newspaper. Many more Mexican Americans had access to the stories or legends because of the *corridos*. Music, therefore, has often accompanied the stories told in the Mexican American community about their favorite folk heroes. Many of the stories in the *corridos* were never printed but were known only through song. Before television and the ritual of watching the evening news became a daily event in most households, these *corridos* were a means by which the members of a community shared their experiences and formed bonds across geographical areas. *Corridos* have continued to flourish in the Mexican American community. Even today, these popular songs remain part of the repertoire of many musical groups. The ballads often have a clearly stated moral value and a musical beat that is catchy and repetitive.

The story that was the basis for the movie *The Ballad of Gregorio Cortéz* was originally told as a *corrido*. Américo Paredes, a renowned folklorist who established the folklore program at the University of Texas in Austin, used the *corrido* to document the story in his book *With His Pistol in His Hand* (1958). The movie was first shown on National Public Television and was then featured in movie theaters. The *corrido* tells the story of a Mexican man, Gregorio Cortéz, who, because of an error in language usage during the translation from English to Spanish, was initially accused of stealing a mare, then of killing the sheriff. He suffered the injustice of a racist judicial system. He escaped and was persecuted by the Texas Rangers but eluded their chase for a while. The story is based on a real event that occurred during a period in Texas that was especially difficult for Mexicans. At this time (the 1950s), the Texas Rangers, though venerated by the American English-language media, were detested by the Mexican American community. The Texas Rangers were racists who were known for their harsh, brutal, and unjust treatment of Mexicans. Gregorio Cortéz was a simple Mexican man, but his astuteness, nerves of steel, and horsemanship helped him evade the Texas Rangers and many other law officers. The legend has been retold many times through the "El Corrido de Gregorio Cortéz," the well-known border ballad.

One can study the *corridos* to learn the history and struggles of the Mexican immigrants. Novels and other genre written by Mexican-American authors, however, can also be studied to understand the ethnic community. When someone shares his or her story, the listener is being given the privilege of entering that person's life and thereby experiencing the world from that point of view. The cultural base of the *corridos* during the turn of the century and that of today's Mexican American novels are very similar; they have relied on the critical experiences of a people to tell Mexican American stories.

## The Stories Behind the Story

There are many life stories behind the stories that are finally documented in typical history books. The stories of disenfranchised communities, such as Mexican immigrants in the United States, have mostly remained unknown and absent from the writings of traditional historians, and they have not surfaced in the literature of mainstream America. The cultural life stories of the Mexican American community have almost never made it to the typical public school classroom. Through the decades, however, familial storytelling events within the Mexican American community have made it possible for many children today to listen to these stories outside the classroom. These stories have contributed to the cultural knowledge base needed by the younger generation to understand themselves in this society. Mexican American authors, like all authors, use known life stories to better understand the significant cultural themes impacting a community. In general, Mexican American authors use the printed word to disseminate the stories that reflect the rich heritage of their culture. These authors are the modern day *cuentistas*, or storytellers, who in the past would often relate their stories in small-group, familial gatherings or in larger gatherings by singing the *corridos* that chronicled the community's history and struggles. By reading their novels and short stories, one can learn about the Mexican American culture from an insider's perspective. Without an understanding of the cultural and sociohistorical background of the Mexican American community, however, the literature may not be understood and stereotypes may even be fomented.

There are three prevalent recurring themes in Mexican American novels, which can help readers understand a story and its cultural base. The underlying threads that bind the stories found in novels are (a) the impact of the sociohistorical experiences of the larger Mexican American community on the lives of ordinary citizens, (b) the key cultural value concerning the family, and (c) the connection with the spiritual world or the sense of metaphysical awareness existing in the community. These three themes or threads are often used singularly or in combination with each other to develop the plot of a story. Therefore, to enjoy the literature and to facilitate the interpretation of the significance of a novel or short story, readers should examine the underpinnings of the story's recurring themes.

First, however, it will benefit teachers and students to consider the legacy of the Mexican American novel. This background knowledge will further add to the understanding of the complexity, depth, and richness of the story behind the stories shared by this ethnic community.

## The Legacy of Chicano Literature

Several terms, such as *Mexican American, Latino, Chicano,* or *Hispanic* can be found in the literature written by Mexican American authors; however, in this chapter, the terms *Mexican American* and *Chicano* will be used to identify the U.S. population of Mexican descent who was born and raised in the United States. The term *Mexican* will be used to describe the population that was born and primarily raised in Mexico.

Much of the discussion concerning ethnic labels can be traced to the confusion caused by the United States Census Bureau in 1980. At that time, the Census Bureau added a racial/ethnic category that classified all the Spanish-speaking communities in the United States as Hispanics. The new label grouped together all the various Spanish-speaking communities, such as the Mexican American, Puerto Rican, Cuban, Salvadorean, Dominican, Peruvian, Panamanian, and Colombian, as well as the community whose origins can be traced immediately to Spain, the Spanish. This caused an often heated dialogue in certain Latino communities, who felt that the unique and historical experience of the various communities was being ignored by the Census Bureau. Many believed that the governmental agency's decision was made out of expediency rather than to gain insight into the unique and common needs of the various ethnic groups living in the United States. Many in the Mexican American community felt that the United States government wanted to emphasize the melting pot theory and deemphasize the ethnic pride gained from the Civil Rights struggle.

The term *Chicano* specifically describes breaking away from the Mexican identity to assert the unique experience of being born and raised in the United States. The term was once considered derogatory in nature; however, during the Civil Rights Movement of the 1960s and 1970s, it began to be used to demonstrate ethnic pride. Many conservative members of the community continue to resent the term, preferring the more traditional label of Mexican American. Nonetheless, the increase in the production of literary works by Chicano authors coincides with the increase in ethnic pride and the asserting of an identity separate from the Mexican experience that occurred during the time of the Civil Rights Movement. For this reason, it is more appropriate to reflect on this literary legacy from the perspective of the Chicano identity.

During the 1960s the oral tradition again played a significant role in stimulating the literary voices of the time. Poetry, along with recitation and declamation, has always been appreciated as a cultural form of expression in the Hispanic world. The writers of this era tapped into this tradition to express their frustration with the political, economic, and educational systems that had failed to respond to their pursuit for equity and rights as citizens of the United States. The two issues that caused most of the frustration and resulted in evoking solidarity among a cross section of the Mexican American community were the Vietnam War and the struggle of the farmworkers.

Although greater numbers of Mexican American youth were entering college at this time, many more were being sent to the front lines in Vietnam. Proportionately, more Mexican Americans were dying in Vietnam than any other ethnic group. At home, farmworkers, who toiled long and arduous hours to put food on the tables of American citizens, often went to bed hungry without the resources to feed, house, educate, or provide health care for their families. When the farmworkers, led by César Chávez and Dolores Huerta, attempted to organize and form a union, the powerful and wealthy farmers resisted violently.

The plight of the migrant worker was well known to the Mexican American community. Many in the community had toiled in the fields. In 1942 the influential agribusiness pushed an agenda that helped establish the Bracero Program. Through an agreement between the U.S. government and the government of Mexico that lasted until the mid-1960s, the growers were allowed to legally bring in thousands of Mexican nationals to work in the fields for very low wages. Mostly men were brought in under contract to work under the most crude and inhumane conditions. Truckloads of *braceros* (the term comes from the word for "arms") could be seen traveling to the growers' fields as a constant source of cheap labor. Many Mexican American families eager to find work also followed the migrant trails. Most of the children of migrant families dropped out of school at an early age, and most began working in the fields before they ever attended school. The situation of this invisible minority united the Mexican American community and contributed to the frustration felt by its youth. The struggles of the migrant farmworker impelled creative voices to emerge. Plays, poetry, songs, declamation, and recitation were presented orally in *campesino* (farmer) theaters, rallies, and even churches. The fervor and spirit of awakening also gave rise to many other written forms of expression.

Community and organization newspapers as well as journals and magazines proliferated during this period. Two publishers that influenced the resurgence of Chicano literature during the late 1960s were the magazine *El Grito* and the publishing house Editorial Quinto Sol. Together they helped launch the careers of the most influential Chicano writers of the time. They published the works of authors who used their ethnic identity as the basis for their creations. Chicano language, history, and culture were the focal point of this literature. Tomás Rivera's *..y no se lo tragó la tierra/...And the Earth Did Not Part* (1971) and Rudolfo Anaya's *Bless Me, Ultima* (1972) exemplify the Chicano novel of that period.

Both books won the national award for Chicano literature, Premio Quinto Sol. The authors wrote about themes that were familiar to working class Mexican Americans, especially men. Their novels continue to serve as models of Chicano literature and to be relevant today as many Mexican Americans persevere in their search for identity. Female writers, however, were not evident in those early years. Most of the early recognition was given to men. The first female writer to win the Premio Quinto Sol Award was Estela Portillo Trambley in 1975 for her collection of short stories in *Rain of Scorpions*. In the 1980s, however, the once-unheard voices of *Chicana women* changed the character of Chicano literature. Currently, *Chicana literature* is a term that is used to acknowledge the uniqueness of the perspectives of Mexican American women. Rebolledo (1995) proposes that Chicana women have used the power of the *cuentos* (stories) shared by their great-grandmothers, grandmothers, and mothers to cross the symbolic literary border that once respected only male writers. She considers Chicana writers to be in the process of articulating the various translations of the lives they live, including the foreign and domestic ones. Many of their stories remain unheard. Although there are many prolific female writers, few are published by the large mainstream publishers but rather are published by small presses and their works are at times difficult to find. Moreover, most of the literary presses of the 1970s have disappeared, including Editorial Quinto Sol. Other publishers, such as Arte Público Press, Aunt Lute, Third Woman Press, and Bilingual Press, have emerged as supporters of this vibrant literature. They publish a large percentage of the works of a growing number of Mexican American writers, especially women.

## Sociohistorical Experiences

The impact of the sociohistorical experiences of the larger Mexican American community on the lives of ordinary citizens is one of the most powerful themes in the literature. The vast migration from Mexico between the years of the Mexican Revolution of 1910 and World War II was initially a reaction to the instability caused by the war between the peasants demanding agrarian reform and the Mexican government attempting to stay in power. Many Mexicans who crossed the border into the United States were expecting to return once the political and economic systems stabilized. However, the overthrow of the Mexican president, Porfirio Diaz, did not end the instability.

Among those who came during this period were a significant number from the upper class and the educated professionals. They came fleeing the crossfire between the troops and the peasants. A majority of those who crossed the border, however, were poor and uneducated. Those who entered the United States expected to find a better life than the one they had left behind, yet what they found was a life that was equally as difficult.

Across regions and class, Mexicans suffered the same conditions: segregated neighborhoods and schools, racism that equated Mexicans to dogs and prevented them from entering many restaurants and swimming pools, lack of employment opportunities, and injustices at the hands of the courts and law enforcement officers. During this period it was a common experience for Mexican doctors, reporters, and political refugees to live in the same neighborhoods as the migrant workers and working-class people. Most of the newly arrived settled in the Southwest and the Midwest. This close proximity among the various classes made many of the elite think of themselves as part of a community in exile, and to a degree they even championed the rights of the poor Mexican immigrant (Kanellos, 1995).

During the Depression, however, there was a tremendous anti-immigrant backlash, and many Mexicans were either voluntarily or unwillingly deported. Families were separated, often picked up on raids, and sent by train to Mexico. Many Mexicans who left had always felt stronger ties to Mexico and espoused the ideology of a Mexican community in exile because they had always expected to return. During their years in the United States, they resented the Americanization of the Mexican immigrant; they often made fun of the peasant who was trying to make sense of the modern American world or was thinking that the United States was better than Mexico and of women who were trying to become more independent, which they felt was at the expense of Mexican men. During the period of repatriation, a large number of those who willingly returned to Mexico belonged to the upper class; however, of those who fought to stay, many belonged to the working class and had children who were born and raised in the United States.

Although the acts of repatriation during the Depression were repressive and abusive on the part of the United States government, Mexicans were nonetheless reaffirming their loyalty to the American government in overwhelming numbers by joining the armed forces and becoming American citizens. During World War II, Mexican Americans proportionately suffered more casualties and won more medals than any other ethnic group in the United States. At the end of the war, they expected to return home and be afforded the same rights as all other citizens; however, discriminatory practices against them continued (Acuña, 1988).

During this same period, Mexican Americans were also undergoing a shift in defining their ethnic identity. Civil rights organizations were formed, such as the G. I. Forum established by Mexican American veterans and the League of United Latin American Citizens (LULAC), which acknowledged the group's ethnic identity as based on the unique experiences in the United States as well as the not-too-distant tie to Mexico. The organizations reflected the fact that the ethnic community was not leaving the United States and returning to Mexico; rather, its members should be considered citizens of the United States and not of Mexico. It was extremely important for the Mexican American leaders of that era to be seen by the larger society as citizens, so even the names of the organizations served as reminders that they were first and foremost American citizens. The ethnic labels most often used by these civil rights organizations were *Latin American* or *Spanish American*, without reference to Mexico. To them, it further reaffirmed the separateness from the Mexican experience and their pursuit of equal access to the rights and privileges available to them as citizens of the United States. Although civil rights organizations like the G.I. Forum and LULAC were initially established to advocate for the community living in the United States, many have consistently supported the rights of all community members, including the immigrant population.

In juxtaposition to the efforts of the mostly older, more conservative members of the community who were striving for equity as American citizens, another phenomenon was developing among the youth. Male youth in particular were demonstrating their alienation from both Mexican and American cultures, primarily through their attire and their language. One of the first identifiable examples of this was among the Zoot Suiters. In the 1940s, the Zoot Suiters wore wide-shouldered suits or drapes with trouser cuffs tight around the ankles, broad-rimmed hats, duck-tailed haircuts, and used a unique dialect that borrowed from Spanish and English, including Spanish slang. Many considered their mode of dressing and jargon to be anti-American. Anti-Zoot Suit sentiment was expressed freely in the press, led by the Hearst media (McWilliams, 1968). In Los Angeles, gangs of servicemen took it upon themselves to rid the downtown area of the Zoot Suiters. In a weeklong riot, the gangs of servicemen targeted and assaulted Mexican American youth.

The *pachucos* of the 1950s also relied on a distinctive dress style to differentiate themselves from the rest of the Mexican American community; they wore Stacy-Adams shoes with thick front leather soles that made the shoes curl up, a white T-shirt and khaki pants, and they spoke *caló* jargon. In the 1960s, the low-riders became more evident as they customized their cars and continued using some of the speech patterns from the *pachucos*, but they also began to use more English. Most of the alienation that has been expressed through their unique attire and speech has been directed inwardly. The Zoot Suiters, the *pachucos*, and the low riders have maintained their lifestyle within the protective confines of the Mexican American community. They have not tried to influence the mainstream community. The Chicano youth of the 1960s and 1970s created a civil rights movement that was directed at gaining the attention of the political and economic system, and therefore they were going outside the community to deliver a message of frustration.

As a significant number of first-generation Mexican American youth began attending institutions of higher education and actively participating in the Civil Rights, farmworker, and anti-Vietnam War movements, they questioned whether the educational, political, and economic systems that their parents and young peers had so valiantly protected during wartime were really providing equity for all citizens (Acuña, 1988). Many became involved in grassroots movements such as registering voters, establishing a community school for the children of undocumented workers, promoting Chicano history and ethnic pride in educational institutions, promoting bilingual education in schools, and establishing bilingual theaters. From the ranks of these youth have come many of today's most respected members of the Mexican American community.

In 1974 Willie Velásquez established the Southwest Voter Registration and Education Project (SVREP), which has been credited with changing the faces in the political arena. Thousands of Mexican Americans now hold elected offices and, together with the Mexican American Legal Defense and Education Fund (MALDEF), have brought hundreds of lawsuits challenging biased practices in education and voting rights. Francisca Flores published *Regeneración*, an activist magazine focusing on women's issues, and founded the Chicana Service Action Center, one of the first community agencies dedicated to serving poor Chicanas (Acuña, 1988). Isaías Torres, a young Tejano lawyer and community activist in the 1970s, led the 1982 court struggle that repealed the Texas law prohibiting the children of undocumented workers from receiving a free education. In 1965 Luis Valdéz established El Teatro Campesino/The Farmworkers Theater to support the organizing efforts of the National Farm Workers of America. His one-act play and use of *corridos* popularized the struggle of the farmworkers and inspired many to mobilize and join the boycott in support of the migrant workers. Valdéz has been instrumental in presenting Chicano history and issues that educate the larger community. His understanding of the themes in Mexican American stories has been manifested throughout his professional life as a Hollywood director and playwright. Early in his career, Valdéz adapted the story of the Zoot Suit Riots and the case of Sleepy Lagoon to the Broadway stage and to film. He also directed *The Ballad of Gregorio Cortéz*, the movie based on Américo Paredes' book (1958) on the *corrido* of Gregorio Cortéz. Both of Valdéz's films are based on true, significant events in the Mexican American community.

These sociohistorical experiences of the Mexican American community continue to be used as the background for individual stories. The experiences associated with immigration, racism, ethnic identity, indigenous roots, gender, language bias, and war have certainly impacted the Mexican American community, but how these forces have influenced the lives of a family or an individual is equally pivotal in Mexican American history. The stories personalize the experiences and elucidate where the Mexican American community has been and where it is going as a people. The thinking and emotional processes of the community, as seen through the stories of common people, is restated and reexamined, and new generations learn from these sociohistorical experiences. All cultures use stories to help new generations understand the group's unique world, socialize according to the group's norms, and maintain its cultural heritage.

## The Family

The second major theme underlying the stories written by Mexican American authors is related to the family. The family as an institution in the Mexican American community continues to be strong, and the cultural value of interrelatedness continues to be meaningful. This cultural value is evident in most families and has long been cited by social scientists (Ramirez & Arce, 1981; Alvirez, Bean, & Williams, 1981). The beliefs, norms, and practices of the community support the family as a significant cultural institution; therefore, stories written by

Mexican American authors would naturally involve the family as a reflection of daily community life.

Most Mexican Americans consider the family as a highly significant contributor to the quality of their lives. Whether the family is rich or poor, the family is often identified as being a positive force in the lives of Mexican Americans. Even when the basic tenets of other institutions in the Mexican American community were being questioned in the 1960s and 1970s, the family remained a fairly stable institution. It has, however, undergone changes in more recent decades. The social and economic forces impacting the larger majority community have also had an effect on the Mexican American family—for example, the changing role of women, the high rate of teenage pregnancies, and the switch in roles that may occur between immigrant parents and their children as the child learns English while the parent does not.

The Mexican American family may be composed of the traditional nuclear members, intergenerational members, and/or non-blood-related individuals, including godparents. Friendships also form strong bonds to families; close intimate friends are often identified as family members rather than as just friends. Social and emotional support within the Mexican American community is primarily available through familial relationships (Keefe & Padilla, 1987). The most significant dimension of the children's psychosocial development has been found to be directly related to the family and social support networks (Zambrana, 1995). It is therefore typical for family members to live in close geographical proximity to each other. The view that children must be raised to be independent of their families is more of a North American value; in the Mexican American family and community, interdependence is much more fundamental and esteemed as a cultural value.

Often a family saga is the central theme of a novel, as in *Rain of Gold* (Villaseñor, 1991). Villaseñor narrates the story of his family through three generations as they face the powerful forces of poverty, immigration, and prejudice. Sandra Cisneros' *The House on Mango Street* (1991) uses the family home as the setting that allows us to see her world and where she lived as a young girl. Her family, the neighbors, and her friends are all involved in the stories that describe the foundation she will use to build her later successes.

# Spirituality

The third theme recurring in Mexican American literature involves an acceptance of the link to the metaphysical world. The Anglo-Saxon Protestant churches viewed much of the relationship with the metaphysical world as emanating from evil forces or witchcraft, and many considered it their duty as missionaries to eradicate any beliefs and traditions held by indigenous people that might be perceived as having a basis in or a link to the spiritual world. The Spanish Catholic missionaries, on the other hand, did not emphasize the elimination of indigenous mythology and beliefs associated with the metaphysical world; rather, they attempted to syncretize the ancestral cultural traditions concerning birth, life, and death with the practices of Catholicism. The concepts associated with Spanish Catholicism became intermixed with the beliefs of the indigenous peoples.

Death in Mexican culture is viewed not as a final act to be feared but rather as part of life. It is seen as a transition between earthly life and life in the spiritual world. Funerals, therefore, are viewed more as a social gathering involving the opportunity for family and friends to remember the dead and, more importantly, provide a supportive experience for the bereaved and pray for the deceased's safe passage to heaven. Spirits that remain on the earthly plane can cause harm to the living. The celebration of the Day of the Dead, a national holiday in Mexico, demonstrates how the metaphysical world is clearly connected to the three-dimensional world. On that day, the spirits return to the earthly homes of their families to share in the festivities. The favorite foods of the deceased are prepared, and an altar is created to honor the deceased family members. Special bread, cookies, and candies are decorated with skulls and other death-related artifacts. Families go to the cemetery on this day to spruce up the graveside and picnic.

*The Legend of La Llorono* (Anaya, 1984), or the weeping/hollering woman, is a story reminding children that roaming spirits are part of this world. There are many variations of the legend; the story told in New Mexico will vary somewhat from the variations told in south Texas, but both are accepted as authentic versions. Since the oral tradition allows each storyteller, or *cuentista*, to add, delete, or embellish parts of a story, the stories have a life of their own. In his short novel, Anaya retells the legend and bridges it to the sociohistorical experience of the Mexican people.

Another legend that is part of the cultural heritage that bridges the indigenous roots to the daily lives of the Mexican people, and is one of the first stories that most schoolchildren in Mexico are told, is represented in the flag of Mexico. In the center of the red, white, and green flag, one can see an eagle holding a serpent in its beak and claws as it majestically perches on top of a cactus plant. The story told in all Mexican schools is of the journey that brought the Aztecs to the land called Mexico. It describes how the Aztecs left Aztlán, their place of origin that is supposedly located in the Southwest United States, in search of the land the gods had selected for them. The gods told them to watch for the sign of an eagle holding a serpent to know where to settle and build their empire. The Aztecs saw the eagle in the center of a lake and proceeded to build their empire and pyramids on the marshy land that is known today as Mexico City. Of course, whether it is myth, folklore, or history can be debated by the scholars, but the story is a powerful one for Mexicans and Mexican Americans alike. It ties the land called the United States to the indigenous people of Mexico. Aztlán may be a mythical concept for some, but for many Mexican Americans it also explains why most of its population can today be found living in the Southwest.

Because of the cultural understanding that supports the link between the metaphysical and the real world, a woman in Ana Castillo's novel *So Far From God* (1994) can die and return to life. The death that occurs early in the novel allows one of the main characters to move back and forth between the spiritual and the physical world through magical realism. In this story of a New Mexican mother and her four daughters, the Mexican American author uses this cognizance to take the reader through a cultural journey. Many Mexican American novelists similarly move their characters between the two worlds. For North American readers, this thread will certainly be challenging but exciting.

## Summary

The goal in writing this chapter has been to help teachers gain some basic cultural insight into the Mexican American experience that will facilitate the interpretation of the literature as well as provide teachers and students with some of the background information on the legacy of the Mexican American novel. Mexican American literature is rich, diverse, and therefore complex. Mexican American authors continue the tradition of the ancestral storytellers as they focus on a good story that also mirrors the real life of the community. However, to interpret some of the recurring themes found in the stories, it is important to be familiar with the group's history and significant cultural values and traditions. One does not have to belong to the ethnic community to gain an appreciation for the literature. As a matter of fact, whether the reader is Mexican American may not be significant to understanding the literature. Because the group's history is not routinely taught in schools, Mexican American readers may not be familiar with the group's history and may need the support of an informed person to help them interpret the story. Moreover, not all members of the Mexican American community experience shared events in the same way. Within all ethnic groups there exist familial, cultural, and individual forces that impact people's lives. Readers need to recognize that not all members of the Mexican American community share the same outlook on life. Understanding this cross-cultural principle avoids cultivating stereotypes about Mexican Americans. Readers may need to reflect on their own unique or family cultural view and compare it to others in their ethnic community to more clearly grasp the understanding that diversity exists in all cultural groups.

Teachers should start to incorporate Mexican American novels by becoming familiar with their students' interests. Providing students with a wide array of choices may trigger their interest and involve them in further exploration of Mexican American novels. The teacher may need to read many of the novels mentioned in this chapter and do a preliminary selection to best match the choices to the community of students. The Reading List at the end of this chapter is limited but cuts across the vast diverse genre known as Mexican American young adult literature. Teachers should also be familiar with the publishing houses, such as Arte Público Press, that print many of the current Mexican American novels. Piñata Books is a division of Arte Público Press that specializes in books for children and young adults. Contact these nontraditional presses, including Bilingual Press, and ask to be placed on their mailing lists. Consider visiting your local university and browsing through its bookstore. Many universities, such as the University of Arizona and the University of New Mexico, have supported their faculty through their presses and have published Mexican American authors, or they have departments in Mexican American/Latin American/Folklore Studies that consistently order novels written by Mexican American authors. Use the resources available through your local library and favorite bookstore for recommendations on current publications. Anthologies are excellent resources for a beginner exploring Mexican American literature. Consider examining the works of Cherrie Moraga and Gloria Anzaldúa, editors of *This Bridge Called My Back: Writings by Radical Women of Color* (1983); Roberta Fernández, editor of *In other words: Literature by Latinas of the United States* (1994); Ramon Gutierrez and Genaro Padilla, editors of *Recovering the U.S. Hispanic Literary Heritage* (1993); Nicolas Kanellos, editor of *Reference Library of Hispanic America, Vol. 2* (1995); Bryce Milligan, Mary Guerrero Milligan, and Angela de Hoyos, editors of *Daughters of the Fifth Sun* (1995); Evangelina Vigil-Piñon, editor of *Women of Their Word: Hispanic Women Write* (1987); and Tey Diana Rebolledo and Eliana S. Rivero, editors of *Infinite Divisions: An Anthology of Chicana Literature* (1993).

Additionally, whereas many of the classic Mexican American novels annotated in the Reading List are written by men, who are among the better known literary figures, Chicana or Mexican American female authors are currently the most exciting and prolific storytellers emerging through the publishing industry maze. It has been doubly difficult for the voices of Chicanas to emerge in literary circles. Not only are they associated with minority literature, but Mexican American women are telling stories that have traditionally been viewed as not worthy of being told, such as those embodying femaleness, home, food and song, wives, service, lesbianism, and violence against women. According to Rebolledo (1995), these themes, which are evident in the work of many Chicana authors, center women and their concepts within the backdrop of a scenario depicting the larger social and cultural forces. Although similar to male Mexican American authors, these women are also primarily published by nonmainstream publishers, but their voices and stories represent issues not typically prized by either the publishing world or the ethnic community (Milligan et al., 1995). Because the Reading List is not an exhaustive list of all the significant Mexican American novels, but only a sampling, and because of the proliferation of written works especially from female authors, teachers should watch for the most recent publications of the following Chicana authors: Gloria Anzaldúa, Irene Beltrán Hernández, Norma Cantu, Ana Castillo, Debra Castillo, Denise Chávez, Sandra Cisneros, Lucha Corpi, Pat Mora, Mary Helen Ponce, and Carmen Tafolla. Many of these authors are better known for their poetry, short stories, essays, or children's books, genres that can greatly enhance a variety of units of study. *Dichos* sayings, songs, oral histories, and poetry are often interwoven into the memories of the cultural traditions and themes that are the backdrop of the stories (Rebolledo, 1995) and can be used as cultural links across ethnic groups.

Students can explore their own cultural oral traditions to tell their stories and comprehend the significance of storytelling in their lives. The use of the personal narrative to tell the story of a community can help us bridge cultures. Storytelling helps us to understand what memorizing dates and names of national heroes or viewing inanimate statues in city parks can never do, which is to help us understand each others' shared humanity, including the joys, fears, grief, dilemmas, hopes, and dreams of individuals and communities living next to us.

Through their novels, the Mexican American *cuentistas* (storytellers) offer their audiences a peek into the insiders' world of the Mexican American community. As these authors take the reader on a cultural journey, remember the story behind the stories. The authors will help you to better understand the cultural themes that include of the role of the family, the acceptance of a spiritual or mythical world, and the impact of the sociocultural history on the individual and larger community. Today's classrooms have the opportunity to reach out and listen to the different voices of the ethnic communities found in our pluralistic society. Consider inviting the Mexican American community into school by exploring the rich literature that expresses the multifaceted identity of this diverse group.

# Reading List

Anaya, R. (1972). *Bless me, Ultima.* Berkeley, CA: Tonatiuh-Quinto Sol.

> This is a sensitive story of a young boy, Antonio, and his relationship with Ultima, a *curandera* or healer. The oral traditions of their rural community are portrayed in this book. A well-known classic in Mexican American litreature.

Anaya, R. (1984). *The legend of La Llorono.* Berkeley, CA: Tonatiuh-Quinto Sol.

> One of very few books written about this well-known Mexican legend. Since many students will be familiar with different versions, it will be a good opportunity to compare and contrast the various versions as well as gain some insight on the origins of this tale.

Anaya, R. (1992). *Albuquerque.* New York: Warner Books.

> Albuquerque is the setting for this novel of a young boxer who learns of his past and about what could be his future. The Southwest's history and traditions are background for this bicultural experience. Recommended for more mature readers.

Castillo, A. (1994). *So far from God.* New York: Norton.

> The story of a New Mexico mother and her four fated daughters. The reader is taken back and forth between the real and the surreal worlds of this family. The author is a skillful storyteller that can engage the young as well as the more mature reader.

Chávez, D. (1994). *Face of an angel.* New York: Warner Books.

> This book is the winner of the Puerto del Sol fiction award and the 1994 Premio Aztlán award. This saga involving the Dosamantes family takes place in rural New Mexico. You get to know the small town of Agua Oscura and the family through the stories narrated by a waitress. Many reviewers have described this book as "delicious."

Cisneros, S. (1991). *The house on Mango Street*. New York: Vintage Books.

A young girl's journey of coming-of-age and knowing herself. The book is organized in vignettes and may reflect the author's experiences growing up in the Latino section of Chicago. It is easy to read, and some powerful issues are presented that can lead to excellent discussions. This author is also well known as a poet and a short-story writer. Her books are excellent for reading aloud.

Gonzales, B. D. (1995). *Sweet fifteen*. Houston, TX: Piñata Books.

The traditional coming-of-age ritual for Latinas is celebrated in a modern setting. A young girl experiences the conflicts of growing up and adjusting to a new family situation when her father dies just before her 15th birthday.

Hernández, I. B. (1995). *Across the great river*. Houston, TX: Piñata Books.

The story of the hardships faced by a young girl whose family is separated while illegally crossing the border into the United States. A moving story that is recommended for the young adult.

Hernández, I. B. (1995). *The secret of two brothers*. Houston, TX: Piñata Books.

Two brothers face some of life's most devastating events, including a mother's death. They rely on their love for each other and their combined strength to overcome some challenging situations. This book is targeted to the young adult reader.

Rivera, T. (1971). *...y no se lo trago la tierra/...an the earth did not part*. Berkeley, CA: Quinto Sol.

A must-read bilingual book that can be used with students who have varying levels of proficiency in English, Spanish or both. The book is organized by 12 short stories that represent the months of the year. The harsh sociocultural reality of the Mexican American experience is presented in this classic. The overriding theme, however, is hope and freedom, not despair.

Trambley, E. (1975). *Rain of scorpions*. Berkeley, CA: Tonatiuah International.

Velásquez, G. (1994). *Juanita fights the school board*. Houston, TX: Piñata Books.

> Juanita fights for her rights and for fairness. She wants to graduate and be the first in her family to earn a high school diploma. She learns to organize with others in order to stand up to the politically powerful school board. The author also introduces us to Juanita's friend, Maya, a protagonist in a later, young adult novel.

Villaseñor, V. (1991). *Rain of gold*. Houston, TX: Arte Público Press.

# References

Acuña, R. (1988). *Occupied America: A history of Chicanos*. New York: HarperCollins.

Alvirez, D., Bean, F. D., & Williams, D. (1981). The Mexican American family. In C. H. Mindel & R. W. Habenstein (Eds.), *Ethnic families in America: Patterns and variation* (pp. 271–292). New York: Elsevier.

Fernández, R. (1994). *In other words: Literature by Latinas of the United States*. Houston, TX: Arte Público Press.

Gutierrez, R., & Padilla, G. (Eds.). (1993). *Recovering the U.S. Hispanic literary heritage*. Houston, TX: Arte Público Press.

Herrera-Sobek, M. (1990). *The Mexican corrido: A feminist analysis*. Bloomington, IN: Indiana University Press.

Kanellos, N. (1995). *Reference library of Hispanic America*, Vol. 2. Detroit, MI: Gale Research.

Keefe, S. E., & Padilla, A. M. (1987). *Chicano ethnicity*. Albuquerque, NM: University of New Mexico Press.

McWilliams, C. (1968). *North from Mexico*. New York: Greenwood Press.

Milligan, B., Milligan, M. G., & de Hoyos, A. (1995). *Daughters of the fifth sun*. New York: Riverhead Books.

Moraga, C., & Anzaldúa, G. (Eds.). (1983). *This bridge called my back: Writings by radical women of color*. Watertown, MA: Persephone Press.

Paredes, A. (1958). *With his pistol in his hand: A border ballad and its hero.* Austin, TX: University of Texas Press.

Ramirez, O., & Arce, C. (1981). The contemporary Chicano family: An empirically based review. In A. Barron, Jr., (Ed.), *Explorations in Chicano psychology.* New York: Praeger.

Rebolledo, T. D. (1995). *Women singing in the snow.* Tucson, AZ: University of Arizona Press.

Rebolledo, T. D., & Rivero, E. S. (Eds.). (1993). *Infinite divisions: An anthology of Chicana literature.* Tucson, AZ: University of Arizona Press.

Vigil-Piñon, E. (Ed.) (1987). *Women of their word: Hispanic women write.* Houston, TX: Arte Público Press.

Zambrana, R. E. (1995). *Understanding Latino families.* Thousand Oaks, CA: Sage.

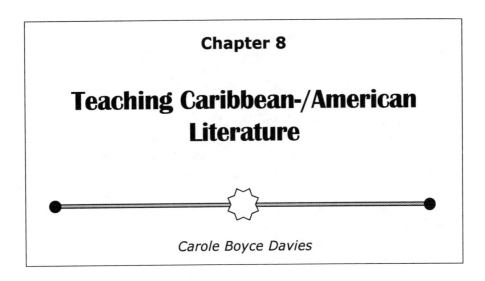

**Chapter 8**

# Teaching Caribbean-/American Literature

*Carole Boyce Davies*

## Introduction

Caribbean-/American literature is a particular type of American literature, as it is possessed with its own Caribbean-generated specificities. The dance between the two poles necessitates the diacritical marking (-/) between Caribbean and American—a hyphenation and a slash, indicating an assertion of belonging, connectedness, and association as well as independence. By this means I am asserting the simultaneity of a conjunction and disjunction of Americanness and Caribbeanness in this literature.

This assertion challenges the very limited understanding of American literature as only North American literature and contests the hegemonic equivalence of "United States" with "American" literature. Thus, it relocates the other Americas as a tangible presence in the larger understanding of "America" and so makes space for Caribbean literature. American Studies programs (1996) and organizations are beginning to confront this issue of what constitutes "America," for otherwise they would remain border-bound and U.S.-centric, vulnerable to the persistent charge of exclusion.

There has been a consistent presence of Caribbean peoples in North America just as there has been a persistent migration of peoples in different North-South directions (Davies, 1994). This idea of persistent migration replaces the narrative of a singular northward migration to one of a series of multidirectional crossings of peoples. A few texts in the American canon are appropriately mentioned here. Martin Delaney's *Blake or the Huts of America* (1861/1970) in the African American literary canon elaborates on the issue of moving outside U.S. borders. The works of Zora Neale Hurston, especially her own research into Caribbean culture, are creative explorations of the associative relationship with the United States—for example, allowing Janie, the lead character in *Their Eyes Were Watching God* (1990), to travel southward subverts the logic of northward migration. All of Paule Marshall's works demonstrate, at aesthetic and political levels, a deliberate and consistent claiming of the Caribbean and a movement in either direction for reconnection (Brathwaite, 1974).

One of the first texts in the African diaspora literary canon—Olaudah Equiano's *The Interesting Narrative of the Life of Olaudah Equiano or Gustavus Vassa, the African* (1789/1996)—with the narrator's variety of stopping points, contests this unidirectional logic of northward migration. Persistent migration, though rooted in slavery-based forced migrations, also includes a variety of subsequent economic and demographic shifts. These range from the construction of the Panama Canal; colonially constructed displacements and desires; contemporary migrations of Haitian and Cuban peoples to the United States at different points in history for political, economic, and familial reasons; and migrations that resulted from ecological disasters such as hurricanes and volcanoes, the most recent being the large-scale shifting of people on the island of Montserrat. All of these movements have produced the people who are both the subject matter and the speaking subjects of this literature, and therefore the only ones with authority over their existences.

The question of immediate location makes Caribbean literature and culture one that is possibly familiar if one moves beyond tourist constructions. For this reason, Caribbean literature is much more culturally accessible to students and teachers and thus more easily acquirable than the much more geographically distant European culture and literature. While many Americans have European ancestry, these heritages are sometimes generations away and lack any reconnection, except that which is invoked at the level of ideology and mythology and which has at times been the foundation of racism. For many African Americans, the question of heritage is also one of history and ideology, but there can be an unwitting narrowness as the Caribbean heritage is omitted from this frame even though it is part of the cultural history and reality of many Black Americans.

Caribbean-/American literature embeds in its very formation the issue of multiculturalism and thus makes it appropriately raised in discussions on this topic. Caribbean literature is born of a variety of ethnic and cultural conjunctions. Thus, Caribbean literature, as it engages North American exercises in multicultural living, already brings to the table its own practice of a distinct Caribbean multiculturality (Goulbourne, 1993).

Throughout this discussion, I propose to locate a series of teaching projects that allow students and teachers to think practically through the process on which we are embarking as we explore some questions specific to the teaching of Caribbean literature. The aim is to relocate the issue of familiarity so that the process of reading Caribbean-/American literature in this way and pursuing this topic becomes a conscious exercise in knowledge transformation. The epistemological logic allows a movement from the known to the unknown; that is, from Caribbean-/American literature to what is understood as mainstream Caribbean literature. (Even the idea of one "mainstream" Caribbean literature is very island-bound and easily contested.)

Caribbean literature is a type of American literature if we understand "American literature" in its broader sense of "literature of the Americas." Still, this is not an argument for subsuming Caribbean literature under the umbrella of American literature as it is understood in the academy. Rather, it is an argument for seeing this literature relationally, using the logic of "critical relationality" (Davies, 1994, pp. 54–56) to produce accessibility. Thus, if we work with Caribbean-/American literature as a category, we can identify it as an important strand of North American literature as well as an important strand of Caribbean literature.

Caribbean-/American literature is produced by writers of Caribbean descent who are any or all of the following:

1. They were born in the Caribbean and write from the United States today.

2. They were born in the United States of Caribbean parents and see familial and cultural connections as critical and name themselves Caribbean.

3. They define themselves as Caribbean, although they were born in the United States, through ancestry and cultural practices and an emphasis on the Caribbean aspects of their identity.

The latter two groups are perhaps the most important in this discussion, for they refer to a whole generation of people who were born in the United States of Caribbean families and who, while they partook of the North American cultural contexts in the larger community, operated in their immediate and familial contexts as Caribbean. These are also the groups that teachers will most likely encounter in their classrooms. Often they and their cultural contexts remain unaccounted for in a variety of North American and Caribbean institutional arrangements, except when they themselves assert that identity.

---

## Teaching Project 1

Have students identify the Caribbean holdings in their library or bookstore and explain what the constraints are in terms of identification, location, access, and knowledge. Have students do family histories.

---

## Caribbean Locations

Sheer proximity alone, at least in the North American context, establishes the relevance of studying Caribbean literature and giving it a more prominent place in North American literary curricula. The question of immediate geography, then, raises a variety of questions as to why the Caribbean is constructed as culturally and intellectually distant. It is quicker, for example, to travel from New York or Miami to Jamaica or Puerto Rico than to Colorado. And, indeed, the Caribbean is sometimes conveniently relocated within the U.S. "sphere of interest" for political, military, and business reasons but not for intellectual ones.

The series of migrations from the Caribbean to various locations in North America and the growth of Caribbean communities there challenge this logic of distance. Additionally, the numerous business, military, and other political relations that North America has had with the Caribbean has fostered a clear sense of an American presence in the Caribbean just as much as a Caribbean presence in North America.

So while one may have difficulty entering the field of Caribbean literature without some basic knowledge, one avenue for some access is an identification and rereading of Caribbean-/American literature to identify both the Caribbean and American themes.

An important reference point is the meaning of the rise of the various Caribbean carnivals, which have become emblematic of the movement of these communities and their establishment of cultural institutions. Some cities, like Miami; Brooklyn, New York; Hartford, Connecticut; Baltimore, Maryland; Washington, D.C.; Toronto; Paris; Montreal; and even Brixton, England, have strong Caribbean populations that make the particular curricular visibility of Caribbean literature absolutely necessary. A Caribbean diaspora has therefore been identified (James & Harris, 1993) that speaks to the reality of migration or the second-level dispersion of Caribbean peoples to diverse locations.

Much of the thinking on the idea of a Caribbean diaspora has come out of activists and intellectuals in England. Being the primary Black population in England, Caribbeans have had to assert their own identities and pursue some relevant cultural meanings as part of contesting state exclusion and disrespect. For example, they have identified the question of belonging as central to this articulation. A helpful exploration of this aspect of identity appears in *Where You Belong* (1992), edited by Alrick X. Cambridge and Stephan Feuchtwang of the Race and Culture Policy Research Unit, London. The text *Inside Babylon: The Caribbean Diaspora in Britain* (James & Harris, 1993) contains several explorations of issues like immigration, racism, activism, Black women, and carnival culture.

As an area, the Caribbean is seen in its most limited understanding through discourses of fragmentation as simply "the islands." In its broader and more appropriate understanding, the Caribbean refers to the entire geographical area touching the Caribbean Sea, thus including the circum-Caribbean areas of Belize, Guyana, Venezuela, and Honduras. If one were to work with geography alone, areas like Miami have a particularly contiguous and cultural relationship with the Caribbean and are seen, in some understandings, as Caribbean culturally. This logic of a "continental Caribbean" is now being advanced. Furthermore, because of secondary migrations beginning in the 1920s with the development of the Panama Canal, Caribbean migration to the United States and European centers like London, Paris, and Amsterdam mean that one can talk of a Caribbean diaspora in the same way that one talks of an African diaspora. This Caribbean diaspora traces the migrations of various Caribbean peoples, but it is a multiracial diaspora, unlike the African and Indian diasporas, which have their identities in singular racial histories.

Caribbean locations include the Caribbean islands as well as the continental Caribbean, such as the Guyanas, Surinam, Venezuela, portions of Mexico and Central America, Miami, and New Orleans. The locations of Caribbean diasporic communities—products of migration to North America, Europe, and Canada, and other geographical locations such as Africa and Asia, with communities that live in a Caribbean cultural reality—are identified as the reaches of the Caribbean diaspora.

---

### Teaching Project 2

Have students identify the Caribbean in terms of a series of mapping exercises identifying locations in relation to the United States and to each other.

---

## Popular-Culture Connections

The ongoing interest of youth cultures in Caribbean music like reggae, soca, and zouk provide another popular-culture reference for this presence. The Afro-Caribbean history and interaction of rap and hip-hop cultures has already been established (Cooper, 1995; Walcott, 1995). Contemporary elements and hairstyles such as dreadlocks reveal a Caribbean influence as they become elements in hip-hop culture, Walcott argues well. One can observe clear generational shifts in North American popular-culture connections with the Caribbean. For the preceding and current generations it has been Bob Marley and Rastafarian music and culture; before that, Harry Belafonte or Desi Arnaz provided that cultural reference. Jazz musicians like Dizzy Gillespie consistently engaged in musical exchanges with Cuban players.

It is important to identify then, that through popular culture youth have often been able to pursue different knowledge bases, which the classroom sometimes seems to work against or at least never acknowledge. Literary study, in my view, has an obligation to engage the student's information base and work toward expanding it. This means that those who teach Caribbean-/American literature to young people may already be working within a cultural field that they and their students are somewhat familiar with or can access through popular culture. Teachers can get students involved in projects that identify Caribbean music and dance and their histories and thereby help to contextualize the literature.

Caribbean literature's accessibility because of proximity, and the demographics of Caribbean migration to the various metropoles, reveals another nexus of interaction through Caribbean popular culture. The film tradition—especially the Hollywood stereotypes and the counterdiscourse of the development of Caribbean film—is another way to provide for a certain kind of learning to take place (Cham, 1991; Martin, 1995).

---

## Teaching Project 3

Have students trace the history and origins of contemporary hairstyles, the languages of the cultures they express, the dance forms, the music, and the style. Pursue an Internet search of Caribbean popular culture.

---

## Historical Meanings

The Caribbean was named for the Carib Indians, one of the Native American groups that populated this area (Walker, 1991). The name *West Indies* is a misnomer, an error of Columbus, yet it identifies one of the most important foundational moments in modern Caribbean history: the period of colonial conquest, domination of the Native peoples, large-scale import of African slaves and Southeast Asian indentured workers for sugar production, and hundreds of years of colonial exploitation of Caribbean resources for the enrichment of Europe. This pattern, which stayed in place until the independence movements of the 1950s, often fails to account for consistent United States involvement in the form of military invasions, political influence, appropriation of labor (domestic for household maintenance and migrant for harvesting crops), and formation of cheap markets for United States goods through the present. The Caribbean has also become one of the sites for the cheap factory-production of goods by United States companies seeking to circumvent the labor demands of the United States unions and thereby maximize their profits.

These important historical movements and events mark the Caribbean and have a direct relationship with the literature. They include the history of Native peoples, slavery and plantation systems, and resistance in the form of maroon settlements, uprisings and rebellions, colonialism and anticolonial movements, decolonization, federation and independence movements, labor movements, outward migrations, and a variety of struggles to develop independent political and economic systems and gain internal control of the Caribbean (Cuba, Grenada, Jamaica, etc.).

Helpful background information can be found in texts like *The Modern Caribbean* (Knight & Palmer, 1989), which includes chapters on some of the major movements in Caribbean history, such as the Haitian Revolution, racial movements in the Caribbean, the question of Cuban and Puerto Rican independence, and various migrations. Similarly, Beckles, Hilary and Verne Shepherd (1991) give a more contemporary reading of some of the questions of Caribbean history. Janet H. Momsen (1993) provides several important essays on gender as a category of analysis in studying Caribbean history.

---

### Teaching Project 4

One can work with islands and pursue specific histories in terms of projects and literature in class. Students working on Jamaica, for example, can identify the place, the language, the music, and the literature.

---

## Multiplicity, Multiculturalism, and Multilingualism

The multiplicity of ethnicities, languages, and cultures of the Caribbean is a primary area to address in teaching Caribbean literature. This is one context in which the practice of multiculturalism has tangible manifestations. The Caribbean thrives on the logics of multiethnic, multiracial, and multicultural communities that nevertheless find ways to live in relative harmony (Goulbourne, 1993). Thus, in teaching Caribbean literature it is important not to approach this as a single racial or ethnic literature but as one which East Indian, African, Asian, and European peoples (and the various Caribbean mixtures of these) have had important roles in shaping, along with its Caribbean cultural meanings.

The Caribbean islands have had various colonial ownerships and therefore carry the stamp of language diversity. The primary languages are English, Spanish, French, Dutch and a variety of creoles, pidgins, and Papiamento. These languages are the remaining sign of the variety of colonizing enterprises. An important reference point for the discussion of language and colonialism is Shakespeare's *Tempest*, in which Caliban becomes the representative dispossessed Caribbean man, losing his language and his island and being reduced to a deformed version of his prior self. A number of Caribbean writers have found it important to reevaluate Caliban, making him a figure of the colonized "other" and an essential stopping point in terms of language (Lamming, 1992).

Caribbean writers have developed a variety of strategies to make these languages their own as they attempted to articulate their cultures. Edward Kamau Brathwaite (1984) defined "nation language" as a way of representing the various linguistic strands that make up the Caribbean language. Similarly, Edouard Glissant (1992) and his discussion of creolité in the Francophone Caribbean identifies the ways that creole languages define a Caribbean reality outside of dominance. Marlene Nourbese Philip (1990), in "The Absence of Writing or How I Almost Became a Spy," speaks eloquently to the question of language and colonialism in the fracturing of the "i-mage" and the strategies to reconstitute it in the writing "I-maging" self of the Caribbean writer. Various writers from different locations articulate in various texts this question of language, from the use of creoles and pidgins to bilingualism in a single text, especially in the Spanish-speaking context, and playing with syntactic and other linguistic structures in ways that reflect the indigenous language patterns of the writer and his or her potential primary audiences.

The question of language is therefore very central in teaching Caribbean literature and provides the means for a variety of entry points into it. Bilingualism, or the assertion of Spanish in the same way that

English is asserted as a given, is important for the Spanish Caribbean. In lieu of translation, several writers have experimented with placing Spanish and English texts in juxtaposition, in repetition, or in different locations to signal the need for an awareness of multiple audiences. For the Francophone Caribbean, Haitian creole is important.The French language, the primary vehicle of French colonialism in Martinique and Guadeloupe, and an assortment of French *patois* in islands in the Eastern Caribbean (such as St. Lucia) provide an interesting range of language forms in the Caribbean. Thus, along with the European languages that appear in the Caribbean (French, Spanish, or Dutch)—which can therefore include Caribbean literatures in their language studies—an awareness of the existence of creole provides another teaching opportunity, a way of simultaneously employing the literature to opening the multicultural meanings of that language and its literature.

Caribbean writers often demonstrate an amazing range of language usage in a single text, which may make reading a tricky enterprise in terms of pursuing meaning. Also, several writers, such as Dionne Brand (1988) or Earl Lovelace (1979), deliberately write in the Caribbean idiom and cadence of a specific island, in this case Trinidadian English. Others, like Merle Collins (1987), incorporate creole and *patois* phraseology, as does Edwidge Danticat (1996) of Haiti. The Yoruba background is seen in Cristina Garcia's *Dreaming in Cuban* (1992).

The poetic discourse may be one of the best places to observe that range. *Voiceprint: An Anthology of Oral and Related Poetry From the Caribbean* (Brown, Rohlehr, & Morris, 1989) has a range of poetic styles, genres, and languages following an interesting introductory essay in this area. This text captures the indigenous poetic traditions—the lyric, dub poetry with its connections to the Rastafarian cultural tradition and reggae music—and the written tradition with its perennial question of the search for voice and audience.

---

### Teaching Project 5

Have students pursue the meanings of colonialism. What are the various ethnicities in the Caribbean? Find a piece of Caribbean creole and work toward a translation. Consult Native speakers who can help.

---

# Caribbean-/American Literature Abroad

Caribbean-/American literature can be said to have begun with writers of the Harlem Renaissance, like Claude McKay and Eric Walrond. Indeed, Tony Martin (1983) argues that the Harlem Renaissance is a kind of "literary Garveyism" in that the philosophy of Marcus Garvey runs solidly through all the philosophical movements of that period. It may be helpful, as I did in "Writing Home: Gender and Heritage in the Works of Afro-Caribbean/American Women Writers" (Davies & Fido, 1990, pp. 59–74) to point to generations of Caribbean-/American writers. Thus, the following writers began their work in the 1940s and 1950s and spoke to Caribbean realities: Paule Marshall, Audre Lorde, and Rosa Guy. In the 1970s and later, writers like Ntozake Shange claim a Caribbean heritage, as does June Jordan. It is significant that these are, in reality, first-generation American writers who see their Caribbean parentage as leading to a more expansive vision. June Jordan, in *Technical Difficulties* (1992), is clear about how this Caribbean familial background shaped her political and cultural sensibilities. Malcolm X also had a Caribbean family history that he considered influential.

The Nuyorican poets of New York; the writers of Caribbean birth like Michelle Cliff, Jamaica Kincaid, Opal Palmer Adisa, Nicholasa Mohr, Carmen Esteves, and Cristina Garcia; and a host of younger writers and rap artists like The Fugees continue to build these generational sequences. Their presence represents the various migrations from Puerto Rico, Anglophone Caribbean (Barbados, Trinidad, Jamaica, Antigua), Cuba, Haiti, and the Dominican Republic.

## Seeing America

One of the most important themes in this group of writers is the way they see America. A few representative texts will suffice as examples. Claude McKay's poem "America" (1928/1992) captures the tension he feels living in North America, struggling with racism, and deciding to directly confront its edifices. His love is born of anguish and tension: "I love this cultured hell which tests my youth" (line 4). For him, "America" becomes a challenge that energizes him to resist it. His "If We Must Die" sonnet takes this question of resistance to terror and domination even further; it becomes a representative poem of many situations that have necessitated an assertive response. Another oft-cited McKay poem, "The Tropics in New York," identifies the range of Caribbean fruits and vegetables that become living memories of a home of "fruit trees laden by low-singing rills" (line 6) and creates the nostalgia for home, which ends the poem. The mood at the end of the poem is much like his "White Houses," in which he captures the edifices of racism and foreign bias that bar his entry. Still, in his larger relations to North America, McKay asserts a certain belonging to a Black community, which he recognizes in his *Home to Harlem* (1928). This has an interesting titular intertextuality with his autobiography, *A Long Way From Home* (1937/1970). The various "homes" in his titles speak to the question of migration, displacement, and the redefinition of home, which is a central theme in Caribbean literature.

Audre Lorde and Rosa Guy have made significant contributions to this definition of Caribbean-/American writers. Guy's adolescent novels are very important in addressing questions of migration, sexuality, friendship, and life in a North American urban community. Several teachers already assign *Ruby* (1983) and *The Friends* (1973) as adolescent literature, but often not as Caribbean literature. Guy's works are another group of texts that fall between the lines because of this dual nature as Caribbean and American.

Perhaps Paule Marshall goes the furthest in accepting this location. Each of her texts, from *Brown Girl, Brownstones* (1959) to *The Chosen Place, The Timeless People* (1969), *Praisesong for the Widow* (1983), and *Daughters* (1991) confronts this movement between the Caribbean and North America—emotionally, physically, and politically. Her first novel, *Brown Girl, Brownstones* is about coming of age in a Barbadian family in New York as it explores the meaning of cultural differences, the relationship between mother and daughter, capitalism, and a more communal way of living. Students can read this novel or pursue some of the same questions in one of Marshall's most representative stories in this theme, "To Da-Duh, in Memoriam" (Andrews, 1992, pp. 499–508). In this story a young girl raised in New York, with its skyscrapers, subways, and physical might, must learn from her grandmother in Barbados about her experiences with canefields and a plantation economy as well as a certain dignity and heritage. The representations of America are presented through the child's eyes as she informs her grandmother, whose information is grounded in history, survival, and ancestry. It is a careful and poignant story as a little girl learns to respect what the past represents and to put it and differing landscapes into a perspective that allows respect and caring. Although Da-duh, the grandmother, dies toward the end of the narrative, her passing has the drama of a quiet dignity and its detailing of the past. Da-duh dies in the midst of a show of British military might, and the grand-daughter exiles herself, almost, to live above a noisy factory as a way of confronting the destructiveness of a certain misuse of power. Marshall often employs a female ancestor figure in her works to make the link between past and present, Africa and the New World, youth and age. Images of might, steel, factory production, technological cold-ness, and alienation appear as counterpoints.

Jamaica Kincaid represents the generation after Marshall. Many of her works are set in the Caribbean, but the novel *Lucy* (1991) de-scribes the life of a young Caribbean domestic worker in the house of a White New England couple whose marriage is falling apart. We see through her eyes the unraveling of a certain American dream that she had inevitably been fed. Kincaid's short collection, *At the Bottom of the River* (1993), and *Annie John* (1985), her novel of coming of age, are perhaps the most easily accessible to young people beginning to read this literature. The introductory piece "Girl" provides extensive dis-cussion of the codes that direct the coming-of-age of young women in numerous cultures. Some of the pieces in that early collection are well representative of magical realism. *Annie John*'s strength is that it re-turns to that model of colonial schooling and youth's various struggles to challenge its meanings, escape it, or in the worst cases make it theirs. Annie is a willfully smart child who challenges the meaning of Co-lumbus to her island, much to the teacher's chagrin. Michelle Cliff also explores some of these issues, locating most of her work in the Caribbean. *The Land of Look Behind* (1985), with prose and poetry, is an accessible text for students and teachers.

A much younger writer, Edwidge Danticat, explores well in *Breath, Eyes, Memory* (1995) the generational responses to living in Haiti at different junctures in history and migrating to North America as one still confronts the past. Woven into it is a young girl's responses to a variety of these experiences, ending with her involvement in contem-porary North American issues and contexts and witness to her mother's deterioration, which is also linked to the traumatic past.

Yanick Francois, in her poem "Amputee" (Davies & Ogundipe, 1995a), identifies being cut off from cultural knowledge and having to reclaim it through deliberate education.

Among Spanish-speaking Caribbean writers, various of takes on this relationship with the United States are also expressed. Nicholasa Mohr's *Rituals of Survival* (1986) describes a variety of Puerto Rican encounters with North America, some triumphant, others tragic. And in many ways Cristina Garcia's (1992) *Dreaming in Cuban* shares elements with Danticat regarding migration and the generational responses to it as well as the way that America is imagined and lived. The mother, Lourdes, becomes the epitome of the Cuban who buys into the North American "stars and stripes and Uncle Sam" narrative to the extreme acceptance of the capitalist ethos. She becomes a bloated, overfed, and distorted person who, in her passionate hatred of Castro, adopts the worst capitalist conduct, policing the neighborhood and her workers, enjoying the cold, and expressing dislike for her mother, who was a daughter of the revolution.

Perhaps it is in the voices of the Nuyorican poets that one gets the more direct versions of American identity. Tato Laviera's poem "AmeRican" (Lauter, 1990) plays with the idea of being Puerto Rican, as in "I Am a Rican," as it plays cleverly with American identity. It is an interesting counterpoint to Claude McKay's "America," with which this section began, and has echoes of Langston Hughes, "I Too Sing America." Louise Bennet's "Colonization in Reverse" and "America," about the various Jamaicans migrating to England and the United States, provide other aspects of this discussion. Filled with Whitmanesque cataloging and detail, the poem salutes the fact that "we gave birth to a new generation" full of diversity, bilingualism, and cultural richness that wants to speak and name itself—"defining myself my own way, any way, many ways." Still, Tato Laviera closes with a gesture of dual belonging, which has much the same tension as a "double consciousness," in the following lines:

> AmeRícan, yes, for now, for I love this, my second
>
> land, and I dream to take the accent from
>
> the altercation, and be proud to call
>
> myself American, in the U.S. sense of the
>
> word, AmeRícan, America.

## Teaching Project 6

How do you define "America?" Have students develop their own version of an "American" poem.

## Seeing the Caribbean

Scholars of Caribbean literature have identified a range of common themes that anyone encountering this literature confronts immediately. These include questions of exile, migration, colonial encounters through education and coming-of-age, and class encounters, which are often imbricated with the rural-urban movements. Kenneth Ramchand, in *The West Indian Novel and Its Background* (1970), identifies many of the traditional themes and historical issues in the development of Caribbean literature; he is an important resource in this area. Additionally, Lloyd Brown's *West Indian Poetry* (1978) is helpful as an introductory text.

Questions of identity are perennial and were initially generated from the issues of exile and displacement. A variety of early works addressed the issues of enslavement, and although there has not been a "slave narrative" tradition as there was in the United States, several texts, including the already mentioned *Equiano's Travels*, provide the context of slavery. An important text in this area is in the Spanish-speaking Caribbean *Biografia de un Cimarron* (1966), published in English as *Autobiography of a Runaway Slave* (1968), edited by anthropologist Miguel Barnet and based on the oral life story of Esteban Montejo.

The major literary movements included the early work of the Euro-Caribbean writers like H.G. de Lisser and Thomas Henry Macdermott; the precursors of the Negritude Movement in the 1920s; the work of C.L.R. James, Alfred Mendes, and others in the 1920s and 1930s, generated by their journal *New Beacon* in Trinidad; the Harlem Renaissance of the 1920s, with McKay's voice being critical; the Negritude Movement in the 1930s in France, with Leon Gontran Damas from French Guyana and Aime Cesaire of Martinique, who both provided important Caribbean responses to French colonialism and deracination; the Negrismo Movement in the Spanish Caribbean, also in the 1930s; and the tremendous outpouring of creative work beginning in the 1940s with Vic Reid's *New Day* (1949) and moving through the 1950s with George Lamming and others who migrated to London and wrote from that British context of decolonization movements. In Cuba, Nicolas Guillen's important poetic contributions would span the 1930s and 1960s, as would Alejo Carpentier's contributions. Just as significant would be Nancy Morejon's poetry in the succeeding generation, particularly with her links to African American writers in the United States and to the Anglophone Caribbean through Grenada.

The most significant development in the 1980s, in my view, is the rise of a body of Caribbean female authors, writing both at home and in a variety of locations abroad, brought together by a desire for full articulation of the variety of issues that beset the Caribbean today. Maryse Conde won the most prestigious prize, The Prix Goncourt in France for *Segu* (1987). A helpful foundational text is *Out of the Kumbla: Caribbean Women and Literature* (1990), edited by Carole Boyce Davies and Elaine Savory Fido, which first signaled this growing presence of Caribbean women's literature. Papers from the Caribbean Women Writers Conferences, such as Selwyn Cudjoe's *Caribbean Women Writers* (1990) and one forthcoming by Helen Pyne Timothy, carry a range of essays by writers and critics that has significantly expanded the contours of this literature.

It was a major landmark in the recognition of Caribbean literature when Derek Walcott, one of the Caribbean's most respected dramatists and poets, won the Nobel Prize for Literature in 1992. Whereas Walcott is significant for maintaining one version of a Caribbean aesthetic, Edward Kamau Brathwaite has been extremely significant in presenting another way of entering and recognizing Caribbean folk culture—rhythmically, with orality and voice being very significant. A number of writers in the years following Brathwaite—such as Linton Kwesi Johnson in England, Mutabaruka in Jamaica, Marlene Nourbese Philip in Toronto, and a range of other contemporary poets—have experimented with the "word."

# The Caribbean *Bildungsroman:*
# Coming of Age Under Colonialism

Among the genres, the Caribbean *bildungsroman* will perhaps provide teachers with the most reward in terms of having students exposed to the meaning of education in their and other contexts. The colonial childhood is a very common theme in Caribbean literature. Merle Hodge's *Crick Crack Monkey* (1970), which has been excerpted in *African-American Literature: Voices in a Tradition* (Andrews, 1992), explores the alienation of a young girl, Tee, who is torn between the poles of her working-class, culturally rooted family, which includes her grandmother's line from the rural area of Pointe d'Espoir (Point of Hope) and her Aunt Beatrice, a citied colonist who tries to remove Tee from that early behavior. The death of Tee's mother ushers in a crisis for her, and in the end she moves into full alienation as she migrates to England to join her father.

Another version of this Caribbean *bildungsroman* from Guyana is that of Janice Shinebourne (of Asian-Caribbean ancestry), who in *The Last English Plantation* (1988) offers an amazing exploration of colonialism, language, labor movements, and the interactions of the Indian, Asian and African populations in rural Guyana. Shinebourne's narrator is a wise young girl, June, who becomes a witness to important changes taking place in Guyana. Colonially run plantations have ended, but the residue of colonial education is brutal. Physical abuse is common in the schools and is usually meted out to poor Indian students. June rides to school and on her way takes in the landscape, the historical changes, the economic movements. She also listens to the various political debates and demonstrates an acute political sensibility, which leads her to reject her mother's prescriptions and gravitate instead to the mythology of the Indian grandmother figure, Nani, who celebrates and tells the narrative that describes Diwali, the Hindu "festival of lights." The lights, or small paper lanterns, symbolically light the path of return to the ancestral homeland in myth and history. A time at which East Indians pay off all their debts, scrub their homes from top to bottom, and settle disputes, Diwali ushers in the new year with a ritual of cleansing and rejuvenation. Above all, the holiday emphasizes the importance of exile and return. Celebrated by Hindus internationally, it is a time at which Hindu myths of gods and royalty are told. In the Caribbean, the performance of the rituals connected with Diwali functions as a way to keep the history and culture of India alive in the minds of generations of descendants of indentured laborers in the region. It is communal ritual that allows Caribbeans of East Indian descents to recall the experience of exile while simultaneously emphasizing the prospect of return through mythology, culture, history, and a commitment to survive. The work of Caribbean Asian writers is not well known but is an important portion of the literature.

More well known is the work of Indo-Caribbean writer Vidia Naipaul, including *The Mimic Men* (1967) and *A House for Mr. Biswas* (1964). These works are often taken as representative of Caribbean literature by Caribbean Indian writers. Caribbean Indian women, like Ramabai Espinet, are articulating specific questions of their gender identities as well as deploying some interesting themes in their writing (Espinet, 1992).

If multiculturalism presupposes the recognition of a variety of ethnic and cultural communities in some relational and nonhierarchical way, then it is possible to read Caribbean-/American literature as an important contribution to this discussion. Teachers, like their students, have to become informed readers, consistently expanding the horizons of their knowledge base with an increasing body of knowledge. Thus, this presupposes a point of entry through which one advances with study, conferences, workshops, and reading groups. The relationship explored here between seeing America and seeing the Caribbean—one examining texts that confront the American reality, the other examining texts that focus on the Caribbean—is what produces the ability to read Caribbean literature.

---

## Teaching Project 7

Identify one branch of Caribbean literature (linguistic, country, thematic, genre, gender, popular) and find as many writers who fit it as you can. Create a bibliography for further reading.

---

# References

*American Studies* (1996). Conference. Global Migration, American Cultures, and the State.

Andrews, W. (1992). *African American Literature: Voices in a tradition.* New York: Holt, Rinehart, & Winston.

Barnet, M. (Ed.), (1968). *Autobiography of a runaway slave.* New York: Pantheon Books.

Beckles, H., & Shepherd, V., (Eds.). (1991). *Caribbean slave society and economy.* New York: New Press.

*Biografia de un Cimaroon.* (1966). Mexico: Siglo Veintiuno Editores.

Brand, D. (1988). *Sans Souci and other stories.* Toronto, Canada: Williams Wallace.

Brathwaite, E. K. (1974, Spring). The African presence in Caribbean literature. *Daedalus, 103* (2), 73–109.

Brathwaite, E. K. (1984). *History of the voice: The development of national language in the Anglophone Caribbean.* London: New Beacon Books.

Brown, L. (1978). *West Indian poetry.* Boston: Twayne.

Brown, S. (1992). *Caribbean new wave anthology: Contemporary short stories.* Portsmouth, NH: Heinemann.

Brown, S., Morris, M., & Rohlehr, R. (Eds.). (1989). *Voiceprint. An anthology of oral and related poetry from the Caribbean.* Harlow, England: Longman.

Busby, M. (1992). *Daughters of Africa: An international anthology of words and writings by women of African descent from ancient Egypt to the present.* New York: Pantheon Books.

Cambridge, A., & Feuchtwang, S. (1992). *Where you belong.* Aldershot, England and Brookfields, MA: Avebury.

Cham, M. (Ed.) (1991). *Ex-iles: Essays on Caribbean cinema.* Trenton, NJ: Africa World Press.

Cliff, M. (1985). *The land of book behind.* New York: Firebrand Books.

Collins, M. (1987). *Angel.* Seattle: Seal Press.

Conde, M. (1987). *Segu.* New York: Viking.

Cooper, C. (1995). *Noises in the blood: Orality, gender, and the "vulgar" body of Jamaican popular culture.* Durham, NC: Duke University Press.

Cudjoe, S. (1990). *Caribbean women writers: Essays from the First International Conference.* Wellesley, MA: Calaloux.

Dabydeen, D., & Tagoe, N. W. (1987). *A reader's guide to West Indian and Black British literature.* Coventry, England: Rutherford/Dangaroo Press.

Danticat, E. (1995). *Breath, eyes, memory.* New York: Vintage.

Danticat, E. (1996). *Krik? Krak!* New York: Vintage.

Davies, C. B. (1994). *Migrations of the subject. Black women, writing and identity.* New York: Routledge.

Davies, C. B., & Fido, E. S. (1990). *Out of the Kumbla: Caribbean women and literature.* Trenton, NJ: Africa World Press.

Davies, C. B., & Ogundipe, L. M. (1995a). *Moving beyond boundaries: International dimensions of Black women's writing.* London: Pluto Press.

Davies, C. B., & Ogundipe, L. M. (1995b). *Moving beyond boundaries: Black women's diasporas.* New York: New York University Press.

Delaney, M. (1861/1970). *Blake or the huts of America.* Boston: Beacon Press.

Donnell, A., & Welsh, S. L. (1996). *The Routledge reader in Caribbean literature.* New York: Routledge.

Espinet, R. (Ed.). (1992). *Creation fire. A CAFRA anthology of Caribbean women's poetry.* Toronto, Canada: Sister Vision Press.

Equiano, O. (1789/1996). *The interesting narrative of the life of Olaudah Equiano, or Gustavus Vassa, the African.* Portsmouth, NH: Heinemann.

Garcia, C. (1992). *Dreaming in Cuban.* New York: Knopf.

Glissant, E. (1992). *Caribbean discourse: Selected essays.* Charlottesville, VA: University Press of Virginia.

Goulbourne, H. (1993). *Ethnicity and nationalism in post-imperial Britain.* Cambridge, England: Cambridge University Press.

Guy, R. (1973). *Friends.* New York: Bantam.

Guy, R. (1983). *Ruby.* New York: Bantam.

Herdeck, D.E. (1979). *Caribbean writers: A bio-bibliographical critical encyclopedia.* Washington, DC: Three Continents Press.

Hurston, Z. (1990). *Their eyes were watching God.* New York: Perennial Library.

James, W., & Harris, C. (1993). *Inside Babylon: The Caribbean diaspora in Britain.* New York: Verso.

Jordan, J. (1992). *Technical difficulties: African-American notes on the state of the Union.* New York: Pantheon Books.

Kincaid, J. (1985). *Annie John.* New York: Farrar, Straus, Giroux.

Kincaid, J. (1991). *Lucy.* New York: Farrar, Straus, Giroux.

Kincaid, J. (1993). *At the bottom of the river.* New York: Farrar, Straus, Giroux.

Knight, F., & Palmer, C. (Eds.). (1989). *The modern Caribbean.* Chapel Hill, NC: University of North Carolina Press.

Lamming, G. (1992). *The pleasures of exile.* Ann Arbor, MI: University of Michigan Press.

Lauter, P. (Ed.). (1990). *The Heath anthology of American literature.* Lexington, MA: Heath.

Lovelace, E. (1979). *The wine of astonishment*. Portsmouth, NH: Heinemann.

Marshall, P. (1959). *Brown girl, brownstones*. New York: Random House.

Marshall, P. (1969). *The chosen place, the timeless people*. New York: Vintage.

Marshall, P. (1983a). *Praisesong for the widow*. New York: Putnam.

Marshall, P. (1983b). *Reena and other stories*. New York: Feminist Press.

Marshall, P. (1983c). *Soul clap hands and sing*. Washington, D. C.: Howard University Press.

Marshall, P. (1991). *Daughters*. New York: Plume.

Martin, M. (Ed.). (1995). *Cinemas of the Black diaspora*. Detroit, MI: Wayne State University Press.

Martin, T. (1983). *Literary Garveyism: Garvey, Black arts and the Harlem renaissance*. Dover, MA: Majority Press.

Mbye, C. (Ed). (1992). *Ex-Iles: Essays on Caribbean cinema*. Trenton, NJ: Africa World Press.

McKay, C. (1928). *Home to Harlem*. New York: Harper.

McKay, C. (1937/1970). *A long way from home*. New York: Harcourt, Brace, & World.

McKay, C. (1928/1992). America. In W. Andrews, *African American Literature: Voices in a tradition* (p. 298). New York: Holt, Rinehart, & Winston.

Mohr, N. (1986). *Rituals of survival: A woman's portfolio*. Houston, TX: Arté Publico Press.

Momsen, J. H. (Ed.). (1993). *Women and change in the Caribbean*. London: James Currey.

Mordecai, P., & Wilson, B. (1989). *Her true-true name: An anthology of women's writing from the Caribbean*. Portsmouth, NH: Heinemann.

Naipaul, V. (1964). *A house for Mr. Biswas*. London: Deutsch.

Naipaul, V. (1967). *The mimic men*. New York: Macmillan.

Philip, M. N. (1990). The abscence of writing or how I almost became a spy. In C.B. Davies & Fido, E. S. (Eds.). *Out of the Kumbla: Caribbean women and literature*. (pp. 217–278). Trenton, NJ: Africa World Press.

Ramchand, K. (1970). *The West Indian novel and its background*. London: Heinemann.

Samuel, W. (1977). Five Afro-Caribbean voices in American culture, 1917–1929: Hubert H. Harrison, Wildred A. Domingo, Richard B. Moore, Cyril V. Briggs, and Claude McKay. (Doctoral dissertation, University of Iowa, 1990). *Dissertation Abstracts International, 38-07A,* 4324, 00181.

Shohat, E., & Stam, R. (1994). *Unthinking Eurocentricism: Multiculturalism and the media.* New York: Routledge.

Shinebourne, J. (1988). *The last English plantation.* Leeds, England: Peepal Tree Press.

Smorkaloff, P. (Ed.). (1994). *If I could write this in fire: An anthology of literature from the Caribbean.* New York: New Press.

Walcott, R. (1995). Performing the postmodern: Black Atlantic rap and identity in North America. (Doctoral dissertation, University of Toronto, 1995). *Dissertation Abstracts International, 57–08A,* 3695, 00266.

Walker, D. J. R. (1991). *Columbus and the golden world of the island Arawaks: The story of the first Americans and their Caribbean environment.* Kingston, Jamaica: Ian Randle.

## Chapter 9

# Negotiating the Classroom: Learning and Teaching Multicultural Literature

*Arlette Ingram Willis* and *Marlen Diane Palmer*

Despite its rich and varied history, multicultural literature has not become a substantive portion of the required reading in either university teacher preparation or secondary curricula (Applebee, 1989; Graff, 1992). The English curricula in both reflect the Western canon and are not representative of the lives of all Americans. Nationwide critics of the exclusive use of canonical literature have called for the inclusion of multicultural literature. This chapter will not continue the debate but offers ways to move beyond the canon by suggesting ways in which multicultural literature can be approached. The chapter is divided into two distinct sections. The first section, by Willis, offers a model for approaching the teaching of multicultural literature in a college course. The second section, by Palmer, describes one high school English teacher's quest from learning to teaching multicultural literature. Both sections are designed as "starting points" for instructors to begin to think about and create their own multicultural literature courses.

## A University Methods Course in Teaching Multicultural Literature

Over the last several years, I have taken a critical look at the learning and teaching of multicultural literature. It is widely acknowledged that "teachers need additional cultural and social knowledge as they work with increasing numbers of students from varied cultural and linguistic backgrounds" (Diamond & Moore, 1995, p. xi). Where will teachers get such knowledge? bell hooks (1993) suggests:

> Most of us were taught in classrooms where styles of teaching reflected the notion of a single norm of thought and experience, which we were encouraged to believe was a universal norm. This has been just as true for non-White teachers as for White teachers. Most of us learned to teach emulating this model. As a consequence many teachers are disturbed by the political implications of a multicultural education because they fear losing control in the classroom where there is no one way to approach a subject but multiple ways with multiple references. (p. 91)

Preservice education appears to many educators to be the optimal time and place to start training future teachers to broaden their understanding, awareness, and sensitivities to the rich diversity that makes America such a unique country. In this section I share the lessons that I have learned as I have watchfully learned and taught multicultural literature to English education majors for several years. There are no mysteries or big secrets here; there is a real call, however, for respect, responsibility, and relevance. Teaching multicultural literature requires (a) a greater understanding of self, history, and the interwoven nature of culture, language, and literature than is found in either a syllabus or a list of readings; (b) an understanding of the sociohistorical and sociocultural events that have given rise to multicultural literature; (c) a willingness to unlearn biases, prejudices, and stereotypes; (d) developing a cultural consciousness that responses to difference in a sensitive and thoughtful manner; (e) addressing a history of dominant ideologies and White privilege in educational circles; and (f) a commitment to teaching and using multicultural literature for improved educational equity. hooks (1993) is correct; there is a great deal of fear associated with teaching multicultural education courses and literature. To begin anew demands the reconceptualization of the teaching of literature and the selection of a new body of literature; it suggests that the current literature is not sufficient to meet everyone's needs. Moreover, there is the tacit assumption that the past hegemonic forces that have helped to retain the canon must be dismantled and replaced with new, more democratic, inclusive forces. There are, of course, opposing points of view on how to best proceed or if there is even a need to proceed at all. At the center of the controversy is literature itself.

## The Canon Is Alive and Well

Within the literacy education community, there has been an ongoing, heated debate on the literature to be used in the classroom. The debate, which has occurred at the high school and college levels, has outspoken proponents of retaining the canon (Bloom, 1987; Hirsch, 1987; D'Sousa, 1991) and opponents who suggest a multicultural list of alternative works (Applebee, 1989; Gates, 1992; Harris, 1992; Au, 1993). At issue is the retention of the traditional canon or its expansion to include works by women and people of color. Retention of the canon means the continued use of the same "classic" literature that has been the staple for nearly a century. Reconceptualization of the canon means, among other things, the inclusion of what is commonly defined as multicultural literature. Multicultural literature is written by African, Asian, Native, Caribbean, and Latino Americans and offers a broad range of gender, class, language, geographical, and age representations. How far have we come as a community of literacy educators to creating a more inclusive body of literature? Let's look to what research has to say about what books have been read and will continue to be read as the core of the English/Language Arts curriculum.

We'll begin this journey by reviewing the research at the college level that has examined the literature in the English Language Arts curriculum. Gerald Graff's nationwide survey (1992) of undergraduate English curricula suggests that there has been little substantive change in the literature offered to English majors in the last 20 years. In addition, Sustein and Smith (1994), in a review of English methods courses, found that decisions on whether to teach the canon have been ongoing for more than 75 years. Karen Peterson's article (1994) on a recent survey by The College Board found the following 20 books were most frequently recommended for high school seniors and college freshmen: *The Scarlet Letter, Huckleberry Finn, The Great Gatsby, Lord of the Flies, Great Expectations, Hamlet, To Kill a Mockingbird, The Grapes of Wrath, The Odyssey, Wuthering Heights, The Catcher in the Rye, The Crucible, Gulliver's Travels, Julius Caesar, Of Mice and Men, The Old Man and the Sea, Pride and Prejudice, The Red Badge of Courage, Romeo and Juliet,* and *Death of a Salesman.* A quick glance at the titles reveals that the list favors the literature of European or European-American men and includes only three titles by women. The list does not include any works by authors from historically underrepresented groups.

At the secondary level, the most current and comprehensive look at literature in the curriculum was completed by Arthur Applebee in *Literature in the Secondary School: Studies of Curriculum and Instruction in the United States* (1993). In the paper he shares portions of the findings from his nationwide survey of the literature taught in our nation's high schools. He observed the continual use of works by Shakespeare, Steinbeck, Dickens, and Twain yet few works by women and minority authors. Further analysis by Applebee of his findings reveals only one European American female author and two African American authors (one female, one male) among the top 50 listed authors. Applebee (1991) suggests that "whether intentional or not, schools have chosen to ignore diversity and assimilate everyone to the 'classical' culture that found its way into schools before the turn of the century" (p. 235). Applebee's suggestions for change include the challenge of expanding the canon to be more reflective of the history, life experiences, culture, and literature of all Americans. He argues that the expansion of the canon begin with preservice programs that require students to read and discuss book-length works written by authors of underrepresented groups. Moreover, Applebee suggests that preservice English courses may help students develop a repertoire of effective teaching strategies to use when teaching the literature.

While in agreement with Applebee, I submit that his suggestions for canon expansion do not acknowledge the need for an increased understanding of the role of history, culture, and ideology in multicultural literature instruction. I suggest that although it is important to expand the canon, expansion without a sufficient understanding of the role of the hegemonic forces that have disserved people of color and women will mislead students and offer preservice teachers inadequate knowledge, understanding, and sensitivities by which to instruct students. Further, I believe that such knowledge must become an integral part of the methodology used to teach multicultural literature. There is a growing body of research that suggests there are distinct understandings, knowledge, and skills that need to be nurtured before teachers attempt to teach multicultural literature. The research indicates that preservice education offers an ideal time for fostering the multicultural awareness, understanding, and sensitivities needed for teaching multicultural literature.

# Teaching Multicultural Literature

Katherine Au (1993) has observed that most preservice teacher education courses are dominated by traditional transmission models of literacy instruction that support a mainstream middle-class perspective of literacy and inadequately address the needs of culturally or linguistically diverse students. Several researchers—Barrera (1992), Ladson-Billings (1994), and Diamond and Moore (1995), among others—have conducted studies that examine the use of multicultural literature in schools. The research on teaching and learning multicultural literature more frequently raises questions and concerns than offers solutions. Enciso (1997) articulates some of the key questions as centering on "how we construct differences and how we enacted and continue to enact social practices related to differences" (p. 14). A review of the studies that focus on the use of multicultural literature during preservice education reveals that researchers have examined the use of reader response to multicultural literature as a means of increasing individual and multicultural awareness, understanding, and sensitivities.

The findings from this body of literature are far from conclusive. On the one hand, some researchers (Flood, Lapp, & VanDyke 1996; Klinger, 1996; Willis, 1997), using reader response approaches to multicultural literature, have found that college students who read multicultural literature during preservice education have increased their awareness, understanding, and sensitivity to multicultural literature as a result of participating in reader response approaches. These researchers suggest that reading multicultural literature can (a) improve understanding of self and others, (b) foster acceptance of multiple interpretations of literature, (c) lead to behavioral and attitudinal changes, and (d) enable preservice teachers to effectively teach multicultural literature. On the other hand, some researchers (Beach, 1994; Jordan & Purves, 1993) also using reader response approaches to multicultural literature have noted enhanced biases and resistance by participants in responding to multicultural literature. These researchers suggest that the resistance of some students may be due to instructional approaches to teaching multicultural literature and insufficient teacher knowledge.

## Selected Activities and Instructional Strategies for Learning and Teaching Multicultural Literature

Literacy methods courses in learning and teaching multicultural literature during preservice education can offer an excellent starting point to develop this understanding, knowledge, and skill. In such courses prospective teachers can learn to examine their own cultural and linguistic assumptions, confront their biases, and learn skills and practices that will enable them to respond to the literacy needs of all children in culturally sensitive and responsive ways. Banks (1994) describes the exposure to a multicultural perspective during preservice training as a way "to examine and clarify their recall and ethnic attitudes, and to develop the pedagogical knowledge and skills needed to work effectively with students from diverse cultural and ethnic groups" (p. vi). Students are encouraged to move beyond generic references to culture and learn about the specific historical, cultural, social, and ideological contexts that have given rise to minority cultures' languages and literature. Banks (1994) suggests:

> When teachers have gained knowledge about cultural and ethnic diversity themselves, looked at that knowledge from different ethnic and cultural perspectives, and taken action to make their own lives and communities more culturally sensitive and diverse, they will have the knowledge and skills needed to help transform the curriculum canon as well as the hearts and minds of their students. (p. 28)

Banks is not alone in his desire to acknowledge the need for increased understanding in teaching children from linguistically and culturally diverse backgrounds. The recent National Council of Teachers of English/International Reading Association (1996) national standards for the English Language Arts make several important suggestions regarding the teaching of literacy that are in concert with more inclusive literature and literacy instruction. Specifically, standard numbers

1, 2, 3, 9, and 10 acknowledge and ask for greater understanding of the languages, prior experiences, and literature of all the cultures that are part of the cultural fabric of the United States:

1. Students read a wide range of print and nonprint texts to build an understanding of texts, of themselves, and of the cultures of the United States and the world; to acquire new information; to respond to the needs and demands of society and the workplace; and for personal fulfillment. Among these texts are fiction and nonfiction, classic and contemporary works.

2. Students read a wide range of multicultural literature from many periods in many genres to build an understanding of the many dimensions (e.g., philosophical, ethical, aesthetic) of human experience.

3. Students apply a wide range of strategies to comprehend, interpret, evaluate, and appreciate texts. They draw on their prior experience, their interactions with other readers and writers, their knowledge of word meaning and of other texts, their word identification strategies, and their understanding of textual features (e.g., sound-letter correspondence, sentence structure, context, graphics).

9. Students develop an understanding of and respect for diversity in language use, patterns, and dialects across cultures, ethnic groups, geographic regions, and social roles.

10. Students whose first language is not English make use of their first language to develop competency in English-language arts and to develop an understanding of content across the curriculum.

How can university courses in literacy methods begin to address the multiple interwoven needs of preservice teacher educators? Below I offer a suggestion; it is, at best, a place to start. Many of the instructional strategies and activities outlined can be used at the high school level as well. There is no magic formula and no secret potions; there are only people who have a broader sense of vision, who are willing to take risks, and who really care about changing the status quo so that all students and their backgrounds are affirmed, welcomed, celebrated, and honored.

## The University Classroom: A Place to Start

The literacy courses I teach offer a variety of learning experiences for students designed and sequenced to nurture the ability to think critically and reflectively about the integrated nature of culture, knowledge, language, and literature. Learning about and teaching multicultural literature requires much more than the accumulation of cultural knowledge, literacy knowledge, and literacy strategies and activities. The course begins by encouraging students to understand themselves as cultural beings within a multicultural society and what that understanding means as they look forward to teaching literacy and literature. I take a decidedly critical, theoretical and pedagogical approach to learning and teaching multicultural literature. The approach itself speaks to the need to consider the multiple discourses on literacy education available to teachers. The following literacy strategies have been gleaned from the research of several leaders in the field of literacy education. A word of caution is needed, however, for I am not suggesting a set of "how-to" rules for teaching multicultural literature. I am sharing instructional strategies and activities that have proven helpful in encouraging students to adopt a more critical understanding of multicultural literature. Listed below are several such literacy strategies and activities:

1. I begin by creating an atmosphere where it is safe to share who you are and what you believe without fear of reprisal. Next, I work at creating an understanding of colearnership within the classroom. I understand that my roles as teacher, colearner, and listener are exemplified in the term *facilitator*. I do not adopt an explicit nonauthoritative stance, for I have not progressed to a point where I can completely relinquish my roles or responsibilities as teacher and teacher educator. However, a conscious effort is made to create a safe, comfortable atmosphere during the first few weeks so that students can share with each other in an environment in which all will listen and respond in supportive manners.

2. Students begin by participating in the course during the first few moments of class. They are called upon to rearrange the furniture and write their names on the board. Each student is encouraged to participate in all classroom activities (Shor, 1987). I too partici-

pate in all classroom activities from the first day. I move among groups throughout the semester and become a learner when literacy lessons are taught. Participatory dialogue among class members begins on the first day of class. I clearly state that we are all learners and teachers, with different backgrounds, experiences, values, and beliefs to share. Later in the course, I gradually transfer much of the responsibility for class content and discussion to the students. Thus, students become active, critical constructors of our multicultural community.

3. Students respond to the following question on the first day of class: "How do your cultural perspectives affect the students you teach?" Following Hansen-Krening's technique (1992), students are asked to respond to the same question on the final day of class. The responses are later compared to chart changes in perspective as a result of participation in the course.

4. Students are asked to explore their own ethnicities through writing an autobiographical essay that becomes part of classroom discussions over the next few weeks. Research by Shor (1987) and Stimac and Hughes (1995) suggests that this practice is useful in helping students to better understand their own and others' cultural heritage. In addition, the autobiographical essays are used to help students begin to address their sense of cultural consciousness. Bennett (1995) defines *cultural consciousness* as "an awareness of one's own worldview and how it has developed and an understanding that one's personal view of the world is profoundly different from the views of people from different cultures" (p. 261). Moreover, I use dialogue strategies to help students demystify notions of cultural neutrality among Whites and cultural inferiority of people of color as students share their cultural heritage in small groups. It is difficult to move students to begin to publicly share private conversations about race, class, and gender, but it is one of the most important tasks in a multicultural course.

5. Students are also asked to write a biography of the school literacy experience. Research by Britzman (1986), Delpit (1988), and King (1991) has shown that many preservice teachers are unaware of the role that dominant values have played in privileging some groups over others in school literacy acquisition.

6. Students are asked to individually define commonly used yet often misunderstood terms in multicultural education. This activity is followed by small-group and large-group discussions of their definitions. Next, students are asked to canvass the campus, seeking definitions of the same words from the "person on the street." Students return to class and share their respondents' definitions. Finally, definitions are compared and contrasted with those offered by experts in the field. This is another opportunity for students to talk about notions of difference and to learn to communicate their ideas.

7. Students select a "popular" text on the issues of race, culture, or multicultural education. Students select from works by Bell, Eldman, Delany, Giovanni, Kotlowitz, Kozol, Ladson-Billings, Pipher, Schleisinger, and West.

8. After writing, reading, talking, and viewing issues of diversity, we move into a theoretical discussion of teaching literature. For example, students read works by Atwell, Au, Delpit, Freire, Heath, and Rosenblatt, among others.

9. I adapted a method of literature exploration created by Dorothy Mathews, an award-winning college instructor at the University of Illinois at Urbana-Champaign. Mathews allowed one entire semester for the study of a selected novel. In my classes, students begin their reading of the multicultural literature after small groups (four or five students) select novels to be read from a predetermined list created by the instructor. The list of novels consist of titles written by male and female representatives of each domestic minority group. Student selections have to be balanced by gender and cultural group. Literature written by European Americans is also included. It is important not to dismiss the ethnic diversity of European Americans.

    Much like Nanci Atwell's students' choice of novels (1987), the group choice allows small groups of readers to come to consensus about the multicultural novels to be read. However, unlike Atwell's notion, I use an approach I call "freedom within structure." Using a slightly altered set of guidelines for selecting multicultural literature (adjusted to the high school level, written by Rudine Sims Bishop in 1992), I create a list of multicultural titles from which small groups select 10 novels to read. The titles are gleaned from my own reading or suggested by local high school teachers. The freedom comes in student choice, and the structure comes from the guidelines and my own reading of multicultural literature. This format allows me to be able to respond, if only mentally, to student reader responses. In addition, in making my selections I include novels that have been banned in some areas or are considered controversial in nature. I "plant" these novels on my list in an effort to elicit classroom discussion about developmental appropriateness, censorship, and cultural boundaries.

10. The literature groups read and respond to the novels they have collectively agreed to read. Students share their written reader responses with one another in their small group. It is important that students are given opportunities to discuss their responses to the readings with others who have read the same novel. This small-group discussion also allows students to hear multiple interpretations of the same novel.

    Students may alter their written responses if they so desire after the small group has shared and discussed the novel. Research by Flood, Lapp, and Ranck-Buhr (1995) and Spears-Bunton (1992), among others, has shown that dialogue helps to foster a greater understanding of multicultural literature.

11. Preservice teachers need more than a list of multicultural books to read and discuss; they also need specific information about the historical, social, cultural, and ideological contexts in which to understand multicultural literature. In my courses students learn this information as part of their teaching responsibilities. Each member of the literature groups is responsible for helping to create a packet of information on the novel for their classmates. The novel packet consists of a summary of the novel, a biography of the author, a list of pertinent historical facts and events that occurred when the novel was written and that cover the time period discussed in the novel, cultural information that may improve understanding of the novel, at least two book reviews of the novel, and a literacy lesson about the novel with supporting materials. The novel packets become a quick resource of activities and information on multicultural literature. The titles listed are merely representative of the plethora of multicultural literature available. I have divided the titles according to cultural groups because I be-

lieve that learning about multicultural literature requires that students read widely in the literature of each domestic minority group before they begin to approach the more popular notions of thematic literature study.

What do students take from this course? An excerpt from a letter written by one of my former Euro-American male students during his student teaching illustrates an outcome:

> My two senior American Literature classes are studying *Huck Finn* this week. An important point that needs be mentioned here is that there are no African-Americans in either of my classes. On Monday, to start out the week, since I knew at some time the issues of race and ethnicity and the banning of the book would come out, I decided to have the class define a few terms: *prejudice, stereotype, race, discrimination, racist,* and *racism.* This was not meant to be a complete treatment of all words that connote racism, but a start. Both classes had interesting discussions of the terms and the variety of definitions was huge . . . as I expected. It served the point of the lesson well.
>
> Tuesday began with a review of the definitions that the students discussed and then an open floor discussion. In both classes the whole-class discussions got into fairly heated exchanges about race, affirmative action, and how people can get out of a bad situation (e.g., the projects, the ghetto). What came out of this was an us-them mentality, and many students were blaming the African-Americans and saying the African-Americans were blaming them. It appeared (and I could be wrong) that they have no idea what it's like to experience racism or what it's like to be continually beat down time and again. Wednesday, we continued the Tuesday discussion and moved into why *Huck Finn* should or should not be banned. One class, in discussing the banning of *Huck Finn* because of the term "nigger," discussed whether the power is from the speaker or the listener, as well as numerous other things. My second class discussed racial problems at our high school and the sexism they've encountered. The students also said there was a double standard based on race, where minorities can get away with things that Whites can not. There was even more us-them attitude.

Tomorrow my co-op and I arranged to have a guest speaker in both of the classes. The main things that I have stressed these last three days are to open a dialogue about racial and ethnic issues so that people can feel comfortable talking, and if they are experiencing racism or sexism directed toward them, they should do whatever is necessary to stop it, even if it means going to court.

I don't think I would have been able to have these discussions in my literature classes had it not been for our class in multicultural literature. I knew how I wanted to approach the text, what information needed to be discussed early on and in a straightforward manner, and how to respond to students who did not share my opinions.

In conclusion, I hope others will begin to make changes in how they approach, select, and teach multicultural literature at every level. My use of each of the above literacy strategies and activities has proven successful in expanding preservice educators' sense of vision. As I warn them, this is merely a starting point. Their challenge is to take what they've learned into their classrooms and create a more just and democratic learning environment.

# Multicultural Literature for High School Freshmen

In school, students learn that America is a "melting pot," a land that has embraced people from many different lands as well as those indigenous to the land. The non-European immigrants came for various reasons, ranging from abject poverty to slavery. While they became part of the fabric of this country, they also retained much of their culture through successive generations. The same is true for Native Americans; they too have struggled to retain their cultural heritages, often under adverse conditions. These rich and varied cultures make these groups unique and, as such, often misunderstood. Unfortunately, misunderstanding can lead to fear and prejudice, especially in populations with little or no exposure to these cultures.

To combat this fear and prejudice and to increase the understanding and appreciation of cultural differences, schools need to educate students about our domestic minority cultures. One way this can be accomplished is through a careful selection of multicultural literature to teach in the English classroom. When selecting literature, a teacher needs to find material that represents a given culture, provides an avenue for meaningful discussion, and is age-appropriate.

The following model for research is the technique taught by my coauthor, Dr. Willis. As part of the teacher's research into a piece of literature, he or she should compile a biographical sketch of the author, a historical review of the setting, a historical review of the period in which the author wrote, and a listing of cultural footnotes to enhance an understanding of the novel. An author's biography can reveal, at least in part, why an author has written about a particular group of people. The historical review of the setting can help to explain why certain events are recounted or how they happened within the context of the times. The historical review of the period in which a piece of literature is written may possibly help a teacher to understand if events of the time motivate or color an author's literary expression. Finally, cultural footnotes provide teachers with an in-depth understanding of an unfamiliar culture and allow teachers to provide themselves and their students with a better understanding of the culture under study.

What follows is my search for multicultural literature for high school freshmen in a rural Midwest school, using the aforementioned format. Novels by African American, Latino American, Asian/Pacific American, and Native American authors were chosen as a starting point for the selection of a novel for my freshman class because these cultures represent the four largest non-European groups, according to the 1990 U.S. census. Tom Poston's autobiographical short stories, *The Dark Side of Hopkinsville* (1991) edited by K. Hauke, tells of growing up Black in a small Kentucky town prior to World War I. In *Bless Me, Ultima* (1972), Rudolpho Anaya recounts the story of a young Mexican boy's struggle to understand his Catholic faith and his familial heritage at the end of World War II. Jeanne Wakatsuki Houston and her husband James tell of Jeanne's childhood experiences at the Manzanar internment camp during World War II in *Farewell to Manzanar* (1973). The final novel, *Two Old Women* (1993) by Velma Wallis, is an Athabascan tale of indomitable courage and survival in Alaska prior to the advent of European culture.

# My Quest

My search for appropriate multicultural literature was inspired by the rural setting in which I teach. While I have been exposed to many cultures over the years, my students have not. I am a secondary school English teacher in a small agricultural community in east central Illinois, 120 miles from the closest large metropolis. The student population averages between 250 and 300 students. Typically, many of these students will remain within the area as adults. Because of this and because the community is virtually devoid of ethnic diversity, I feel that it is particularly important that my students are exposed to other cultures through literature.

The view that America is a "melting pot" has been reinforced by governmental policies and religious fervor as a vision of assimilation. However, this vision has done a disservice to minority populations. Too often minorities have been denied their cultural heritages for the sake of conformity. In a land that prides itself on individuality, this is ironic. Perhaps it would be better if America were thought of as a "rich, flavorful stew," with each ingredient enriching the broth yet remaining distinct from the other ingredients.

Fortunately, over the past several decades educational institutions have slowly acknowledged the importance of ethnic pride and the retention of ethnic heritage. They also acknowledge that it is important for students to learn tolerance and respect for other cultures. At the college level, ethnic studies have been initiated and courses with multicultural literature have been introduced. In the public school system, students are now beginning to read multicultural literature. Certainly, schools are an excellent vehicle to begin developing an appreciation of individual cultures in students; however, teachers need to carefully select appropriate literature and then become "comfortable" with the culture.

Granted, the demands on a teacher's time are great, and he or she needs to use discretion when investing time in classroom preparation. But teaching literature about another culture requires an investment of time. In the past, I have used and depended upon publishers for materials to present literature in the classroom. While this has worked for Western literature, I have discovered that, though helpful, this material is insufficient when teaching literature of other cultures.

The effective presentation of a particular piece of multicultural literature requires more than a superficial knowledge of the author's background and the times in which the novel is set and was written. Through my study of these novels, I discovered a sense of time, place, and people that I had never experienced before. I have found my "comfort" level and have discovered novels appropriate for freshmen English students.

Poston's short story collection has humorous appeal. The stories read much like episodes of Bill Cosby's "Fat Albert." On one level, Poston recounts the innocent escapades of his youth. Male students in particular can relate to the adventures of the young boys. Yet on a more subtle level, Poston presents a firsthand or insider account of the life of the African American community; the "darker side of Hopkinsville." His experiences growing up in a racially segregated town depict life in the segregated Black community and his understanding of life in the segregated White community. The author's deft handling of these issues presents ample opportunity for topical discussion without bludgeoning the students. This humor can open minds which might otherwise remain closed. Unfortunately, the collection is no longer in print. However, the local library does have it. With a borrowed copy, teachers can present the collection in its historical context and then read one or more stories aloud for an effective presentation and cultural discussion of Poston's work.

Like Poston's work, Anaya's *Bless Me, Ultima* would be an excellent addition to a suggested reading list for high school students, but I do not think it is appropriate for freshman classroom study. Certainly, the maturation theme and the cultural insights would work well at this level, but the unique blending of Latin American Catholicism and superstition as another major theme limits the novel's use in the classroom. This is especially true in the rural setting in which I teach, because a significant number of my students are Catholics. Although I would feel comfortable suggesting that mature students read the novel, I would not feel comfortable teaching it. Therefore, I will continue my search for appropriate Latino literature.

Of the four novels I researched, *Farewell to Manzanar* is the most timely. The year 1995 marked the 50th anniversary of the Japanese surrender in World War II. It also marks the freeing of Japanese Americans from American detention camps, ending a shameful moment in

American history. However, it is not just timely in a historical sense but in a modern sense as well. The novel shows students that the Constitution, although written to protect the rights of the individual, has not always guaranteed protection. Thus, as future voters and responsible citizens, they need to examine issues rationally to avoid ethnocentric hysteria. Much like literature about the Holocaust, stories like this need to be read and discussed by students "lest we forget" the lessons of the past.

The final novel, *Two Old Women,* also deals with topical subjects. On the most obvious level, it is an adventure story similar to Jack London's tales of survival. However, it is much more than an adventure, for interwoven throughout the text are themes that offer rich discussion for high school students at any level. Although the tale is of another time and people, Wallis presents themes pertinent to today. Perhaps the most obvious theme is the treatment of the elderly in a Native American culture that can be compared with the treatment of the elderly in mainstream American society. A second theme is gender roles in both societies, and the similarities in each. The final theme reflects a contemporary concern for the value of community and its importance to the survival of a society. Overall, the novel is an enjoyable reading experience, rich in themes for classroom discussion.

Having found good literature, it was time to make the final selection. For me, the selection chosen needed to provide the greatest potential for ties within my freshman curriculum and to the school's curriculum. For these reasons I chose *Farewell to Manzanar.* Because of my research, I knew that media and institutional propaganda was an integral part of the Japanese American experience during World War II. *Farewell to Manzanar* was a natural choice to follow my unit on media propaganda. The novel also presented a different facet of the events of World War II from those presented in Modern American History courses or in senior English's study of Holocaust literature. In addition, I found another cross-curricular tie—the state-mandated Constitution course taken by my students either at freshman or sophomore level. Thus, *Farewell to Manzanar* suited my criteria best. The fall 1995 semester was my first foray into teaching multicultural literature in my classroom with the inclusion of *Farewell to Manzanar* by Jeanne Wakatsuki Houston and James D. Houston.

*Biography*   This biographical sketch will focus on Jeanne and not her husband, for it is her story under study. According to *Contemporary Authors* (1990), Jeanne, one of 10 children, was born to Ko and Riku Wakatsuki in September of 1934. Her father immigrated to the United States in 1904 and was therefore an *issei*, or first-generation person, whose occupation was fisherman. Her mother was a *nisei*, or second-generation person, the daughter of an Oregon farmer.

Until 1942 Jeanne attended the local school in Ocean Park, California, where her father fished in the coastal waters (Houston & Houston, 1973). From 1942 unto 1945, Jeanne was educated in the internment camp at Manzanar. She reentered public school in Long Beach, California, after release from the camp. Jeanne received her bachelor's degree from the University of San Jose, where she studied sociology and journalism. This is also where she met her husband, James. According to the short biographical notes at the end of the novel, Jeanne and James attended the Sorbonne in Paris after he finished his service in the military.

Jeanne has worked as both a probation officer and a college administrator. She is also a writer and playwright. Although best known for her work on the novel and the screenplay, *Farewell to Manzanar*, she has also written a teleplay, *Barrio*, with James and several nonfiction works. Jeanne, the mother of three, currently resides in Santa Cruz, California, with James.

*Historical Review of the Setting*   The autobiographical novel opens on the morning of the attack on Pearl Harbor as the Wakatsuki men leave the harbor for a day of fishing. As the story progresses the reader learns how one Japanese family is affected by this event and the ensuing isolation by internment and the years immediately following World War II. However, the story does not follow a completely chronological chain of events, for interspersed throughout are short vignettes touching on prior family history. This history is important, for it explains not only the actions and attitudes of various family members but also the history of the Japanese, from *issei* to *sensei* (immigrant to third-generation Japanese American). Therefore, what follows is not a recounting of just the war years but also the earlier years, when attitudes and patterns were established.

According to Marsha James and Cecelia Munzenmaier (1993), the Japanese immigration that began in the late 1800s peaked between the years of 1900 and 1920. People were lured to America by promises of land and a bright future (Hamanaka, 1990). However, the Euro-Americans on the West Coast were enraged by the Asian immigration, perceiving them as the "Yellow Peril." To avoid an international incident and to counteract the wave of immigration, President Roosevelt entered into "a Gentleman's Agreement with Japan to limit immigration to the United States" in 1908 (James & Munzenmaier, 1993, p. 15).

This agreement did not end or lessen the prejudice. In fact, it increased it. In 1913 the Alien Land Bill was passed, denying the right to own land or a business in California to anyone not eligible to be an American citizen (Hamanaka, 1990). The bill, directly affecting Japanese immigrants, was based on the federal Naturalization Law of 1790, which stated that only White immigrants could become U.S. citizens. By 1924 negative attitudes toward Asian immigration became so entrenched that Congress denied citizenship to aliens and passed the Immigration Exclusion Act. This act closed the door to Asian immigration for many years (James & Munzenmaier, 1993). In effect, these events barred the *issei* from participating in the "American Dream" and attempted to relegate them to menial occupations, especially in California.

These discriminatory laws, however, did not prevent the *issei* and later the *nisei* from gaining some economic success under these adverse conditions. They circumvented restrictions by leasing land and developing truck farming, which became a fairly lucrative business. They also began service occupations in urban areas. The majority of these businesses took the form of lunch counters, laundries, cleaners, barber shops, and gardening (Kitano, 1976). The success of all these ventures was based upon the unique family and community solidarity which the Japanese maintained in this country.

Japanese ethics demanded that individuals support each other. This support system was a cultural phenomenon incorporated in all facets of life, not just in economics. At the center of this philosophy was religion and family. The Buddhist religion, unlike Christianity, was not an institution but the teachings of an ethical code of behavior. This ethical code focused on behavior toward others including duty, obligation, responsibility, and ethnic identity. The expected loyalty to the patriarchal family system and to the Japanese community drew them together to work for the common good. Husbands, wives, children, and extended family members worked long hours for minimal return on the land and in the business, sacrificing to establish economic stability (Kitano, 1976). In addition to the family support system, the community provided both financial and labor support as needed.

This code of ethics extended into the area of education as well. Because four years of education were mandatory and four years were optional in Japan, many *issei* arrived in the United States with "an understanding of, familiarity with, and respect for the educational process" (Kitano, 1976, p. 25). The Japanese code of behavior demanded that children accept unquestioningly all that teachers said and that the children behave as models of decorum. They were also expected to do well in school because their success directly reflected on the family pride. With the denial of citizenship to the *issei*, the American education of the children (*nisei*) became critical to the future of the Japanese in America. The behavior and attitude of Japanese children helped ensure their admittance in local schools but did not overcome the reluctance of Caucasians to mingle with them socially outside the classroom (O'Brien & Fugita, 1991). Thus, education during this period allowed Japanese students to learn the culture but not assimilate it.

Relations with Japan were strained throughout this period, peaking in the 1930s because of the Japanese invasion of Asian territories. Inouye notes in the foreword to *Japanese American History* (1993) that in 1923 the United States Army recommended surveillance of the Japanese in Hawaii to maintain national security. This suspicious attitude never truly abated, and in 1936 President Roosevelt echoed these sentiments. After the attack on Pearl Harbor in December 1941, the climate was such that, ignoring the majority of his advisors, President Roosevelt allowed leading *issei* to be detained. In February 1942 he passed Executive Order 9066, which allowed the military to incarcerate Japanese in detention camps throughout the United States, ignoring the constitutional rights of the *nisei* and *sensei* as citizens. The Japanese were quickly rounded up and shipped off to the camps, leaving their property and many of their belongings behind. They lost their homes and possessions, most of which were never regained.

While friends and family remained in the camps, many young men sought to prove their loyalty and preserve their honor by joining the armed services. Initially and ironically, these jobs meant serving in an intelligence unit, monitoring radio transmissions and translating documents from Japan (James & Munzenmaier, 1995). As the war intensified, the government allowed combat recruitment after they signed a loyalty oath (Carnes, 1995). In 1943, two Japanese American combat units were formed to fight in the European theater. In both capacities, these men served with honor and distinction.

Ignoring loyalty oaths and honorable military service, in 1944 the Supreme Court upheld the decision for the exclusion of Japanese Americans by evacuation to internment camps. Without legal recourse, they remained in the camps until the dropping of the atomic bombs and Japan's surrender on August 14, 1945. Slowly, the internment camps were closed. The internees were given $25 and released to resume their lives (Inouye, 1993). They had come full circle, once again seeking to start a new life. While some returned to their communities on the West Coast, many Japanese headed East in search of a new start (Kitano, 1976). This response was understandable in that returning meant a reminder of the humiliation that they had undergone. Wherever they went, they began to pick up the threads of their lives and to reestablish ethnic communities.

The facts surrounding Japanese American life in the United States during World War II are woven seamlessly into the novel, until it is not just the history of one family but of an entire people. In this novel, history is everything. The author in straightforward prose recounts a despicable action taken against 112,000 people, two-thirds of whom were American citizens. While the study of the period before World War II explains why it happened, it does not excuse its racist roots. Through her personal narrative, the author allows the reader to experience how the lives of so many people changed in a very short span of time, how family treasures had to be abandoned or sold for a pittance, how families were separated, and how the question of loyalty could destroy the honorable. The author also demonstrates how the ethical code of duty, obligation, responsibility, and ethnic identity worked both for and against Japanese Americans, during this period. It is an accurate picture of history through the eyes of a child who lived through it.

*Historical Review of the Time of Writing*   In the foreword to the novel, the author states that it took her 25 years to discuss freely what happened at Manzanar, which would date the writing around 1970, with the publication in 1973. The 1960s were a time of political unrest and minority protest. A look at the events leading up to the early 1970s may, in part, explain why Jeanne Houston finally broke her self-imposed silence about those years. What follows is an overview of national events followed by events that directly touched Japanese Americans.

The 1960s were a time of political upheaval and protest in the United States. Leading political and social figures were assassinated. The Vietnam War was tearing the nation apart. Hippies and others advocated peace. Draft protesters burned their draft cards and were imprisoned or fled to Canada. Drug experimentation was common, especially among college students. During this period, minorities protested social and political discrimination, and Japanese Americans were no exception. They too chose a public forum, seeking redress for earlier wrongs.

The Asian American Movement originated on the West Coast in the 1960s and included youths from various Asian countries, most notably China and Japan (Kitayama, 1993a). They based their organization on Asian pride and unity. The Asian American Political Alliance (AAPA), like other militant minority groups, was concerned with the lack of minority studies at the college level. Their renewed pride in their ethnic heritage and identity spurred them to demand ethnic studies at the university level. Their efforts resulted in the establishment of programs across the nation by 1970. The AAPA also became involved in the antiwar movement. Not surprisingly, Asian American youths felt strongly about the U.S. involvement in Vietnam and became very vocal in their demands for withdrawal by participating in peace marches and rallies (Niiya, 1993). This involvement raised fears of government and police reprisals, especially in light of the Emergency Detention Act of 1950 (EDA). As a result, their most significant political activity became the petition drive for the repeal of EDA in 1968. What began as a relatively small action took on national significance when the most politically powerful Asian association, the Japanese American Citizen League (JACL), took up the cause.

JACL had more political clout because it included members of all ages and occupations. JACL's main purpose was to protect the rights of Japanese Americans through legal channels and political activism.

Though reluctant at first to become involved in the fight for repeal of EDA, JACL soon made it a national cause. Memories of the detention camps of the 1940s were still very fresh for many members, and the EDA loomed as a very real threat to the camps' revival. The fear of this threat seemed justified because EDA allowed the government to establish detention camps for any persons who the government thought might engage in sabotage or espionage (Kitayama, 1993a). The act was eventually rescinded in 1971.

Two significant offshoots of this effort were the campaign for re-dress and the Manzanar Pilgrimage. The demand for redress and repa-rations began in 1970 (Kitayama, 1993b). This campaign sought acknowledgment of the grave injustice done to Japanese Americans in World War II and financial compensation commensurate with the economic losses they experienced. This was a long-fought battle that did not end until 1988 (Carnes, 1995). The Manzanar Pilgrimage be-gan in 1969 "to clean and restore the cemetery grounds . . . and also to highlight the campaign to repeal" EDA (Kitayama, 1993c, p. 225). This prompted pilgrimages to other camps and became an annual event that continues today. These efforts became significant reminders of past indignities and brought national attention to the wrongs com-mitted against Japanese Americans during World War II.

Looking at the events and political actions of Japanese Americans during this period, it seems significant that Houston felt compelled to write her story at this time. Certainly, Houston, who resided in Cali-fornia, was aware of Japanese American political activism as both a college administrator and a Japanese American. In chapter 22 of the novel, Houston explains how she slowly began to discuss her experi-ences in 1966 when she met a photographer from Manzanar (Hous-ton, & Houston, 1973). This meeting awakened memories that she had long suppressed. From these memories she, in collaboration with her husband, composed her autobiographical novel, which gives life to the published facts concerning Manzanar. Although Houston does not allude to this, it is significant that Houston's eldest child, a daughter, was at the time the same age as Houston was during her internment. Perhaps the story was, in part, written for her children so that they could understand their cultural heritage and history and the part both played in this country's history.

### Cultural Footnotes

1. **Patriarch**   The Japanese family is ruled by males, usually the father.
2. **Shikata ga nai**   It means something cannot be helped. The Japan strongly believe in fate and that events are often beyond control.
3. **Buddhism**   It is a code of ethics and, unlike Christianity, not an institution with weekly organized rituals.
4. **The samurai class**   This was the military class in Japan, an elite ruling class in earlier centuries.
5. **Nippon**   The Japanese word for Japan.
6. **Bonsai**   A word that can be a battle cry, greeting, or a cheer, which means "May you live ten thousand years."
7. **Geisha**   A woman who was trained in the "appropriate" way to provide company to men.

## Farewell to Manzanar: The Unit

In teaching this unit, I have a number of goals and objectives. My two primary goals are that the students increase their understanding of and develop an appreciation for another culture and that the students understand how propaganda can be used to manipulate the general public. To meet these goals, I have established the following five objectives:

1. Involve the mind and feelings in the active experience of reading the novel.
2. Visualize the people, settings, and actions while reading.
3. Share the experience of Japanese Americans, perceiving their motivations and values and analyzing their problems and solutions.
4. Participate in honest and thoughtful discussion, using personal experience and insight.
5. Demonstrate through classroom discussion, written responses, and tests an understanding of the Japanese American experience.

The following is a partial list of the activities used to meet these goals and objectives.

1. My unit on the Japanese internment follows a unit that I teach on propaganda. I make a bridge between the two units by beginning a discussion of ethnocentric hysteria created by biased media coverage.

2. Following our discussion, I show a video that outlines the history of intolerance in America, from the arrival of the first Europeans through today. I encourage open class discussion and evaluation of what has been viewed.

3. Next, I ask my class what they know about Japanese immigration to America, the role of Japanese Americans in World War II, and their knowledge of Japanese culture.

4. The students are give a Japanese American time line, and we discuss the events and sort fact from fiction. As a class we discuss the time line, and I present additional information about Japanese culture, the Japanese American culture and experience, and political events pertinent to World War II.

5. We then begin reading the novel. I provide throughout the reading a set of teacher-developed questions that focus on both the literal and inferential levels of understanding. As we read, I draw from the students how Jeanne's family fits the historical and cultural presentation given prior to reading. Vocabulary from the novel is presented on a chapter-by-chapter basis with a discussion of possible meanings gained from the context.

6. Students are required to write a paper after reading the first three chapters. The paper is a minimum of five paragraphs, detailing what personal items they would take to an internment camp and why they chose each particular item. This activity is designed to help students make a reading and writing connection as well as a personal connection to the text.

7. The postreading activity comes in the form of a test that includes an assessment of knowledge, application, and analysis.

For the final writing assignment of the year, I asked my students to write a personal response to the unit. While the responses varied, several thoughts were expressed repeatedly. Some students were angered and dismayed that American citizens were interned (*imprisoned* often replaced *interned* in student writings) on American soil. Others mentioned their admiration and respect for the Japanese culture. The more thoughtful wrote of the parallel they found between the treatment of Japanese Americans of 50 years ago and the treatment of those groups who are considered "different" in today's society. Finally, one young man expressed his fear that no one is safe if the U.S. Constitution cannot protect a group of Americans from discrimination. Because of my success with this technique for teaching multicultural literature, I would recommend this approach to all teachers who are contemplating introducing literature from a culture other than their own.

Over the past three years, opportunities to enrich the students' experience while reading this novel have presented themselves. For instance, a chance discussion with a colleague provided the name of a local individual whose parents had been interned during the war. Mr. H. spoke to each of my classes frankly and openly about his personal experience and that of his parents, making history come alive for them. He also invited student questions as he spoke, encouraging all of us to feel as if we were engaging in a personal conversation. The high school principal joined us during one session, and the visit was the topic of conversation in the teachers' lunchroom. This past year a number of my students attended a Japanese tea ceremony and/or visited a Kabuki theater performance at a local college, making a more personal cultural connection with the unit. Now I find myself actively seeking fresh opportunities for student enrichment. Because of my research, I can honestly say that my enthusiasm for the project has increased. Obviously, I derived benefits from this research-based approach as I found my "comfort level" with the culture; more important, however, my students benefited as well.

# Reading List

Following are five lists of recommended novels for multicultural high school students to read, selected by the author in order of preference, for European Americans, African Americans, Asian Americans, Latino Americans, and Native Americans.

## European American

1. *Growing Up*, Russell Baker
2. *Death of a Salesman*, Arthur Miller
3. *The Great Gatsby*, F. S. Fitzgerald
4. *Fahrenheit 451*, Ray Bradbury
5. *Schindler's List*, Thomas Keneally
6. *The Scarlet Letter*, Nathaniel Hawthorne
7. *The Glass Menagerie*, Tennessee Williams
8. *As We Are Now*, Mary Sarton
9. *My Antonia, O Pioneers*, Willa Cather
10. *To Kill a Mocking Bird*, Harper Lee
11. *The Chosen*, Chaim Potok
12. *Night*, Elie Wiesel
13. *Two or Three Things I Know for Sure*, Dorothy Allison
14. *Chasing Grace: Reflections of a Catholic Girl, Grown Up*, Martha Manning
15. *Spoon River Anthology*, Edgar L. Marsh
16. *Sophie's Choice*, William Styron
17. *The Prince of Tides*, Pat Conroy
18. *Heart of Darkness*, Joseph Conrad
19. *A Separate Peace*, John Knowles
20. *One Writer's Beginnings*, Eudora Welty
21. *Cold Sassy Tree*, Olive Ann Burns
22. *The Loneliness of the Long Distance Runner*, Alan Sillitoe
23. *To Dance with the White Dog*, Terry Kay
24. *The Old Man and the Sea*, Ernsest Hemingway
25. *The Drowning of Stephan Jones*, Bette Greene
26. *The Things They Carried*, Tim O'Brien
27. *Puddin'head Wilson*, Mark Twain
28. *Ethan Frome*, Edith Wharton
29. *Cry the Beloved Country*, Alan Patton

30. *The Heart is a Lonely Hunter,* Carson McCullers
31. *The Awakening,* Kate Chopin
32. *Catcher in the Rye,* J. D. Salinger
33. *The Grapes of Wrath,* John Steinbeck
34. *Diary of a Young Girl,* Anne Frank
35. *The Chronicles of Narnia,* C. S. Lewis
36. *Herland,* Charlotte Perkins Gilman
37. *The Red Badge of Courage,* Stephen Crane
38. *Grendel,* John Gardner
39. *Winesburg, Ohio,* Sherwood Anderson
40. *Ragtime,* E. L. Doctorow

# African American

1. *Their Eyes Were Watching God,* Zora Neal Hurston
2. *I Know Why the Caged Bird Sings,* Maya Angelou
3. *Narrative of the Life of an American Slave,* Frederick Douglass
4. *Fallen Angels,* Walter Dean Myers
5. *Black Ice,* Lorene Cary
6. *Long Distance Life,* Marita Golden
7. *Native Son,* Richard Wright
8. *The Autobiography of Malcolm X,* Malcolm X with Alex Haley
9. *Beloved,* Toni Morrison
10. *The Darkside of Hopkinsville; Stories by Ted Poston,* K. Hauke
11. *Quicksand and Passing,* Nella Larsen
12. *The autobiography of Miss Jane Pittman,* Ernest Gaines
13. *Roll of Thunder, Hear My Cry,* Mildred Taylor
14. *Brown Girl, Brownstones,* Paule Marshall
15. *Marked by Fire,* Joyce Carol Thomas
16. *Warriors Don't Cry,* Melba Beale
17. *The Color Purple,* Alice Walker
18. *A Lesson Before Dying,* Ernest Gaines
19. *Mississippi Solo,* Eddy L. Harris
20. *The House of Dries Drear,* Virginia Hamilton
21. *Sweet Summer,* Bebe Moore Campbell
22. *Kindred,* Octavia Butler
23. *The Wedding,* Dorothy West
24. *The Autobiography of an Ex-colored Man,* James Weldon Johnson

25. *Praisesong for the Widow*, Paule Marshall
26. *Every Goodbye Ain't Gone*, Itabari Njeri
27. *The President's Daughter*, Barbara Chase-Riboud
28. *Devil in a Blue Dress*, Walter Mosely
29. *Coming of Age in Mississippi*, Anne Moody
30. *The Color of Water*, James McBride
31. *Life on the Color Line*, Gregory Howard Williams
32. *The Ditchdiggers Daughter*, Yvonne S. Thornton
33. *Tuskegee's Hero's*, Charlie and Ann Cooper
34. *Sankofu: Stories, Proverbs, and Poems of an African Childhood*, David Abdulai
35. *The Watsons go to Birmingham*, Christopher Paul Curtis
36. *Rosewood*, Michael D'Orso
37. *A Gathering of Old Men*, Ernest Gaines
38. *This Strange New Feeling*, Julius Lester
39. *These Same Long Bones*, Gwendolyn M. Parker
40. *Daughters of the Dust*, Julie Dash

# Asian American

1. *The Joy Luck Club*, Amy Tan
2. *Nisei Daughter*, Monica Sone
3. *No-No Boy*, John Okada
4. *When Heaven and Earth Changed Places*, Lely Hayslip with Jay Wurts
5. *The Floating World*, Cynthia Kadohata
6. *China Boy*, Gus Lee
7. *One Bird*, Kyoko Mori
8. *The Rollerbirds of Ramur*, India Rana
9. *Molly by Any Other Name*, Jean Davis Okimoto
10. *Yokohama, California*, Toshio Mori
11. *Warrior Woman: Memoirs of a Girlhood Among Ghosts*, Maxine H. Kingston
12. *Obasan*, Joy Kogawa
13. *America is in the Heart*, Carlos Bulosan
14. *Farewell My Concubine*, Lillian Lee
15. *Farewell to Manzanar*, Jeanne Wakatsuki Houston and James D. Houston
16. *Saying Good-bye*, Maria G. Lee

17. *Native Speaker*, Chang-Rae Lee
18. *The Hundred Secret Senses*, Amy Tan
19. *Red Azalea*, Anchee Min
20. *Middle Heart*, Bette Bao Lord
21. *The Concubine's Children*, Denise Chang
22. *On Gold Mountain*, Lisa See
23. *What the Scarecrow Said*, Stewart D. Ikeda
24. *Mona in the Promised Land*, Gish Jen
25. *In the Heart of the Valley of Love*, Cynthia Kadohata
26. *A Bridge Between Us*, Julie Shigekuni
27. *Fifth Chinese Daughter*, Jade Snow Wong
28. *Bound Feet and Western Dress*, Pang-Mei Natasha Chang
29. *Eat a Bowl of Tea*, Louis Chu
30. *Issie, Nessi, Ward Brides*, Evelyn Glenn
31. *Year of impossible good-byes*, Sook Nyul Choi
32. *The clay marble*, Minfong Ho
33. *Donald Duk*, Frank Chin
34. *Rape in Nanjing*, Iris Chang
35. *Hiroshima*, Ronald Takaki
36. *From a Native Daughter*, Haunanh K. Trask
37. *Running in the Family*, Michael Ondaatje
38. *A Healing Family*, Kenzaburo Oe
39. *Raise the Red Lantern*, Su Tong
40. *Journey to Topaz*, Yoshiko Uchida

# Latino American

1. *The Last of the Menu Girls*, Denise Chavez
2. *So Far from God*, Ana Castillo
3. *Chronicle of a Death Foretold*, Gabriel Garcia-Marquez
4. *Like Water for Chocolate*, Laura Esquirvel
5. *How the Garcia Girls Lost Their Accent*, Julia Alvarez
6. *House on Mango Street*, Sandra Cisneros
7. *Love in the Time of Cholera*, Gabriel Garcia-Marquez
8. *The House of the Spirits*, Isabelle Allende
9. *Days of Obligation*, Richard Rodriquez
10. *Albuquerque*, Rudolfo Anaya
11. *A Time for Wedding Cake*, Salvatore La Puma
12. *Cantora*, Sylvia Lopez-Medina

13. *The Fourteen Sisters of Emilio Montez O'Brien*, Oscar Hijuelos
14. *And the Earth Did not Devour Him*, Tomas Rivera trans. Evangelina Vigil-Pinton
15. *Pocho*, Jose Antonio Villarreal
16. *Sweet Fifteen*, Diane Gonzales Bertrand
17. *An Island Like You: Stories from the Barrio*, Judith Ortiz Cofer
18. *Sonnets to Human Beings: And Other Selected Works, Second Edition*, Carman Tafolla
19. *Taratuta ~ Still Life with Pipe*, Jose Donoso
20. *Under the feet of Jesus*, Helen Maria Viramontes
21. *Jalamanta: A Message from the Desert*, Rudolofo Anaya
22. *Bless me Ultima*, Rudolofo Anaya
23. *Enchiladas, Rice, and Beans*, Daniel Reveles
24. *Always Running*, Luis J. Rodriguez
25. *Silent Dancing*, Judith Ortiz Cofer
26. *Hoyt Street: An Autobiography*, Mary Helen Ponce
27. *The Autobiography of a Brown Buffalo*, Oscar Zeta Acosta
28. *Hunger of Memory*, Richard Rodriguez
29. *America is in the Heart*, Carlos Bulosan
30. *Paula*, Isabelle Allende
31. *Child of the Dark*, Carolina Maria De Jesus
32. *Mangos, Bananas and Coconuts*, Himilee Novas
33. *The Man Who Read Love Stories*, Luis Sepulveda
34. *When I was Puerto Rican*, Esmeralda Santiago
35. *A Place in El Paso: A Mexican-American Childhood*, Gloria Lopez-Stafford
36. *El Santo Queso: Cuentos/The Holy Cheese: Stories*, Jim Sagal
37. *Nina Otero-Warren of Santa Fe*, Charlotte Whaley
38. *Eleven days*, Brianda Domecq (trans., Kay S. Garcia)
39. *Face of an Angel*, Denise Chávez
40. *Rain of Gold*, Victor Villaseñor

## Native American

1. *Love Medicine*, Louise Erdich
2. *Ceremony*, Leslie Silko
3. *Owl's Song*, Janet Campbell Hale
4. *Cheyenne Autumn*, Mari Sandoz
5. *Fools Crow*, James Welch

6. *Lakota Woman*, Mary Crowing
7. *A Yellow Raft in Blue Water*, Michael Dorris
8. *A Thief of Time*, Tony Hillerman
9. *Dawn Land*, Joseph Bruchac
10. *Mankiller*, Willa Mankiller
11. *Winter in the Blood*, James Welch
12. *House Made of Dawn*, N. Scott Momaday
13. *Choteau Creek: A Sioux Reminiscence*, Joseph Iron Eye Dudley
14. *Folktales of the Native American*, Dee Brown
15. *Tracks*, Louise Erdrich
16. *Two Old Women*, Velma Wallis
17. *Daughters of Copper Woman*, Anne Cameron
18. *Grand Avenue*, Gary Sarris
19. *The Education of Little Tree*, Forrest Carter
20. *Pigs in Heaven*, Barbara Kingsolver
21. *Indian School Days*, Basil Johnston
22. *Spider Woman's Granddaughters*, Paula Gunn Allen (Ed.)
23. *The Grass Dancer*, Susan Power
24. *The Deaths of Sybil Bolton*, Dennis McAuliffe Jr.
25. *Medicine River*, Thomas King
26. *Thunderheart*, Lowell Charters
27. *Sees Behind Tress*, Michael Dorris
28. *Darkwind*, Tony Hillerman
29. *Indian Killer*, Sherman Alexie
30. *Bloodlines*, Janet Campbell Hale
31. *I. Rigoberta Menchu: An Indian Woman in Guatemala*, Rigoberta Menchu
32. *Geronimo: His Own Story, the Autobiography of a Great Patriot Warrior.* S. Barrett
33. *Ghost singer*, Anna Lee Walters
34. *The Jailing of Cecelia Capture*, Janet Campbell Hale
35. *Bird Girl and the Man Who Followed the Sun*, Velma Wallis
36. *Waterlily*, Ella Cara Deloria
37. *No Turning Back: A Hopi Woman's Struggle to Live in Two Worlds*, Polingaysi Qoyawayma
38. *The Autobiography of a Papago Woman*, Ruth Underhill
39. *Night Flying Woman: An Ojibway Narrative*, Ignatia Broker
40. *We are a People in This world: the Lakota Sioux and the massacre at Wounded Knee*, Conger Beasley Jr.

# References

Anaya, R. (1972). *Bless Me, Ultima*. Berkeley, CA: Tonatiuh International.

Apple, M. (1992). The text and cultural politics. *Educational Researcher, 21*(7), 4–11, 19.

Applebee, A. (1989). *A study of book-length works taught in high school English courses*. Albany, New York: Center for the Learning and Teaching of Literature.

Applebee, A. (1991). Literature: Whose heritage? In E. H. Hiebert (Ed.), *Literacy for a diverse society: Perspectives, practices, and politics* (pp. 228–236). New York: Teachers College Press.

Applebee, A. (1992). Stability and change in the high school canon. *English Journal, 81*(5), 27–32.

Applebee, A. (1993). *Literature in the secondary school: Studies of curriculum and instruction in the United States*. Urbana, IL: National Council of Teachers of English.

Atwell, N. (1987). *In the middle: Writing, reading, and learning with adolescents*. Portsmouth, NH: Boyton/Cook Heinemann.

Au, K. (1993). *Literacy instruction in multicultural settings*. Fort Worth, TX: Harcourt Brace.

Banks, J. (1994). *An introduction to multicultural education*. Boston: Allyn & Bacon.

Barrera, R. (1992). The cultural gap in literature-based literacy instruction. *Education and Urban Society, 24*(2), 227–243.

Beach, R., (1994). *Research on readers' response to multicultural literature*. Paper presented at the Annual Meeting of the American Educational Research Association, New Orleans, LA.

Bennett, C. (1995). Preparing teachers for cultural diversity and national standards of academic excellence. *Journal of Teacher Education, 46*(4), 259–265.

Bishop, R. (1992). Multicultural literature for children: Making informed choices. In V. Harris (Ed.), *Teaching multicultural literature in grades K–8* (pp. 37–54). Norwood, MA: Christopher-Gordon.

Bloom, A. (1987). *The closing of the American mind: How higher education has failed the democracy and impoverished the souls of today's students*. New York: Simon & Schuster.

Britzman, D. (1986). Cultural myths in the making of a teacher: Biography and social structure in teacher education. *Harvard Educational Review, 56*(4), 442–456.

Carnes, J. (1995). Home was a horsestall. *Teaching Tolerance, 4*(1), 50–57.

*Contemporary Authors,* (1990). Vol. 29, p. 207. Detroit, MI: Gale Research.

Delpit, L. (1988). The silenced dialogue: Power and pedagogy in educating other people's children. *Harvard Educational Review, 58,* 280–298.

Diamond, B., & Moore, M. (1995). *Multicultural literacy: Mirroring the reality of the classroom.* New York: Longman.

D'Sousa, D. (1991). *Illiberal education: The politics of race and sex on campus.* New York: Free Press.

Enciso, P. (1997). Negotiating the meaning of difference: Talking back to multicultural literature. In T. Rogers & A. Soter (Eds)., *Reading across cultures: Teaching multicultural literature in a diverse society* (pp. 13–41). New York: Teachers College Press.

Flood, J., Lapp, D., & VanDyke, J. (1996). *The multidimensional uses of multicultural literature in the classroom.* Paper presented at the Annual Meeting of the National Reading Conference, Charleston, SC.

Flood, J., Lapp, D., & Ranck-Buhr, W. (1995). What happens when teachers get together to talk about books? Gaining a multicultural perspective from literature. *Reading Teacher, 48*(8), 720–723.

Gates, H. L., Jr. (1992). *Loose canons: Notes on the culture wars.* New York: Oxford University Press.

Graff, G. (1992). *Beyond the culture wars: How teaching the conflicts can revitalize American education.* New York: Norton.

Hamanaka, S. (1990). *The journey.* New York: Orchard Books.

Hansen-Krening, N. (1992). Authors of color: A multicultural perspective. *Journal of Reading, 36*(2), 124–129.

Harris, V. (1992). *Teaching multicultural literature in grades K–8.* Norwood, MA: Christopher-Gordon Publishers.

Hauke, K. (Ed.). (1991). *Dark side of Hopkinsville: Stories by Ted Poston.* Athens, GA: University of Georgia Press.

Hirsch, E. D., Jr. (1987). *Cultural literacy: What every American needs to know.* New York: Houghton-Mifflin.

hooks, b. (1993). Transformative pedagogy and multiculturalism. In T. Perry & J. Fraser (Eds.), *Freedom's plow: Teaching in the multicultural classroom* (pp. 91–97). New York: Routledge.

Houston, J., & Houston, J. (1973). *Farewell to Manzanar.* New York: Bantam Books.

Inouye, D. (1993). Foreword. In B. Niiya (Ed.) *Japanese American history: An A to Z reference from 1868 to the present.* New York: Facts on File.

James, M., & Munzenmaier, C. (Eds.). (1993). *Latitudes: Farewell to Manzanar.* Logan, IA: Perfection Learning.

Jordan, S. & Purves, A. (1993). *Issues in the responses of students to culturally diverse texts: A preliminary study.* Albany, NY: Center for the Learning and Teaching of Literature.

King, J. E. (1991). Dysconscious racism: Ideology, identity, and the miseducation of teachers. *Journal of Negro Education, 60,* 133–146.

Kitano, H. (1976). *Japanese Americans: The evolution of a subculture* (2nd ed). Englewood Cliffs, NJ: Prentice-Hall.

Kitayama, G. (1993a). Emergency Detention Act of 1950, Repeal of. In B. Niiya (Ed.), *Japanese American history: An A to Z reference from 1868 to the present* (pp. 131–132). New York: Facts on File.

Kitayama, G. (1993b). Japanese American Citizen League. In B. Niiya (Ed.), *Japanese American history: An A to Z reference from 1868 to the present* (pp. 182–184). New York: Facts on File.

Kitayama, G. (1993c). Manzanar Pilgrimage. In B. Niiya (Ed.), *Japanese American history: An A to Z reference from 1868 to the present.* New York: Facts on File.

Klinger, J. (1996). *Changing pre-service teachers' attitudes through multicultural literature.* Paper presented at the Annual Meeting of the National Reading Conference, Charleston, SC.

Ladson-Billings, G. (1994). *The dreamkeepers: Successful teachers of African American children.* San Francisco: Jossey-Bass.

National Council of Teachers of English/International Reading Association (1996). *Standards for the English Language Arts.* Urbana, IL: National Council of Teachers of English.

Niiya, B. (1993). *Japanese American history: An A to Z reference from 1868 to the present.* New York: Facts on File.

O'Brien, D., & Fugita, S. (1991). *The Japanese American experience.* Bloomington, IN: Indiana University Press.

Peterson, K. (1994, December, 27). "Scarlet" has "A" position on reading lists. *USA Today,* p. 16.

Reyes, M. de la Luz (1992). Challenging venerable assumptions: Literacy instruction for linguistically different students. *Harvard Educational Review, 62,* 427–446.

Shor, I. (Ed.). (1987). *Freire for the classroom: A sourcebook for liberatory teaching*. Portsmouth, NH: Boynton/Cook.

Spears-Bunton, L. (1992). Literature, literacy, and resistance to cultural domination. In C. Kinzer & D. Leu (Eds.), *The forty-first yearbook of the National Reading Conference: Literacy research, theory and practice; views from many perspectives* (pp. 393–401). Chicago: National Reading Conference.

Stimac, M., & Hughes, W. (1995). Student reflections on cultural autobiography: A promising curricular practice. *Multicultural Education, 3*(1) 18–20.

Sustein, B., & Smith, J. (1994). Attempting a graceful waltz on a teeter totter: The canon and English methods courses. *English Journal, 83*(8), 47–54.

Turnbull, S. (1989). *Samurai warlords*. London: Blandford Press.

Wallis, V. (1993). *Two old women*. New York: HarperPerennial.

Willis, A. (1997). Exploring multicultural literature as cultural production. In. T. Rogers & A. Soter (Eds.), *Reading across cultures: Teaching literature in a diverse society* (pp. 135–160). New York: Teachers College Press.

# About the Author and Contributors

**Arlette Ingram Willis** is an Assistant Professor with the language and literacy faculty in the Department of Curriculum and Instruction at the University of Illinois at Urbana-Champaign. She teaches graduate and undergraduate courses in literacy and the history of reading research in the United States. Her current research and scholarly interests focus on preparing teachers to teach literacy in a diverse society, multicultural literature for grades 6–12, and historical barriers to literacy acquisition in the United States. Among her published works are "Reading the Worlds of School Literacy" in *Harvard Education Review*; "School Literacy Experiences: How Culturally Narrow Are They?" in *Discourse*; "Break Point: The Challenges of Teaching Multicultural Education Courses" in *The Journal of Assembly for Expanded Perspectives on Learning;"* and "Expanding the Boundaries: A Reaction to the First-Grade Studies," *Reading Research Quarterly* (1997).

**Carol Boyce Davies** is Director of African–New World Studies and Professor of English at Florida International University. She was also Professor of English, Africana Studies, Comparative Literature, and Women Studies at State University of New York–Binghamton. In addition to numerous scholarly articles, she has published the following critical texts: *Ngambika: Studies of Women in African Literature* (1986);
*Out of the Kumbla: Caribbean Women and Literature* (1990), both for Africa World Press; and a two-volume collection of critical and creative writing, *Moving Beyond Boundaries.*—Vol. 1, *International Dimensions of Black Women's Writing* and Vol. 2, *Black Women's Diasporas*. Her most recent book is *Migrations of the Subject: Black Women, Writing Identity.* She has studied, taught, and lectured at universities in Africa, South America, the Caribbean and Europe and has conducted many workshops on cross-cultural knowledge and communication.

**Cameron R. McCarthy** is an Associate Professor of Education and Human Development. He authored *Race and Curriculum* (1990) with Falmer Press, and co-edited *Race, Identity and Representation in Education* (1993) with Routledge. He has written numerous articles on racial inequality and schooling and on the politics of difference regarding contemporary educational research.

**Antonio Nadal** is Chairman of the Department of Puerto Rican and Latino Studies at Brooklyn College. He has taught courses in the Music of Puerto Rico, Puerto Rican Literature, and Bilingual Education. Professor Nadal was the recipient of the Tow Award for excellence in teaching. He has published extensively in the areas of education of Latino students, Caribbean literature, and music. He is a salsa singer and composer.

**Milga Morales-Nadal** is the Program Head of Elementary Education and Bilingual Teacher Education at Brooklyn College. She teaches teachers in the Masters in Education Program. Morales has a Ph.D. from the Ferkauf Graduate School of Psychology. She has published in the areas of critical pedagogy, the teaching of social studies, and bilingual education. She serves as a board mem ber of ASPIRA of New York.

**Marlen Diane Palmer** received her B.S. from Eastern Illinois University, with certification in both English and Special Education, and her master's degree from the University of Illinois. She has taught for eight years and currently teaches high school, in both regular education and special education classrooms. Palmer is involved in a cross-circular writing project in conjunction with high school science teachers, and with another teacher she

has begun a tutoring and mentoring program that matches high school student volunteers with junior high and elementary students. She also serves on the district accreditation committee and represents the high school on the Gifted Student Program Committee.

**Debbie Reese** is a Pueblo Indian woman, currently enrolled in a doctoral program in the Department of Curriculum and Instruction at the University of Illinois at Urbana-Champaign. Her primary research interests focus on the ways in which Native people are presented to young children in the media, the school environment, children's books, and society in general. She conducts workshops on issues related to teaching young children about Native Americans.

**Sylvia Y. Sánchez** earned a B.S. in Education with a specialization in nursery to ninth-grade education. She earned her master's from Brooklyn College, New York, and her doctorate from the University of Houston, Texas. Currently she is an Associate Professor and codirector of the Unified Transformation Early Education Model program at George Mason Uni-versity in Fairfax, Virginia. She was recently awarded a federal grant to develop curriculum and training materials for inservice professionals working with culturally, linguistically, and ability-diverse young children and their families.

**Linda Spears-Bunton** is an Assistant Professor and program director of English Education at Florida International University. She teaches classes in advanced methods of teaching English in the secondary school, masters and doctoral seminars in English education, and classes in adolescent multicultural literature. Her publications include a chapter in *Transforming Curriculum for a Culturally Diverse Society* (Erlbaum) as well as articles in several journals and monographs.

**Anna Lee Walters** received her B. A. and M.F.A. degrees from Goddard College in Vermont. She has worked at Navajo Community College in Tsaile, Arizona, for several years as the Director of the College and as an instructor in the Humanities Division. Walters is an accomplished scholar and author. She has written eight books and contributed to over 60 journals and periodicals. Her work can be found in anthologies and textbooks. Some of her works include: *The Sun is Not Merciful* (1984), *Ghost Singer* (1988), *The Spirit of Native America: Beauty and Mysticism in American Indian Art* (1989), and *Talking Indian: Reflections on Survival and Writing* (1992). Her most recent works include an edited volume, *Neon-Pow-Wow: New Native American Voices of the Southwest*, and the retelling of an Otoe story in the form of a children's book, *The Two-Legged Creature: An Otoe Story* (1993). She also is an independent consultant on American Indian issues.

**Sandra S. Yamate** is a Chicago native who received her A.B. in Political Science and History from the University of Illinois at Urbana-Champaign and was elected to Phi Beta Kappa. She earned a J.D. from Harvard Law School and practiced law in Chicago for ten years. She is a past President of the Asian American Bar Association and was the first Central Region Governor for the National Asian Pacific American Bar Association. In 1990, she helped  found Polychrome Publishing Corporation, the only publishing company in the nation dedicated to producing Asian American children's books. She has taught Asian American Literature at DePaul University in Chicago and facilitated a course in Asian American Women's Issues at Northwestern University. She is the author of two children's books, *Char Siu Bao Boy* and *Ashok by Any Other Name*, as well as numerous papers and presentations, including, "Asian Pacific American Children's Literature: Expanding Perceptions About Who Americans Are" in *Using Multiethnic Literature in the K–8 Classroom*, edited by Violet Harris. Yamate reviews books for the Asian Pacific American Librarians' Association Newsletter and is the President of the Japanese American Service Committee as well as a member of the boards of the Multicultural Publishing & Education Council and the Asian Pacific American Women's Leadership Institute.

# Author Index

# Subject Index

## S

St. Lucia, 202
Salem witch trials, 54
Salish, 159
Salvadoreans, 174
Schomberg Library of Nine-
    teenth-Century Black
    Women Writers, 50
School system, 5, 10–11, 12–13
Science, 3
Second Renaissance of African
    American Literature, 69–71
Semple, Jesse B., 57, 65
Short stories, xviii, 25–26, 228,
    230
    African American, 49, 51, 56,
        58, 60, 62, 65, 66
    Asian/Pacific American, 115,
        127
    Caribbean-/American, 204,
        205
    Mexican American, 169, 170,
        173, 174, 176, 187
    Native American, 158, 159,
        161, 162
    Puerto Rican, 94, 96
Simon, Paul, 1
Sioux, 146
Slavery, 29, 84, 102, 227
    African, 39, 49–48, 57, 66, 67,
        70, 72, 104, 105, 130
    in the Caribbean, 8, 194, 199,
        200, 207
Social studies, 156
    textbooks, 6–8
Social workers, 93
South Africa, 1

South America, 7, 102, 143
Southeast Asians, 113–114, 122,
    129, 199
Southwest Voter Registration
    and Education Project
    (SVREP), 180
Spain, 38, 85, 91, 102, 169, 171,
    174
Spanish-American War, 85
Speeches, 48, 62, 161
Stanton, Elizabeth Cady, 6
Storytelling, xiv, 17, 144, 169,
    171, 173, 183, 185, 187
Students,
    equal instructional
        opportunties for, 12, 13
    impact on, xix, 19, 23
    secondary, xiii, 32, 68
Surinam, 198

## T

Tainos, 85
Takei, George, 121
Teachers
    biases of, xix
    concerns of, 20
    dilemma of, 22–24
    information for, xii
    pivotal role of, 9–10, 12, 14,
        22, 31
    preservice training of, xi–xiii,
        12, 24, 156, 215–227
    repositioning of, 28
    self-assessment by, 25–27
    strategies of, 128–130, 155–
        160
Television, 1, 25, 64, 172
Texas Rangers, 172